Critical Muslim 28

Narratives

Critical Muslim is published quarterly by C. Hurst & Co. (Publishers) Ltd. on behalf of and in conjunction with Critical Muslim Ltd. and the Muslim Institute, London.

All editorial correspondence to Muslim Institute, CAN Mezzanine, 49–51 East Road, London N1 6AH, United Kingdom.
E-mail: editorial@criticalmuslim.com

Critical Muslim acknowledges the support of the Aziz Foundation, London.

C. Hurst & Co (Publishers) Ltd.,41 Great Russell Street, London
WC1B 3PL

ISBN: 978-1-78738-021-9 ISSN: 2048-8475

To subscribe or place an order by credit/debit card or cheque (pounds sterling only) please contact Kathleen May at the Hurst address above or e-mail kathleen@hurstpub.co.uk

Tel: 020 7255 2201

A one-year subscription, inclusive of postage (four issues), costs £50 (UK), £65 (Europe) and £75 (rest of the world), this includes full access to the *Critical Muslim* series and archive online. Digital only subscription is £3.30 per month.

A Cataloguing-in-Publication data record for this book is available from the British Library

Critical Muslim

Subscribe to Critical Muslim

Now in its seventh year in print, *Critical Muslim* is also available online. Users can access the site for just £3.30 per month – or for those with a print subscription it is included as part of the package. In return, you'll get access to everything in the series (including our entire archive), and a clean, accessible reading experience for desktop computers and handheld devices — entirely free of advertising.

Full subscription

The print edition of *Critical Muslim* is published quarterly in January, April, July and October. As a subscriber to the print edition, you'll receive new issues directly to your door, as well as full access to our digital archive.

United Kingdom £50/year
Europe £65/year
Rest of the World £75/year

Digital Only

Immediate online access to *Critical Muslim*

Browse the full *Critical Muslim* archive

Cancel any time

£3.30 per month

www.criticalmuslim.io

CM28

October–December 2018

CONTENTS

NARRATIVES

Merryl Wyn Davies	INTRODUCTION: STORIES WE ARE HEIRS TO	3
Jeremy Henzell-Thomas	SIMPLE STORIES, COMPLEX FACTS	13
James E Montgomery	WRITING TRAVEL	31
Brad Bullock	BIG, BAD, TRUMP	53
Burçin Mustafa	TRANSLATIONS	65
Irna Qureshi	HALWA HISTORIES	79
Leyla Jagiella	'GOD KNOWS BEST'	91
Giles Goddard	EMPIRE AND FREEDOM	101
Nicholas Masterton	BUILDING CHRONICLES	114
Nur Sobers-Khan	DREAMING	128
Sabrina Stallone	THE WOMEN OF RAWABI	138
Onaiza Drabu	BEING MUSLIM	149
C Scott Jordan	POSTNORMAL WORDS	158

ARTS AND LETTERS

Boyd Tonkin	ANTIGONE AND SHAMSI	173
Tam Hussein	SHORT STORY: THREE BLIND MICE	185
Norhayati Kaprawi	KEMBAN AND CALLIGRAPHY	195
Mozibur Rahman Ullah	FIVE POEMS	204

REVIEWS

Shanon Shah	REWORKING IBN KHALDUN	215
Hassan Mahamdallie	SHELLEY'S SHADOW	224

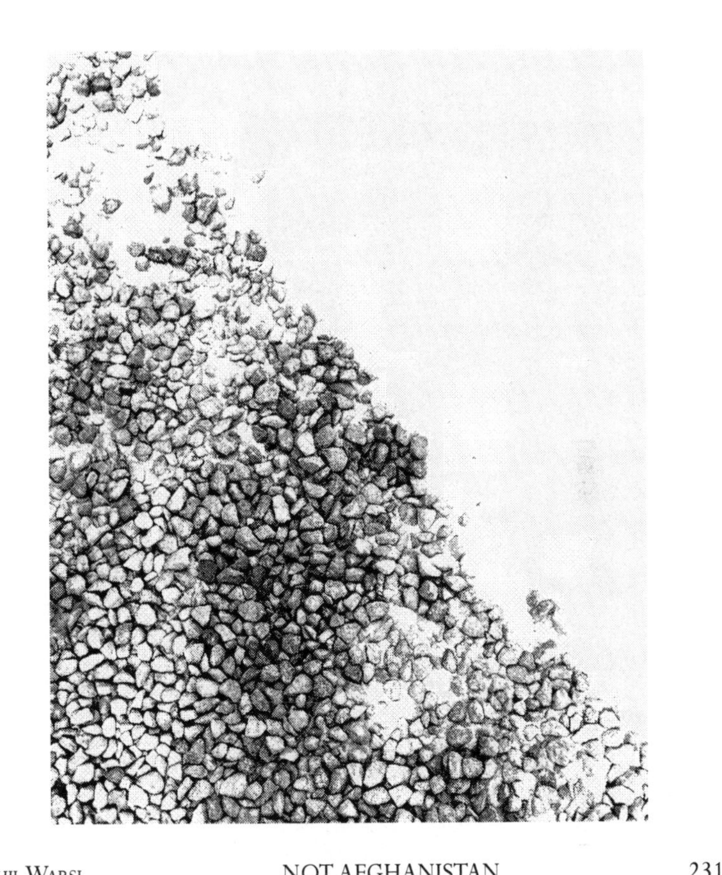

SAHIL WARSI — NOT AFGHANISTAN — 231

MISHA MONAGHAN — BEING BRITISH — 240

ET CETERA

SAMIA RAHMAN — LAST WORD: ON FAMILY NARRATIVES — 247

THE LIST — SHAZIA MIRZA'S COMEDIANS — 254

CITATIONS — 258

CONTRIBUTORS — 269

NARRATIVES

INTRODUCTION: STORIES WE ARE HEIRS TO *by MerrylWyn Davies*
SIMPLE STORIES, COMPLEX FACTS *by Jeremy Henzell-Thomas*
WRITING TRAVEL *by James E Montgomery*
BIG, BAD, TRUMP *by Brad Bullock*
TRANSLATIONS *by Burçin Mustafa*
HALWA HISTORIES *by Irna Qureshi*
'GOD KNOWS BEST' *by Leyla Jagiella*
EMPIRE AND FREEDOM *by Giles Goddard*
BUILDING CHRONICLES *by Nicholas Masterton*
DREAMING *by Nur Sobers-Khan*
THE WOMEN OF RAWABI *by Sabrina Stallone*
BEING MUSLIM *by Onaiza Drabu*
POSTNORMAL WORDS *by C Scott Jordan*

INTRODUCTION: STORIES WE ARE HEIRS TO

Merryl Wyn Davies

Let me tell you a story…

To begin at the beginning. I'll tell you how it was… In the beginning there was talking. 'Where did we come from?' 'It's like this boys … and girls…' 'What happens when you have a baby?' 'Well girls … boys you can cover your ears – it's like this…' Not just babies were born but also narrative. When there were only words the story began. Everything that came after is the continuing saga, the elaborate tracery of intertwining stories. Narrative rules, because by habit, convention, tradition, acculturation, conditioning, programming – whatever term, analogy or reference seems most apposite – all information makes most sense in narrative form. We know what we know when we know how it makes a narrative: coherent, episodic, eclectic, or otherwise.

Human communication began with speech, the development of words to describe things and ideas. All society and culture began and was communicated orally. These words were spun into narratives: parables, fables, myths or legends or just plain speaking that contained the compendium of available knowledge and were designed to do far more than divert and entertain. Whether the narratives came in poetic formula, metred no matter how complexly, to be sung or chanted or whispered or just in plain speech ordered by ancient rote, they taught what needed to be known as well as fuelling the imagination. Narratives were word pictures that served as world pictures, to borrow British philosopher Mary Midgley's felicitous phrase. By descriptive words the world was known, as was the place of each thing within it and its proper nature. Such was the age of orality; nor has that age entirely passed from being, as old narratives never die: they keep on regenerating varied guises. Consider Sophocles' *Antigone*, which, as Boyd Tonkin shows, has been around since 442 BC and 'has travelled the world' ever since, 'and still does'; most recently, reappearing in British-Pakistani author Kamila Shamsie's *Home Fire* as 'a story of jihadi violence, state repression and torn loyalties'. Old stories keep on exerting their power as familiar basic intrinsic patterns of thought, conventions of usage, longstanding adages, conceptual principles and creedal precepts. Believe or don't believe, dissent and criticise, you will do so within a tradition, a convention, a history of concepts and ideas in which old stories wield an influence. We are bound and beholden to the word/world pictures from which we originate, to which we belong.

It is not a case of once upon a time. We are all enmeshed in stories. Indeed the very mention of 'once upon a time' immediately confines and prejudices our appreciation of narrative. The glib assumption/condemnation is that 'once' refers to the long ago when humankind knew little and was easily diverted by awe and wonder, superstition and fear. In this long ago people still needed explanations for all the immensities they could not understand. Thus cosmology, creation myths, legends of superheroes and shape-shifting men/women/beasts/natural force hybrids, grew and religion was born full of stories to fill in the gaps. Of course I paraphrase but explanations of this type, style and implication continue to appear in erudite academic texts to demean the intelligence and purpose of forebears. If such a beginning is given to a story, what can we know or appreciate, in the sense of value, of how particular genres came to exist? What we should know is that if humankind had not interrogated, explored, developed, creatively and innovatively applied the content of these stories we would not be where we are now. The narratives of the long ago are the foundation of all we have become. There is an enormous amount of nonsense continually recycled about the artless, witless, naiveté of early humans which was indissolubly attached to non-Western persons as part of the self-serving supremacist outlook of the self-declared lords and masters of 'mankind': the European colonising bastards. The ability to come to an understanding of the origins of human society, let alone its later stages, begins with the really bad press given to old stories that have survived down the ages or are recovered through excavation and study. 'Simple societies' and their 'simple stories' is too prejudicial in language and intent. Such simplicity includes competence, knowledge and artifice of considerable sophistication that requires the suspension of intentional ignorance to appreciate. Were this not true such societies would never have survived, nor would they have given birth to change, adaptation and divergence that we call the history of humankind. The antidote to the 'simple' syndrome is in the complexity and sophistication of the narratives that typify each society, culture, tribe or grouping of people.

Delinking the complex narratives of 'simple' people marks an important erroneous distinction. Narrative, the weaving of information into world pictures is an extensive and inclusive cultural definition in the anthropological/sociological sense. Complex stories consign narrative to the ambit of high culture in the artistic conceptual sense of 'culture'. So let us not at the outset get derailed by confusion over what we mean by culture. It may be crass but it's pithy and to the point to refer to the classic definition of culture offered by Edward Tylor: 'that complex whole which includes knowledge, belief, art, morals, law, customs, and any other capabilities and habits acquired by man as a member of society'. Admittedly this was written in 1871, so women seem to be overlooked and it was part of a racist hierarchical view of humanity where living societies and cultures were deemed to be mere relics of the stages by which the masters of the universe had risen to their pre-eminence and proper dominance. Ever since, anthropologists and sociologists have played around with the language to show how they are divesting themselves of the relics of Tylor's mode of thought only to end up saying much the same thing about 'culture' in more verbose, round-about jargoned terminology. I downloaded twenty pages of variations on the definition of culture in preparation for this mild excursion into definition. I came out by the same door where I went in. Tylor for all the flaws in his outlook offers a succinct and coherent narration of the comprehensive nature of culture and hence its pervasive influence on all we think and do. And the necessary conclusion is that there is no narrative without culture, and culture gives narrative its nuance, its particularity its *je ne sais quoi* – the essence one has to just know to fully appreciate what is being said not in the lines of words but between them. It is in those spaces, the nuances, the allusions, implications, sideways glances and vague associations that narrative thrives and is most potent. For in those spaces narrative does not so much contain history as it manipulates all the possibilities of what history was and yet could be. It is in the unsaid that narrative is the engine of new thought and as yet undreamt of potential.

The problem we need to wrestle with is the rise of the idea of art as the determinant of civilisation. The idea is replete in the remaking of the BBC television classic series *Civilisation* (1969). In the original, art critic Kenneth Clark offered an erudite essay on the development of Western high culture through the examination of great works of art, architecture and ideas from the Dark Ages to present times. The 2018 remake had to be much more politically correct and was led not by an art historian but bona fide historians: Simon Scharma, Mary Beard and David Olusoga. It is titled *Civilisations*, thus making the transition from the Tylorian view of human history as a unitary upward escalator model to the modern anthropological/sociological view of the multiple paths of human advancement. The new series, instantly forgettable, comes after the postmodern watershed and it is important to recall that a basic definition of postmodernism is the collapse of over-arching narrative. With the removal of inclusive grand patterns, a story into which everything fits, two things are left: doubt and the questing self. Art becomes the medium through which the quest and wrestling with doubt is mediated. The artist becomes the high priest of postmodernity called upon to pontificate or is it bloviate on the state of human affairs. The novelist in particular uses narrative to explore, interrogate and obsess about the self. Thus Martin Amis a novelist of little acquaintance with matters Muslim or Islamic suddenly became a regular commentator on all matters Islamic and Muslim terrorists. His qualification for expertise and special insight was his facility in narrative manipulation of thoughts about the questing self. It makes no sense in terms of actual learning and none with regard to insight but it is emblematic of where we are now.

The turning of the wheel of time has arrived at the point where we are only the story of self, we are all now the narrative of whom or what we choose to be or become. A by-product of this is the growth of autobiography as the only basis for intellectual inquiry. Indeed, autobiographical reaction to the field became a standard trope for anthropological monographs. The exercise was not so much to learn about the other as to reflect upon what the experience of being among otherness elucidated; and that what the researcher brought back from the field was most valuable as knowledge of self. In the postmodern era all things were relative but not necessarily relational. Therefore it should come as no surprise to hear Mary Beard categorically assert (she seldom asserts in any other mode or register) that it is impossible to tell an integrated story of world civilisations, not possible to relate what is happening in one part of the world to what is occurring in another. So we are left with the old familiar separate boxes, fragmented history that misses what I would venture to say should be the real objective: to understand the history of transformative interaction. What is lacking in the narrative of human history is the connective tissue, the fact that we have never been islands sufficient unto ourselves. What we have to learn is how humans have learnt from each other. If we can explore this untrodden path of inquiry we might gain insight into how to better live one with another across and through our differences rather than insisting the only way forward is my way or the highway – the language and interaction of dominance, assimilation and generation of monoculture that is the annihilation of plurality. In other words, the old story of civilisation as a unitary progression has not ceased to be – it has merely been transmuted into a vision of the future, a globalised world modelled on the Western experience.

And yet the insufficiency of old stories is a spur to new kinds of studies. In technical terms it is known as a paradigm shift. A paradigm is a means of fitting facts, theories and hypotheses together to make a coherent narrative of what is understood, what the data indicates. The terminology is most familiar from science and was introduced by the American historian of science Thomas Kuhn in his seminal work, *The Structure of Scientific Revolutions*, to explain how ideas change. Paradigm shifts occur when anomalies are found. Or think of it as a jigsaw where suddenly it seems as if pieces have to be forced, uncomfortably, with fraying and twisting edges to fit into what should be the accommodating apertures. When it becomes more and more difficult to connect the pieces new explanations, new arrangements of facts, will be sought to provide a more elegant and satisfactory descriptive schema or paradigm. This is the point at which we need to recognise that science too translates its insight into narrative and world pictures to present its understanding of how things work. At one level this is a self-evident natural human response to handling information.

On the other hand it can be a dangerously seductive invitation to flights of fancy: think British biologist Richard Dawkins and the lumbering robots he makes of human beings – indeed all biological kind – mere carapaces to carry genes and enable them to fulfil their prime directive to replicate themselves. In the explanatory world pictures of science, it is possible to trace the influence of old stories and their familiar motifs drawn from across the full range of cultural influences. As Mary Midgley demonstrates so elegantly in *Evolution as a Religion,* her dissection of the origins of the world pictures used to present various theories about human evolution, the traces of Biblical exegesis, moral philosophy and ancient classical mythology can all be found mingled to taste to express the trajectory of human evolution as a historic biological process of descent with adaptation. It is just one more example of what American sociologist Margaret Hodgen described as 'the mind's fidelity to the old.' If narrative is how we present explanation, then our explanations draw upon the storehouse of ideas contained in all the old stories we are heirs to. Thus culture rules and includes us all in its capacious embrace.

If narrative is all we have then the question is how responsible and sensible, how apposite and pertinent are the cultural references and narrative tropes that are used to make the world comprehensible. This is a question taken up by Brad Bullock who is concerned less with the epiphenomena of fake news than the long gestation that has prepared the ground. The nationalist narrative of American existence is the democratic spirit. Yet as Bullock demonstrates it is the steady rise of disengagement from politics that created the condition not merely for the election of Donald Trump but the widespread apathy in the face of fake news itself. Fake news is not a new creation. It is part and parcel of the long narrative history of public discourse. From outright propaganda to scurrilous yellow journalism the record of circulating dubious, misleading or downright economical-with-the-truth information is hard to deny. An elected President dubbing the fourth estate 'the enemy of the people' however is something new. The progression from fake news to Trump's assertion people can no longer believe what they see with their own eyes, and presumably what they hear especially from Trump's mouth is summed up neatly by the President's lawyer's assertion that 'truth is not truth'. The point is the swift and largely unchallenged acceptance that we live in a post-truth era came before the 'enemy of the people' and 'truth is not truth' outbursts. The ground had been prepared by a long prehistory of familiarity with the manipulation of information for nefarious ends. The issue is not fake news but the seeming capitulation of society to its establishment as the new norm. George Orwell warned of the dangers in his novel *1984*. When the calendar year 1984 rolled around, I well remember, it was generally thought the worst of his predictions had not materialised because while it might be possible to envision his nightmare scenarios in a centralised command Stalinist society, it could not possibly happen in the open, critical, sceptical territory of a democratic society with a free press and free market in information. Where is that calm complacent self-assurance now? The economy and technology of information generation and dissemination have changed so radically that it is possible to live one's life entirely within the bubble of fake news and never encounter an alternative narrative. The conditions that permit such blinkered existence are most pervasive in the United States but they pose a problem for the whole world. American disengagement from politics heightens the dangers for everyone.

Jeremy Henzell-Thomas is keen to remind us that fake news is merely the tip of an iceberg. Beneath the surface there is the entire undergirding of the substructure of 'false historical narratives.' The enormities of self -serving nationalist history: the vision of a benign empire on which the sun never set or the providential vanishing of native peoples that carried America forward to achieve its manifest destiny, these voices of the victors of history in all their vain glory are not only always there – they are always making a comeback. In the political arena it is always 'hug a flag' week because people want to feel proud of who they are and where they come from – it is human nature. And history concerns times and places unfamiliar to contemporary generations. The truth of what happened in history is usually buried under mountains of fake news and the polite narratives made from such cloth. As Giles Goddard suggests, the sanitised narrative of Great Britain is deeply ingrained in the British psyche; and 'the overall narrative has not changed'. The familiar aspects of the story are repeated again and again, while 'the inconvenient parts' of British colonial 'history are quietly forgotten. The treatment of Ireland, Wales and Scotland. The loss of the United States. The rape of India and the shameful division of Africa. The Suez Crisis. The active encouragement of the slave trade – the campaign to ban it took forty years to achieve success. Britain's imperial past is what makes us great, and no amount of agitation by ex-colonials will change that'. What was worst about history happened to someone else, someone Other, someone not of Us, hence we have no folk memory, no dark narratives of our own culpability. This forgetting is not the same as an inability to learn and know what happened in history. Henzell-Thomas reports that as a good 'iconoclast, subversive, rebel, non-conformist myth buster' he stood up for counter narratives, the alternative facts available. And there is the rub. We have heard of 'alternative facts' more recently – it is the memorable phrase of Kelly-Ann Conway promoting the fake news agenda on behalf of her master Donald J Trump. As Henzell-Thomas puts it: 'a narrative is therefore essentially a top-down cognitive structure, a mindset that facilitates rapid thinking and obviates the need for laborious bottom-up factual inquiry and careful assimilation of complex information. As a simple conceptual framework that is easy to digest analysis, meticulously evidence-based, often inherited or "received" rather than individually constructed, it also acts as a handy "meme" for the transmission of cultural ideas, symbols or practices from one mind to another. Ease of transmission is typically facilitated by distinctive terminology, the use of familiar "mantras" or "loaded" words by which a "narrative" becomes defined and cemented through repetition.' And the trouble is the definition works as well for fake news as for the iconoclastic, subversive non-conformist counter narratives of alternative facts.

The existence of false historical narratives is not in doubt. The quandary is how to redress the problems of mutual misunderstanding and self-ignorance they create. The point is well made by Bullock: 'here's the storyline: declining political participation and a shallower sense of civic responsibility are both cause and effect of our increasingly contentious political climate in the US. Powerful forces have operated on us. Yet, we still live in a functioning democracy. We, ourselves, are ultimately responsible for the political polarisation, unbridled partisanship, and disaffection. This is not a new narrative, but it rarely appears in public discourse even as new chapters are added. Self-implication is never pleasant. Yet, in a very real sense, we are reaping what we have sown, wittingly or not.' For the wider question of false historical narratives, it is the same self-implication that has to be awakened. Other voices, other records, other narratives exist and have to be listened to, allowed their own credibility and be given credence. Only once that willingness and openness is conceded can a conversation begin about what might constitute restorative justice. False historical narrative like fake news has real consequences in the real world. Righting the balance will never be easy because it is hard to imagine just how things can change. Received history, received opinion, received narratives of the way the world is are a burden on imagination. They occupy imaginative space to the exclusion of alternative ideas. Their nuances and silences, nods and winks, do not trend to righting wrongs but always lean towards self-vindication – though that most of us were well-intentioned and good, the few bad apples let the side down and we can regret that but bad people do bad things – what to do lah!

In the final analysis, the existence of false historical narrative is not my greatest concern. I would suggest that to truly see through the inadequacy of received ideas we have to accept and appreciate them – for what they are is an aspect of the totality of possibility. I was reminded of the patience necessary by Shanon Shah's review of Robert Irwin's biography of Ibn Khaldun: 'his work is also a story of the creative and analytical potential of Islamic jurisprudence.' A bold statement and a justified one. Yet it has always irked me in the extreme when Ibn Khaldun is embraced in Western texts as a father of sociology. This is exactly what many would point to as restorative justice, listening to the other and taking on board another view of history and its works. Such attitudes are nothing but fake news in *mardi gras* costume. To be a parent you have to actually produce progenies. Ibn Khaldun's work contributed nothing, alas, to the development of Western social science; the varied disciplines were well past adolescence by the time Ibn Khaldun's work was discovered, translated and ingested by Western scholars. The honorifics bestowed upon him have far more to do with cultural appropriation and glib political correctness. Once appropriated, ideas are stripped of their cultural context, their existence within their own discrete cultural narrative nexus is ignored and that way lies not mutual understanding but further excursion into self-serving manipulation.

If appreciating Ibn Khaldun and paying lip service to his achievements is not the answer, what is? Cultures are narratives, discursive narratives. What we need is to be able to trace the points of contact between cultural narratives to learn how they have touched each other, the ways of interaction and influence one on another. The points of contact have been more profuse than we generally credit because it has been the convention to regard culture as tightly bounded isolates that must be known only in discrete separate compartments. Yet the boundaries have never been as exact, precise and closed as the theory demands. There is a growing trend in many disciplines to explore the intervening spaces, the debatable ground where cultures meet and interact and trace the diffuse acts of diffusion by which mutual influence has taken place. When these lacunae are investigated perhaps it will become possible to see multiple narratives occupying mutual space and all being relevant, contributory, true. It may be possible to accept the possibility of learning more than one genre of cultural narrative so that overlapping creative imaginative spaces open up where it is not necessary or inevitable that one dominates over another but both are acknowledged, credited and mutually respectful of the potential and opportunity they offer each other. How can I describe this glorious visionary world picture, how to give it narrative shape to make it comprehensible and commonplace?

I love old movies. I love John Wayne movies, especially westerns – I always have, I grew up on them. I also grew up abominating the supremacist, appropriating, self-serving attitude that underpinned the entire enterprise contained in the narrative thrust of such movies. I was always unapologetically on the side of the Indians! It is possible to hold at least two and potentially more mutually exclusive ideas at the same time – that is the genius of human imagination and actually the quietest truth to be told about narrative. Building on the potential possibilities of such an understanding is the way forward, beyond the quicksand and swamp of the falsity and fakery in which we are miring ourselves. It the only way I can imagine ever getting to… And they all live happily together for the rest of their days. Or maybe not. As Leyla Jagiella encourages us to say: 'God knows best'.

SIMPLE STORIES, COMPLEX FACTS

Jeremy Henzell-Thomas

When I was studying history at 'A' level in 1964, our syllabus identified 1492 as the year in which 'Modern History' began, the year that Columbus 'discovered' the 'New World'. I was not told that it was also the year in which Columbus, in his relentless search for gold and slaves, instituted shockingly cruel and genocidal policies in the Caribbean islands he had 'discovered', including the rapid decimation of the populations of indigenous Arawak Indians. Neither was I told that it was the year in which Muhammad XII, the last Emir of Granada, surrendered his city to the Catholic Monarchs after a lengthy siege, bringing to an end 780 years of relatively peaceful co-existence under Islamic rule in Al-Andalus. And no mention was made of the Alhambra Decree in the same year, expelling all Jews from Spain unless they converted to Roman Catholicism. Clearly, I was expected to assimilate the dominant 'narrative' from a Eurocentric perspective, a straightforward 'story' about modernity, progress and outreach as pivotal features of Western civilisation and hegemony.

In *Deceit & Self-Deception: Fooling Yourself the Better to Fool Others*, Robert Trivers refers to 'false historical narratives' as 'lies we tell one another about our past. The usual goals are self-glorification and self-justification… False historical narratives act like self-deceptions at the group level, insofar as many people believe the same falsehood', unconscious of the fallacies that went into constructing the narrative. In 'The Power of False Narratives', Robert Parry gives us an example in the defeat of a modest gun-safety bill in the US Senate which is 'further vindication of Orwell's cynical observation that "who controls the past controls the future" since the American Right has persuaded millions of Americans that a false narrative about the Second Amendment is true.' And Trivers is also surely right that 'if a great majority of the population can be raised on the same false narrative, you have a powerful force available to achieve group unity.'

The emotional power of such narratives can easily be harnessed and exploited by leaders in the service of identity politics, corporate power or tribal or national interests. Thus, 'German people have long been denied their rightful space, so *Das Deutsche Volk muss Lebensraum haben!* (German people must have room in which to live!) – neighbours beware. Or the Jewish people have a divine right to Palestine because ancestors living in the general area some two thousand years ago wrote a book about it – non-Jewish occupants and neighbours better beware.'

I was fortunate in having a very enlightened history teacher whose method of teaching was not to teach at all but to ask the class to research the topic at hand. This was very similar to the Harkness method at Phillips Exeter Academy in New Hampshire which I observed in action when I visited the school to investigate the method forty years later. He would ask one of us to give a presentation based on our research, followed by a discussion amongst the class, with little intervention from his side. I recall being asked to give the presentation on Columbus and the 'Age of Discovery'. Budding iconoclast, subversive rebel and non-conformist myth-buster that I was, I delighted in undermining the dominant Eurocentric narrative. I based my counter-narrative on my eye-opening research into the Convivencia in Al-Andalus which was totally new territory not only to me and the class, but also to the teacher, especially since there were so few books on the subject in our school library.

I deliberately use the term 'counter-narrative' to describe my subversive presentation, because, as I realised many years later, my idealised vision of the Convivencia could also be legitimately described as a 'narrative' in itself. This is encapsulated in the title of María Rosa Menocal's book *The Ornament of the World: How Muslims, Jews, and Christians Created a Culture of Tolerance in Medieval Spain*.

Nevertheless, while Amir Hussain is surely right in describing Cordoba in the ninth and tenth centuries as 'one of the most important cities in the history of the world' with Christians and Jews 'involved in the Royal Court and the intellectual life of the city', we also have to acknowledge that the historicity of the supposedly idyllic and harmonious co-existence of Muslims, Jews and Christians has been repeatedly challenged as a 'myth'. In *Communities of Violence: Persecution of Minorities in the Middle Ages,* David Nirenberg claims that 'violence was a central and systemic aspect of the coexistence of majority and minority in medieval Spain' and he even suggests that 'coexistence was in part predicated on such violence'. In *The Myth of the Andalusian Paradise*, Dario Fernandez-Morera describes how, during the Muslim rule of much of the Iberian peninsula, the relationship between the three faith groups was one of uneasy co-existence, marked more often than not by segregation and mutual hostility. He points out that in the massacre of the entire Jewish population of the city of Granada in 1066, the Jewish death toll was higher than in the much-publicised Christian pogroms in the Rhineland thirty years later. The Jewish philosopher Moses Maimonides (1135–1204), depicted today standing alongside Ibn Rushd and Ibn 'Arabi in the museum across the bridge from the Great Mosque in Cordoba, was actually forced to flee from Al-Andalus to avoid conversion by the Almohads, which may have prompted his bitter statement that Islam had inflicted more pain on the Jewish people than any other 'nation'.

In the light of all such correctives and qualifications, we can safely conclude that, however one might choose to interpret the balance of the evidence, common 'narratives' attached to the significance of the year 1492 (whether as the marker of the beginning of the 'modern age' or as the end of the Convivencia) are one-sided to some degree. And this tells us a lot about what a 'narrative' often is. If Fernandez-Morera describes the 'Andalusian Paradise' as a 'myth', we might equally well apply his epithet to the persistent Eurocentric assumption that the European Renaissance and its associated 'Age of Discovery' has a unique and special status at the very heart of our conception of modernity. The title of Jonathan Lyons' book *The House of Wisdom: How the Arabs Transformed Western Civilisation* speaks for itself. In his series of ground-breaking books, Jack Goody has also applied a much-needed corrective to the biased Eurocentric narrative, applying rigorous historical analysis to bring to light the parallel renaissances that took place in other cultural contexts, notably Islam and China.

In his work in comparative and historical sociology, John Hobson has produced a similarly well-researched (and more strongly polemical) challenge to triumphalist European misappropriations of modernity by arguing that one of the chief drivers of Western industrialisation was the adoption of Arab and Chinese knowledge. In doing so, he 'propels the hitherto marginalised Eastern peoples to the forefront of progress in world history.' The idea of modernity pervades what Hobson calls 'the Orientalist construction of the West versus the East'. The exposure and deconstruction of the Orientalist 'narrative' is of course closely associated with Edward Said. As Hamid Dabashi points out, forty years after the publication of Said's seminal masterpiece dismantling 'figurative, tropic and narrative representations' within 'the European project of colonial modernity and all its ideological trappings', Orientalism lives on in other shapes and forms. It was Said's 'magisterial text that turned an entire discipline of scholarship upside down and enabled a mode of thinking hitherto impossible to fathom in postcolonial thinking around the globe. In *Orientalism*, Said unleashed our tongue and unsheathed the sword of our critical thinking.' While Said 'paved the way and pointed us in the right direction', Dabashi advocates an 'even more radical dismantling of the "European project"'.

In Hobson's tabulation of adjectives contrasting the 'dynamic West' with the 'unchanging East', the West characterises itself as 'inventive, ingenious and proactive', and the East as 'imitative, ignorant and passive'. The West is 'rational, scientific, disciplined, ordered, mind-oriented', the East 'superstitious, ritualistic, lazy, chaotic, erratic, emotional, body-oriented, exotic'. The West is 'independent, functional, free, democratic, tolerant, honest', the East 'dependent, dysfunctional, enslaved, despotic, intolerant, corrupt'. Perhaps above all, the West is 'civilised, enlightened and progressive' (morally, intellectually and economically), the East 'savage, barbaric, dark, regressive, and stagnant'. The common 'narrative' denying modernity to non-Western cultures has also come through in recent times in the exploitation of the negative connotation of the term 'medieval' to refer to what is 'dark', 'barbaric' and 'savage' and in its reiteration in the crude ethnocentric polemics underlying what Fred Halliday has called the 'incendiary banalities' of the 'pernicious doctrine' of the 'clash of civilisations' – in particular in Orientalist depictions and caricatures of Muslims as perhaps the chief contemporary expression of Occidentalist bias.

This bias, also expressed in the term 'Dark Ages', has been reflected in various scaremongering stereotypes at different times, perhaps most vividly in the representation of the 'yellow peril' in the caricature of Fu Manchu, the Chinese master criminal of exotic malignance, hatred of the white race, and lust for world domination. This character, created in 1912 by the British writer Sax Rohmer, was depicted in a series of films from 1965 to1969 by Christopher Lee, famous also for his depiction of Dracula in the Hammer horror films. The titles speak for themselves and include *The Brides of Fu Manchu* (1966), *The Vengeance of Fu Manchu* (1967), and *The Blood of Fu Manchu* (1968). Pitted against the Chinese supervillain are Nayland Smith of Scotland Yard and Dr Petrie, who personify the epitome of stolid, wholesome and upstanding Britishness in the face of inscrutable deviousness, ingenious cruelty, and ruthless megalomania. In direct antithesis to the Sinophilia of the European Enlightenment, the scathing racism of Sinophobia (or Chinaphobia) had developed during the high imperialism of the mid- and late-nineteenth century and one of its popular myths is patently evident in Dickens's descriptions of Chinese opium smoking dens in the East End of London with their mysterious and threatening connotations and the moral loathing they evoked.

In fact, it is worth exploring in some depth the wildly exaggerated and sensationalised portrayal of East End opium dens, as imagined not only by Dickens but also by Conan Doyle and Oscar Wilde, because they provide a particularly suggestive and concrete historical example of the distorted lens through which even highly intelligent and creative representatives of one 'civilisation' can make unjust and pernicious judgements about another. Ransom Riggs points out that the Encyclopaedia Britannica's 1888 edition claims that addiction to narcotics 'happens chiefly in individuals who are practically moral imbeciles, often addicted also to other forms of depravity'. Yet, although it was not known exactly how many Londoners slummed it in opium dens, many more Victorians 'partook of and became addicted to opium in the form of laudanum – an alcoholic derivative so popular it was spoon-fed to teething infants – than by smoking it, a practice that suggested exotic danger simply because it was associated with the "alien" culture of Chinese immigrants.'

The fact is, as Riggs notes, that 'the East End's Limehouse district never had more than a few hundred Chinese and about a half-dozen opium dens – if you could even call them that. On the whole, these "dens" were simply rooms where Chinese men gathered to smoke opium, gamble, and gossip; they were more like informal social clubs than dens of desperate iniquity.' Conan Doyle depicts Sherlock Holmes as himself a drug addict with a penchant for shooting up a seven per cent solution of cocaine. He would occasionally indulge in binges that left his 'sinewy forearm and wrist all dotted and scarred with innumerable puncture-marks'. Dr Watson is prepared to excuse Holmes's 'drug mania' as a periodic reaction to the boredom he felt when 'cases were scanty and the papers uninteresting'. Yet, in 'The Man with the Twisted Lip', the good doctor describes his visit to an East End opium den as a descent into Hell, and Holmes himself describes it as 'the vilest murder-trap on the whole riverside'. While Holmes was given to lying on the sofa in a drugged stupor for days on end, 'hardly uttering a word or moving a muscle from morning to night', the 'civilised' reaction to this does not approach the horror and opprobrium expressed by Watson as he enters the opium den: 'Through the gloom one could dimly catch a glimpse of bodies lying in strange fantastic poses, bowed shoulders, bent knees, heads thrown back, and chins pointing upward, with here and there a dark, lack-lustre eye turned upon the newcomer. Out of the black shadows there glimmered little red circles of light... as the burning poison waxed or waned in the bowls of the metal pipes.'

It can be argued that the shadowy or inflammatory imagery, emotive terminology and vehement hyperbole deployed to project the clash of civilisations point very clearly to an underlying psychological problem. One of the ways to describe this problem is to see it in Jungian terms as a projection of those aspects of the self which are unconscious and unrecognised (hence 'dark' or in 'shadow') onto 'the other'. In such a way, the 'other' is feared, denigrated and even demonised or obliterated, whether as a civilisation, culture, race, religion, or any other form of 'identity' perceived to be markedly different. As I have suggested elsewhere, numerous malignant outcomes of this unconsciousness might be mentioned, including the murderous rampages of Boko Haram and Anders Breivik in their respective demonisation either of the 'West' or the 'multiculturalism' which raises for the xenophobes the hideous spectre of the 'Islamification' of Europe.

In his delicious riposte to the woefully ignorant dismissal of the Qur'an by novelist Sebastian Faulks, Ziauddin Sardar points out that 'through a broken mirror one will inevitably see only darkly, imagining distorted figures whose ideas, motivations, beliefs and their relation to actual Islamic sources will be incomprehensible.' Faulks had described the Qur'an (a subject, as Sardar states, that 'demonstrably exists well beyond his grasp') as 'very disappointing', 'one-dimensional', 'barren', a 'depressing book' with 'no ethical dimension'. Sardar asks, if that were the case, 'how could it motivate the believers to develop science and learning, promote reason and experimental method, establish universities and research-based hospitals, and advance philosophical inquiry?' If Faulks had read it with even a modicum of attention and a genuine spirit of open inquiry, how could he have missed

> the abundant statements detailing what constitutes moral and ethical behaviour: distributive social justice that encompasses all spheres of human activity. He ignored the repeated injunctions that roundly condemn oppression, the denial of the rights of others, whoever they maybe, whatever their beliefs. And he overlooked something that would have benefitted him greatly: the Qur'an's frequent advice to be humble and acknowledge the limitations of one's own understanding and insight.

Sardar concludes that 'as a man of letters of our time, Faulks does not disappoint. His literary diagnosis of the Qur'an suggests he is blissfully triumphant in his self-assured ignorance. He has no idea of what he does not know.'

It is important to note here that the kind of epithets used by Faulks to describe the Qur'an are certainly less colourfully sensational as what I have described as the 'shadowy and inflammatory imagery, emotive terminology and vehement hyperbole' associated with the worst excesses of demonisation of the 'other'. But they are revealing all the same as an example of one of the distorting lenses (or broken mirrors) through which one culture or civilisation is prone to resort to judgements about another. In this case it is the conventional lens of the 'man of letters' addicted to literary 'nuances' and culture-bound assumptions about what is 'interesting' and 'creative', and 'disappointed' by any 'style' of discourse that does not fit into his preconceptions. The language of Divine Revelation, a language which reaches to the 'furthest horizons', is a long stretch for someone looking through the wrong end of a telescope. This lens may not have that degree of chromatic aberration that conjures wildly fantastic, bizarre or phantasmagoric images; it is more like a lens with a thick coating of cultural conditioning that effectively blinds even 'sophisticated' viewers to any understanding or perception beyond familiar norms. The clash of civilisations is by no means confined to the vulgar mob heated up by populist rhetoric. If both Sherlock Holmes, the epitome of observational powers, forensic science, and logical reasoning, and Sebastian Faulks, a paragon of literati, can succumb to it, we can infer that the fixed ideas and mindsets, the 'schemata', 'frames', 'scripts' and, indeed, 'narratives' cemented by cultural conditioning, can be highly resistant, even impervious to modification.

Various synonyms for the concept of 'narrative' have emerged in the foregoing discussion: myth, stereotype, caricature, mindset, schema, frame, script, and lens. Most, if not all, of these terms imply some degree of bias, one-sidedness or simplification. We could also include within its semantic field the broader canvas of 'ideology', 'worldview' and 'paradigm'. A particularly useful notion is the 'narrative fallacy' introduced by the trader-philosopher-statistician Nassim Taleb in his popular book, *The Black Swan*. Referring to this at the beginning of the chapter entitled 'The Illusion of Understanding' in his book *Thinking, Fast and Slow,* Nobel Prize winning economist Daniel Kahneman refers to narrative fallacies as 'flawed stories of the past' which 'shape our views of the world and our expectations for the future'. They are simple (even simplistic) but alluring and compelling explanatory stories which arise from our continuous attempt to make sense of the world.

A narrative is therefore essentially a top-down cognitive structure, a mindset that facilitates rapid thinking and obviates the need for laborious bottom-up factual analysis, meticulous evidence-based inquiry and careful assimilation of complex information. As a simple conceptual framework that is easy to digest, often inherited or 'received' rather than individually constructed, it also acts as a handy 'meme' for the transmission of cultural ideas, symbols or practices from one mind to another. Ease of transmission is typically facilitated by distinctive terminology, the use of familiar 'mantras' or 'loaded' words by which a 'narrative' becomes defined and cemented through repetition.

The potential for serious over-simplification, distortion and fallacy in 'narrative' thinking can be illustrated in extreme form in early attempts to develop Artificial Intelligence (AI) programmes for 'reading' and paraphrasing natural language texts. In my doctoral research completed in

1985 into the psychology of learning, in which I investigated the interaction between top-down and bottom-up processes in the comprehension of informative text, I referred, amongst others, to a programme developed to 'read' and summarise texts rapidly for the US Congress by Roger Schank, appointed in 1981 as Chair of Computer Science at Yale and director of the Yale Artificial Intelligence Project. In order to read rapidly, one needs to activate global schemata (background knowledge) which can make predictions about content, because a bottom-up parser analysing every grammatical and syntactic cue, though more accurate, would be very slow. I believe the AI challenge was to discover how to combine top-down with bottom-up data-driven processing, and to determine when the slower data-driven processing should kick in so as to check on the accuracy of the comprehension state. Schank developed an essentially top-down parser so as to enhance speed of processing. The perils of script-driven processing are strikingly illustrated in the way the parser summarised a newspaper article entitled 'Pope's Death Shakes the Western Hemisphere'. It came up with 'Pope killed in an Earthquake'. This is a classic example of top-down processing that accommodates information to an existing schema rather than assimilating what is new and thereby modifying a provisional state of knowledge (the process we call 'learning'). The programme merely sampled lexical items in the text, taking no notice of syntactic structure or range of connotations and generated an 'Earthquake' script from the collocation of 'Shakes' and 'Western Hemisphere'. It then fitted the Pope's death into the Earthquake script.

This is, of course, a very crude example of 'jumping to conclusions' based on minimal input, but, as such, it does illustrate at least one factor behind the popularity of 'narratives' and the fallacies associated with them. The 'fast thinking' described by Kahneman as a preferred cognitive strategy is not so far from the sampling technique of a crude top-down AI parser. A dominant 'narrative', with its familiar buzzwords and collocations, is itself a 'schema' into which we can comfortably fit our assumptions and expectations without having to learn anything new.

AI programmes have of course advanced exponentially since such primitive models, to the extent that the late Stephen Hawking commented at the Web Summit technology conference in Lisbon in 2017 that because 'computers can, in theory, emulate human intelligence, and exceed it' the emergence of AI could be the 'worst event in the history of our civilisation unless society finds a way to control its development.'

Arundhati Roy, interviewed by Tim Lewis in *The Guardian* in June 2018, agrees. 'Perhaps AI can do better surgery than surgeons, write better poetry than poets and better novels than novelists.' It's 'a way of becoming the perfect human being, which fascists have always thought about: the supreme human being.' She says we need to be 'paranoid' about this, because a time will come 'when the masters of the universe will decide that the universe is a better place without most of the population.'

On the other hand, whatever justifiable fears there may be about the future of AI in terms of the big picture, it seems to me that we can learn a lot about the human capacity for learning from AI models of natural language processing within the field of cognitive science. Although I have not kept up with the evolution of AI natural language parsers since their early days at the time of my research, I suspect that huge strides must have been made in integrating both top-down and bottom-up processes to the extent that such programmes are capable of learning through cumulative adjustment of existing schemata. In that sense, AI may be able to model the learning process in ways that positively counteract human fixations on familiar 'narratives'. As such, they can help us to understand the cognitive and linguistic processes involved in critical thinking in the sense employed by Warren Berger, who asks the question 'What is critical thinking, exactly?' in an article aptly entitled 'Want to be a better critical thinker? Here's how to spot false narratives and "weaponised lies"'. Berger maintains that authentic critical thinking, involving 'reasoning, evaluating, and making decisions based on evidence' and driven by 'objectivity, integrity, and fair-mindedness' in the search for truth, is 'fundamentally different from "weak-sense critical thinking" – a term popularised by the late Richard Paul, a co-founder of the Foundation for Critical Thinking.' Weak-sense critical thinking, Berger explains, means 'applying the tools and practices of critical thinking –questioning, investigating, evaluating – but with the sole purpose of confirming one's bias or serving an agenda.' As such, it generally lacks awareness that its reasoning and judgement may be skewed. Berger also suggests that fair-mindedness and objectivity are also probably even harder in the age of social media echo chambers, and there is reason to believe that 'Facebook's newsfeed algorithm actively works against critical thinking by serving up news and information based on our pre-existing preferences and beliefs.'

In *Weaponised Lies: How to Think Critically in the Post-Truth Era,* the psychologist Daniel J. Levitin claims that our capacity for critical thinking also has been weakened by information overload. According to Levitin, this sense of being overwhelmed makes us more vulnerable to 'fake news' – unsubstantiated stories from suspect sources and 'alternative facts' served up by spin doctors. All of this works against the careful evidence-based inquiry germane to Daniel Kahneman's 'slow thinking' and reinforces the tendency for fast thinking that 'goes with the gut' and therefore falls prey to false narratives. According to Levitin, 'research shows that your gut's going to be wrong more than it is right.' Evidence-based decision-making, on the other hand, 'leads to better outcomes' in many areas of life. As Carl Sagan warned in an interview with Charlie Rose just months before his death in 1996: 'If we are not able to ask sceptical questions...to interrogate those who tell us something is true, to be sceptical of those in authority... then we are up for grabs for the next charlatan, political or religious, who comes rambling along.'

In a recent article in *Psychology Today* entitled 'A Passionate Call for a Commitment to the Truth', Gregg Henriques points out that the 'human propensity to simplify data through a predilection for narratives over complex data sets typically leads to narrative fallacy. It is easier for the human mind to remember and make decisions on the basis of stories with meaning, than to remember strings of data' and 'this is one reason why narratives are so powerful'. The way to avoid the narrative fallacy, he asserts, is through principled scholarly research that champions validity and reliability in the collection, analysis and presentation of data. 'To become credible champions of truth, we must first earn our own credibility. And to do so, we must set our integrity to the facts as our first, most non-negotiable moral concern.'

Henriques is also surely right that the process of evidence-based inquiry 'has to begin with self-knowledge, with rigorous awareness of the roots of one's own thinking and the impediments within oneself to unbiased commitment to the Truth.' I would contend that such awareness is intimately related to the language one uses to frame one's thoughts. We have already noted how the common Orientalist 'narrative' denying modernity to non-Western cultures often uses derogatory terms such as 'dark', 'barbaric' and 'savage', and also attaches negative connotations to essentially neutral terms such as 'medieval'. As Norman Cigar has shown in his study of the role of Serbian Orientalists in the justification of genocide against the Muslims of the Balkans, the Serbs differentiated and isolated Bosnian Muslims by creating a caricature, 'a straw-man Islam and Muslim stereotype' and 'setting and emphasising cultural markers' which focused on Islam and the Muslims as reflections of the 'darkness of the past', inimical to modernity, alien, culturally and morally inferior, threatening and perversely exotic. And, as Cigar concludes, 'by bending scholarship and blending it with political rhetoric' they exploited 'the extensive media exposure they enjoyed in Serbia' to define Islam and the local Muslim community in such a way as to contribute significantly to making genocide acceptable.

This is a telling illustration of Sardar's crucially important insight that the source of the 'ultimate power' of the West, 'its worldview with all its axioms and assumptions' does not essentially reside in its economic, military and technological prowess, but in 'its power to define'. This goes against the conventional view that it was military power that ensured the dominance of the West. Ten years before Niall Ferguson's rightwing paean to the 'six killer apps of Western power', in *Civilisation: The West and the Rest*, Victor Hanson had argued in *Why The West Has Won* that although the steady rise of Western power owed much to 'its focus on individualism, democratic political structures, and scientific rationalism', the key factor was the overpowering military might that enabled it to project its 'values' around the globe, though 'sometimes with devastating effects on local cultures which have at times adopted the worst of what European traditions have offered or imposed.' To put this in Ferguson's later terminology, this has been the ultimate 'killer app'. As Hanson shows, the keystone for this military success had been laid in ancient Greece. Unlike the autocratic world of the Persians, the constitutionally governed Greek city-states promoted political participation, equality, and civic freedom. A social and political system in which soldiers had a say in military affairs and small farmers had a right to land ownership had much to do with the creation of a military ethos based on egalitarian camaraderie and individual initiative. The combination of such values with the Greek mastery of technology in producing matchless weapons, their flexibility in tactics, and discipline in planning and execution, produced a fighting force of consummate power and effectiveness.

Yet, as Sardar explains, it is the monopoly on definition held by the West, sustained by academic disciplines providing 'learned, scholarly and rational legitimacy to the defining concepts' that bolsters and disseminates its dominant narratives, and one can legitimately uphold that it is this conceptual power rather than military power that is the ultimate 'killer app'. 'The West defines what is, for example, freedom, progress, civilisation and civil behaviour; democracy and human rights; law, tradition and community; reason, mathematics and science; who is a dictator or a terrorist or a moderate person; what is real and what it means to be human.'

In the same way, the West claims the high ground in its appropriation and ownership of the 'International Community', that grandiose term noted by Nick Gvosdev as 'part of the background noise of political statements.' As Martin Jacques reminds us, we have heard this term a thousand times, slipping off the tongues of newsreaders and correspondents as if we all know exactly what it means. As he says, although 'it is supposedly a broad group of world governments with a common perspective and set of values, especially in relation to political repression and human rights', it means 'the West, of course' and using the term is 'a way of dignifying the West, of globalising it, of making it sound more respectable, more neutral, more highfalutin.' And as he says, 'the great majority of the world (indeed, "the West" constitutes less than one-fifth of the world's population) is, in fact, being tacitly ignored: unless, of course, it happens to agree with the West.' Noam Chomsky goes so far as to narrow its location to the United States and its client states and allies, and even more narrowly to 'Washington', although this is impossible to reconcile with the recent judgement of Donald Tusk, President of the European Commission, that the Trump presidency is 'on a mission' to 'undermine the international rules-based order'.

Perhaps even more insidious than the use of words to claim cultural and moral superiority, is the use of what is described in the field of Critical Discourse Analysis (CDA) as the ploy of 'mitigation and denial', the substitution of mild, polite, saccharine, evasive or roundabout words for more direct and honest ones. Some familiar examples include 'targeted killing' (assassination/murder by death squads/extra-judicial killing/execution), 'enhanced interrogation techniques' (systematic torture), 'collateral damage' (civilian casualties), 'killed in crossfire' (shot by soldiers or snipers), 'settler' (illegal settler), 'suburbs' (illegal settlements), 'disputed territory' (illegally occupied territory), 'provocative act' (criminal act according to international law). The Western media also define who live in 'areas' (Palestinians) and who in 'communities' or 'neighbourhoods' (Israeli 'settlers'), and by so doing reinforce the 'narrative' that the latter are more 'civilised'.

Studies in corpus linguistics have long shown how people are conditioned even at a subliminal level by repeated collocations in the language of the media and political discourse. Drawing on his own meticulous work in this field in order to examine the representation of Islam in the British press, Costas Gabrielatos has revealed the insistent drip-feed of collocations, both explicit and implicit (as in the disproportionate number of collocations between Islam and 'terrorism') which inevitably conditions public attitudes.

The analysis of the clash of civilisations in the form of Sinophobia or Islamophobia needs, of course, to be balanced by an acknowledgement of the counter-narrative of 'Westophobia'. According to Ameer Ali, Westophobia has been provoked by 'the failure of Western secular models to promote democracy and development with justice and equity, and persisting grievances against a West-manufactured world order'. But the blaming of 'the West' for the failures of Muslim societies is itself deeply problematic, in the same way as valid self-criticism and much-needed reform can be avoided by resorting to the label of 'Islamophobia' in response to any criticism from 'the other'.

There is a tricky balance to be found here. Abdullah Faliq argues that many would agree that 'it is right to reject the claim that the term Islamophobia is exploited to stifle legitimate criticism of Muslims, because such a claim legitimises indolent stereotypes and panders to fascist groups and sections of the media.' But the corrective to the overuse of the label of Islamophobia by Muslims as a means of diverting attention from the need for change can itself be taken too far. According to Barry Rubin, 'the key to understanding the Middle East is not Islamophobia in the West, but the region's own Westophobia' and he includes within this broad category, 'many other phobias', including modernity, secularity, democracy, freedom, and gender equality, as well as Judaism and Christianity. On the other hand, the categorical assertion that the chief fault lies in anti-Western phobias is to play into the polarised thinking of the clash of civilisations which seeks to identify what is dysfunctional in only one side of the equation. The 'key' is neither the one-dimensional perspective of one side nor the other, but the human addiction to narratives arising from binary and polarised thinking.

The 'tricky balance' identified by Faliq in steering a course between competing narratives also needs to be navigated in relation to the tension between simple narratives and complex facts, or fast and slow thinking, as I have outlined in other terms in my discussion of the interaction between top-down and bottom-up processes.

As Henriques acknowledges, the question remains how one verifies the veracity or accuracy of the 'facts' one gathers as a means of challenging or applying a corrective to a dominant 'narrative'. As we have already seen, so-called 'evidence-based inquiry' may only go so far as 'weak-sense critical thinking', tending to reflect, in Henriques' terms, 'the existing leanings, interests, perspectives and even ideologies of the "inquirers", to the exclusion of awkward "facts" that undermine such confirmation bias.'

In exploring this propensity for biased thinking in my essay on 'the power of education' in the *Power* issue of *Critical Muslim*, I pointed out that it is well attested that even the very 'rational' scientific community is susceptible to confirmation bias. 'In the same way, we know from the psychology of perception that the human mind tends to see what it wants or expects to see. Perceptual preferences are of course necessary and understandable. Without the rapid automatic routines generated by familiar expectations we would not be able to function in the world, for we would have to analyse everything laboriously from the bottom-up as if we were encountering it for the first time.' The survival benefits of decisive judgement and action facilitated by rapid processing are obvious. 'By contrast, the armchair philosopher who scrutinises the logical minutiae of every proposition, absorbs every qualification, respects every position, and agonises over every minor dissonance and nuance may never get out of his chair.'

By way of balance, it is important to acknowledge that such reservations may be in themselves important correctives to the over-valuation of factual evidence as the only source of truth. In other words, the existence of narrative fallacies should not lead us to the wholesale rejection of narratives as pathways to understanding. In *The Myth Gap: What Happens When Evidence and Arguments aren't Enough*, Alex Evans argues that

> once upon a time our society was rich in stories. They united us and helped us understand the world and ourselves. We called them myths. In this time of global crisis and transition – of mass migration, inequality, resource scarcity and climate change – it is only by finding new myths, those that speak to us of renewal and restoration, that we will navigate our way to a better future. It is stories, rather than facts and pie-charts, that have the power to animate us and bring us together to change the world.

Let me interject the caveat that the unification bestowed by shared narratives is, of course, a double-edged sword. We do not have to look very far in the world today to observe the negative form of *'asabiyyah* (tribal partisanship), roundly condemned by the Prophet Muhammad as 'helping your own people in an unjust cause.' It is that crudely jingoistic or ethnocentric mentality which endorses tribal prejudice and parochial self-interest. It feeds exclusivism, triumphalism and narrow identity politics in the distortion and misappropriation of doctrines and values for cultural, ethnic, religious, national or civilisational superiority.

Ibn Khaldun, however, was aware of the equivocal nature of social bonding in his use of the term *'asabiyyah* and acknowledged that it can be a source of solidarity and social cohesion. It recognises that co-operation and community spirit are hard wired into humanity, and social organisation and community pride are necessary for civilisation to flourish. The tension between the negative and positive aspects of *'asabiyyah* is well illustrated in the titles of consecutive books by Jonathan Sacks, the British Chief Rabbi, philosopher and scholar of Judaism. The titles speak for themselves: the first, *The Dignity of Difference: How to Avoid the Clash of Civilisations* (2002), followed by *The Home We Build Together: Recreating Society* (2007). Here, Sacks navigates from narrative to counter-narrative, moving from a perspective that respects diversity to one that appeals for a 'shared narrative'.

In his review of *The Myth Gap* in *New Scientist,* Fred Pearce agrees with Evans about the need to bring inspiring narratives back to the heart of progressive politics, so that 'the science of the planet and its workings' can be linked to 'real and important human values that we all can share.' Instead of couching environmental challenges in technocratic terms that are owned by a priesthood of experts, 'to the exclusion of millions', we must 'tell stories of passion and conviction about restoring nature. We need myths we can live by. If scientists can't do that, they need to let artists and theologians, playwrights and economists, lawyers and revolutionaries tell it their own way.' Pearce denies that we should regard this as 'post-truth'. Rather, he says, 'it is perhaps post-Enlightenment, or at least a recognition that the Enlightenment was science's own founding myth.'

Pankaj Mishra pulls no punches in his analysis of why 'the Western model is broken', and why 'the West has lost the power to shape the world in its own image – as recent events make all too clear.' Mishra includes 'Ukraine and Iraq' amongst those 'events' but we might also add Libya and Syria. He asks the telling question, 'So why does it still preach the pernicious myth that every society must evolve along Western lines?' and then explodes the myth: 'All of the Western nations are caught in the lie of their pretended humanism; this means the West has no moral authority.' More recently, in the wake of the massacre of Charlie Hebdo journalists in Paris, he makes the telling point that 'we may have to retrieve the Enlightenment, as much as religion, from its fundamentalists...The advocacy of more violence and wars in the face of recurrent failure meets the definition of fanaticism rather than reason. The task for those who cherish freedom is to re-imagine it – through an ethos of criticism combined with compassion and ceaseless self-awareness – in our own irreversibly mixed and highly unequal societies and the larger interdependent world.'

Mishra's passionate appeal for the 're-imagining' of the 'Enlightenment' provides a valuable model for how we might reconcile 'stories' and 'facts', finding value, on the one hand, in inspiring and unifying narratives, and on the other, in factual understanding arising from rigorous and meticulous evidence-based inquiry. To do so we must ensure that narratives and myths do not become cast in stone, but are continually re-assessed and renewed in the light of contemporary needs. On a grander scale, in the broader sweep of history, this is akin to the process of paradigmatic change – what

Jean Gebser has described as the periodic evolutionary advances in the structure of human consciousness, or, in Richard Tarnas's terms, the 'epochal shifts in the contemporary psyche'.

The essence of Mishra's appeal for the re-imagining of narratives is captured so well in the very different language of Ibn 'Arabi in his description in the *Futuhat* of the cumulative and never-ending process of 'self-manifestation' through which one experiences successive revelations of God's nature or activity in the world – an ever-expanding creative process of renewal reaching to the furthest horizons:

For after the first such self-manifestation, then another occurs to them, with still another quality and implication unlike that of the first – even though the divine reality manifesting Itself is undoubtedly the same. After that still other divine self-manifestations follow one another, with their different implications, so that through this ongoing spiritual unveiling one comes to know that this matter has no end at which it might stop.

Although Ibn 'Arabi is referring here to the ever-expanding renewal of Divine revelation in the never-ending spiritual journeying of each unique individual, his description of the discovery of ever-new 'qualities and implications' applies equally to the absolute imperative, applicable to both individuals and communities, to re-imagine the stories that shape their understanding of the world. And it applies equally to the gathering of 'facts', for, as Ibn 'Arabi avers, 'this matter has no end at which it might stop'. Anyone who does serious research these days knows only too well how statistics, ranking systems, pie-charts, and all the other supposedly 'objective' measures of truth, are double-edged swords that can obscure and mislead as much as they can clarify and correct.

It is surely the 'ceaseless self-awareness' advocated by Mishra that must be the guiding principle, for only deep self-knowledge can support a truly transformational 'ethos of criticism' – one that can transcend the kind of 'weak-sense critical thinking' that draws on those biases, preferences, interests, perspectives and ideologies that may be largely unconscious, or at least unadmitted.

WRITING TRAVEL

James E Montgomery

There is a deep affinity between travelling and telling a story. Put in the simplest of terms, both activities require a starting-point, move through a sequence, and, as conclusion of the activity, aim at an ending, a destination. Travel is a lived experience; telling a story is an expression of lived experience. Both activities are intricate, unpredictable, sometimes dangerous, and ambiguous because they entail change, be it to the traveller, the teller or the audience. The process of narrating an account of a voyage is therefore a natural, though not a necessary, consequence of the voyage itself. Such travel accounts are informed by an instability produced by how they intersect fictively with what the traveller's society took to be (often wanted to be) factual – like the traveller on a journey, travel narratives are neither here (at home) nor there (at the destination) but somewhere in-between, engaged in movement towards or from.

Travel and story-telling both require optimism (that the conclusion-destination can and will be reached) and both have at their centre a concern with the self (and how that self relates to the world around the self). Empiricism is foundational to both, irrespective of whether the traveller belongs to a culture and society that assigns greater epistemological weight to auditory knowledge (i.e. things we have been told by others) than it does to visual knowledge (things we have seen for ourselves). It might at first blush appear that travel narratives are essentially parasitic on the activity of travel – the journey I am going to tell the story of must surely take place before I produce my account of it, but then we realise that there are accounts of imaginary journeys, accounts that mimic and replicate the narratives of actual journeys undertaken – in other words, narratives of journeys that have not (or not yet) occurred. It is the fate of many a traveller, upon returning home and telling the tale of the journey, not to be believed. For the story of the voyage to work, we have to believe that the story-teller did not make everything up, and yet at the same time we are unwilling (or unable) to believe unquestioningly in the veracity of the story-teller.

Travel writing is a particular form of the travel account. Many of the Arabic texts surveyed in this article depend on oral, spoken, narratives and incorporate oral testimony into their written strategies. They luxuriate in inhabiting the space between the oral and the written, in porous categories. Like the journeys of which they speak, many of these texts are unpredictable, unusual, unconventional, occasionally maverick, and most tend to defy simple or straightforward categorisations. Travel writings are fascinating products of the society and culture of the traveller, of the landscapes through which the traveller moved, and of the writer who was authorised by society to tell the story of that journey.

There are as many reasons why people travel as there are for telling the story of their travel. In the pre-modern world of the Islamic oikumene, Muslims and non-Muslims, Arabs and non-Arabs, went on journeys, be it to visit learned teachers, holy men, shrines, or institutions; be it as scholars to secure patronage and employment; be it as physicians and others looking for a livelihood; be it as diplomats or soldiers, prisoners of war; be it as merchants or hunters; be it as spies or couriers, part of the intelligence networks that connected the oikumene; be it as exiles, looking to escape persecution or to seek safety, or as banished and ostracised; be it as proselytisers; be it as wives, moving to new homes, be it as slaves, deprived of liberty and forced to move; be it as renunciants, withdrawing physically from the temptations of the world, or spiritually, through the inward ascent of the soul. This article does not attempt a cultural or social history of travel in the pre-modern Islamic world, but rather presents a loosely arranged survey of travel writings in Arabic, based on a single criterion of inclusion – their availability in English translation.

Desert

Travel accounts in Arabic begin in the desert. The desert is a place beyond time, without bounds, without gods, a space where the human has no meaning except in defiance, offering in its seclusion and boundlessness – sovereignty of the spirit, bodily freedom, and an almost overwhelming provocation. The oral poetry of pre-Islamic Arabia is a whirligig of movement, as poets mounted on camels plunge into scorching deserts when the sun is at its hottest, defying death by traversing trackless wastes on starless nights, solitary voyagers on a quest or riding at the head of a raiding party against enemy tribes. These poems breathe the ethos of the desert, abounding with meticulous descriptions of its fauna: camel, horse, onager, oryx, ostrich, antelope, eagle, snake and wolf.

The most famous poem in Arabic, and one of the oldest, the 'suspended' Ode of Imru' al-Qays (called a *mu'allaqa* because it is one of the seven or ten pre-Islamic poems said to have been inscribed on silk and 'suspended' from the walls of the Kaaba), begins with an interrupted journey:

No further, friends. I am crushed by the weight of tears,
memories of love, between Dakhul and Hawmal.

In the 'suspended' ode of 'Antara ibn Shaddad, pre-Islamic Arabia's legendary warrior, composed circa 600 AD, we find a classic narrative formulation of the desert voyage. 'Antara's qasida is driven by a weird energy as the poet pursues his quest for self-realisation through death, a death denied him by Death, reluctant to relinquish such a favourite servant. In this section of the poem, he wonders whether he can reach the woman who has been denied him by her family, mounted on the back of a mighty she-camel described in a series of brilliant, if grotesque, images:

Can I reach her on a shadani camel,
her teats snipped, cursed to be dry?
She's a high-stepper, tail still twitching
after a long night's ride,
feet like mallets as though
I were smashing stones and hills
on the back of a dock-ear pinch-toe
ostrich dashing to his flock
as Yemenis rush to a stuttering stranger,
sprinting to his nest in Dhu l-'Ushayrah,
his crown like a cover draped
over bier posts held high,
tiny head and thin neck,
a dock-eared slave wrapped in furs.
She drinks at Duhrudan and sprints
from Daylam's wells with a mad stare,

swaggering to and fro, groaning
as if fleeing a cat strapped
to her right flank against whose claw
and fang she wheels in a rage.
At the ride's end, she looms, massive
as a fortress, kneeling at the well of Rida',
long legs like hoarse bass-horns,
sweat oozing from her neck like syrup
or the tar blacksmiths boil for pots –
an angry, noble tail-switcher,
bulky, big as a bite-scarred stud.

Sea-faring is perhaps the last form of travel we would expect to encounter in a body of poetry as dominated by the desert landscape as the pre-Islamic corpus. Yet this is exactly what we have in a qasida by Bishr ibn Abi Khazim of the tribe of Asad, a contemporary of Prophet Muhammad:

I sailed to sea on a high-humped, heavily laden ship,
stern kowtowing to the winds, timbers caulked –
compact, sturdy boards secured with oakum and pegs.
When her captain took her out to sea, I pondered
my faults, as the waves dashed against our fleet
of wood, lying low on the water, timbers tightly fitted.
Onboard, we sat with heads bent low, like camels
refusing to drink. The ships' cargo was myrtle, spices,
black musk, weapons. Finally, the wind turned in our favour
and the prows, gleaming-black, skimmed the briny deep.

Bishr, the poet of the desert, concludes a magnificently boastful poem with a tale of his finest achievement – surviving a terrifying voyage by sea.

'The Straight Road' (Q. Fatiha 1:6)

Verses 5–9 of Qur'an 16 (Nahl) teach us, in the context of an enumeration of God's acts as Creator, that God provided man with animals for him to domesticate and beasts of burden for him to travel the earth more easily:

> Livestock – He created them for you; they have warmth, and benefits; you eat of them [5]; ... They carry your burdens to a land which you cannot reach without misery to yourselves, because your Lord is Clement and Merciful [7]; horses, mules and asses, for you to ride ... [8]; It is for God to set the path, and some stray from it; had He wished, He would have guided you all [9].

But note that we are also instructed in verse 9 that it is God who guides man aright and who leads him astray: God's Revelation is itself a path which He determines. In fact, God's religion is revealed in the Qur'an as a form of travelling. The Qur'an is a revelation which was sent down from heaven to earth; God refers to Islam as 'the straight road' and as movement 'in the path of God.' He repeatedly reminds mankind that they will *return* to Him, that His religion is right guidance, and that failure to follow it is to stray from the right way. Muhammad is the man sent with His Message, His Rasul. And the verses of the Qur'an are signs for us to be guided by.

We are so familiar with the notion of 'following a religion' that we might be inclined to consider these formulations dead metaphors. We would, I think, be wrong to do so. Even the semantic range of the word Islam in the Qur'an involves motion. This becomes evident when we look at phrases such as *man aslama wajhahu* (Q. Baqara 2:112), he who submits or surrenders his face, by turning it in God's direction. Islam, submission to God, is manifested through *directing* our face to Him. The Arabic word for divinely revealed law, shari'a, is etymologically connected with *shar'*, a track which leads to a watering-hole. Here is its sole occurrence in the Qur'an (Q. Jathiya 45:18-20):

> Then We placed you on a track (shari'a) in the matter, so follow it and do not follow the desires of those who do not know [18]; ... this is clear sight for the people, a right guidance and a mercy for a folk who are certain.

The message of the Qur'an is therefore: follow God's path. There were various ways in which believers could show that they were following God's path, most significantly the Hajj, the pilgrimage to Mecca. The Hajj as a religious duty lies at the very heart of Islam. Throughout Islam's histories, the Hajj has represented the sacral organisation of space, providing opportunities for believers to reach the spiritual centre of the realm of Islam and come close to God, and for scholars to share and acquire knowledge and ideas. Pilgrim routes and trade routes were often indistinguishable, and the sacred month each year witnessed (and continues to witness) a mass congregation of the faithful as they return to the House of God, the Kaaba, at the heart of the Sacred Precinct, in Mecca.

Movement, thus, is central to Classical Islam's vision of itself as the religion and civilisation of the Qur'an. The foundation of the Islamic community is held to be an act of movement: the Hijra, the emigration of the Prophet Muhammad and the first Muslims from Mecca to the settlement of Yathrib to the north, a city now known as Medina (that is, the *City* of the Prophet). The year of the Hijra (622 AD) is the point at which the Muslim calendar begins. Emigration led eventually to return, when a decade later in the year 632 Prophet Muhammad was powerful enough to return to Mecca to perform the Pilgrimage.

The Hijra did not come to an end with the conquest and return to Mecca, but became one of the principal concepts which informed the universalising mission of the Muslims in a process whereby the religion of the Arabs of the Peninsula became the religion of mankind. As such hijra was virtually synonymous with jihad, complete devotion of the self in the path of God. Hijra, exodus, in the early period means mobilisation, and the conquests of the first two centuries are to be considered among its most convincing manifestations. Within a period of eighty years, the Muslims had conquered territories far in excess of the Roman Empire. Syria was conquered by 640, Iraq and central and western Persia, as well as Egypt, by 642. During the Umayyad caliphate (661-750) the Arab conquerors had reached as far as Tours in France where in 732 they were defeated by the Frankish ruler Charles Martel, and whence they retreated to consolidate their rule in those areas of the Iberian peninsula that came to be known as al-Andalus. The north-eastern frontiers of the caliphate remained a war-zone until its boundaries were fixed in 751 when Muslim and Chinese forces met in the Battle of Talas beyond the Jaxartes River (the Syr Darya) in Central Asia. Fortune favoured the Muslim army but it did not press home its victory, content to remain in possession of most of the Iranian world.

The ideological and narratological paradigm for the conquests was furnished by the expeditions led by Muhammad. The accounts of these expeditions were gathered together in a subgenre of the hadith, and were compiled by Ma'mar ibn Rashid (d. 770) as an early biography of Muhammad. Significantly, this text is not dominated exclusively by military victories and exploits, though they do proliferate throughout the work.

According to Sean Antony, a *maghzah* (the Arabic singular of the plural *maghazi* that he renders as 'expeditions'):

> is ... a place where any memorable event transpired and, by extension, the *maghazi* genre distills all the events and stories of sacred history that left their mark on the collective memory of Muhammad's community of believers.

Nostalgic, cornucopian, numinous, and triumphalist, Ma'mar's *Expeditions* surveys the marvel of Islam's ascendance as the divinely mandated expression of imperial civilisation.

Islam's classical formulations regularly defined it as movement and organised many of its primary ideas in terms of movement. The hadith, the body of sayings and deeds of the Prophet, were gathered together in the ninth century and came to be known as the Sunna, properly *Sunnat Rasul Allah*, the Way of the Messenger of God. With time, this Sunna became one of the two defining components of the shari'a, the divinely revealed path of the law, the other being the Qur'an.

After a period of development and standardisation, the various approaches in Islamic legal thinking to understanding the legislative and practical relationship between Qur'an and Sunna came to be known as the *madhahib*, literally 'the ways of going, moving or proceeding.' The sources often refer to a particular Muslim or group of Muslims as 'going to' a belief which they held, or a theological position which they defended. Within the developed tradition of Sufism, the various articulations are known as *tariqas*, roads. The stations of progression can be known as *mawaqif*, stopping points, or as *rutab*, stages or ranks, the terminology used, for example, by the Syrian Sufi scholar and poet 'A'isha al-Ba'uniyya (d. 1517) in her luminous synopsis *The Principles of Sufism*, an anthology of pious apophthegms clustered around her notion of Sufism as a tree with four roots: repentance, sincerity, remembrance, and love.

Islam, thus, in its classical formulations, reminds us that a belief is not merely an idea to which we give assent but is also a way of acting, a procedure which we must follow.

Seek Knowledge

Movement was central to the acquisition of knowledge. An important saying of Prophet Muhammad exhorts the believer to seek knowledge, a saying that became a powerful motivation for the movement of scholars across the Islamic domains in their thirst to acquire knowledge, principally, though not exclusively, of the sayings and deeds of the Prophet. Let us briefly consider the account of the early life of the Qur'anic scholar, exegete, and legal thinker al-Tabari (d. 923):

> My father, Tabari reminisced, had a dream concerning me. He saw me standing before the Prophet with a bag filled with stones, and I was spreading some of them in front of him. A dream interpreter told my father that the dream signified that I would be a good Muslim as an adult and a strong defender of the religious law of the Prophet. As a consequence, my father was ready to support my quest for knowledge when I was still a small boy.

From his birthplace in Tabaristan, his first port of call was the city of Rayy (Rey, now a suburb of greater Tehran), when he was twelve years of age, and then Baghdad, at the age of seventeen. He pursued his studies in Basra, Kufa and Wasit. In his late twenties, Tabari visited Syria, Palestine and Egypt to complete his studies and probably also to perform the Pilgrimage, where he would have enjoyed a protracted scholarly sojourn in both Mecca and Medina. His education and religious formation complete, he returned to Baghdad, 'to devote himself entirely to teaching and publication.'

Al-Tabari's career is fairly typical of how scholars sought to acquire religious learning and acceptance in the scholarly community. Accounts of how the scholar in search of hadith, seeking to link himself to a chain (*isnad*) of authorities that would securely link him with the past and guarantee the continuation of his participation in this past into the future, are glowing, and fantastical, narratives of dedication, renunciation, hardship, and determination: there are no rigours that the hadith-scholar was not prepared to endure, in order to traverse the community in his quest to learn from, and be accredited by, the great scholars and masters of hadith.

The Great Unknown

A destination both familiar and unfamiliar for Muslim travellers is the Afterlife: familiar because it is described in the Qur'an, unfamiliar to all but the dead. In the ninth century, al-Muhasibi (d. 857), a hadith expert, wrote a 'guidebook' to Heaven for the pious: *The Book of Imagination (Kitab al-Tawahhum)*. It is a spiritual exercise in which the reader is exhorted to imagine what it will be like to be called before God on Judgement Day, to picture the perils of Judgement, the rewards of paradise and the torments of Hell. Al-Muhasibi's book takes the believer on a spiritual tour of the terrors of uncertainty as he is exhorted to imagine crossing the Bridge and then, once admitted into the company of the Elect, seeing with bliss the panoramas of beauty which unfold to the believer rewarded for his good conduct. Page after page of heavenly delights ensue.

It is no surprise that one of the hadith folk should have written such a work: by reading al-Muhasibi's *Book of Imagination* the believer is imitating the practice of the Prophet, for Muhammad, mounted on a fabulous beast called Buraq, is said to have been taken on a journey from Mecca to Jerusalem, a journey known as the *isra'*, 'the night voyage'. From there Muhammad climbed through the seven heavens into the very presence of God, a journey known as the Mi'raj, the celestial ascension, according to some authorities via a ladder, one of the meanings of *mi'raj* in Arabic, or according to others mounted on Buraq. A large number of narratives and poems of the event, inspired by verse 1 of Qur'an 17 (Isra'), were written in Arabic and Persian, and the subject proved especially popular for miniature paintings.

Such Afterlife texts sought to capture in words the delights of Paradise, as well as the abysmal horrors of eternal damnation. In the process of seeking to give voice to what was both indescribable and beyond the parameters of human experience, they fashioned and indulged in a rhetoric of sensory overload. These rhetorical excesses were mercilessly parodied by a remarkable Syrian scholar, poet, epistolographer, and vegan, Abul-'Ala' al-Ma'arri (d. 1057) in one of the most dazzling and imaginative, yet baffling, tours-de-force of Arabic letters: *The Epistle of Forgiveness (Risalat al-Ghufran)*.

Al-Ma'arri tells us how he has received a letter from an ageing grammarian and hadith scholar, Ibn al-Qarih, expressed as a request to secure Ma'arri's interest in introducing him to the scholarly community of Ma'arra, and exonerating himself from accusations of ingratitude to a family that had previously given him patronage. Such letters of introduction would have been commonplace compositions, given that one of the main reasons for the movement of scholars around the Islamic realms was in order to secure patronage. Something about Ibn al-Qarih's letter annoyed al-Ma'arri to the point that he composed one of the strangest ever epistolary replies – a two-part letter, in the first section of which al-Ma'arri imagines Ibn al-Qarih in Paradise, and in the second part of which he masquerades a character assassination of Ibn al-Qarih as an erudite disquisition on hypocrisy, heresy, sins, pilgrimages and repentance.

In the first part of the *Epistle*, al-Ma'arri describes how Ibn al-Qarih dreams that he has died and is at the gates of heaven, composing verses of commonplace panegyric in order to ingratiate himself with the angels, all to no avail. It is only with the intercession of the Prophet who has found Ibn al-Qarih's name in the register of repentance that he can be carried across the Bridging Path, on the back of a servant-girl. Once in Heaven, Ibn al-Qarih seeks out the company of other renowned grammarians and, finally, has the chance to interview the mighty pre-Islamic poets about aspects of their verses that had fuelled so many controversies across the centuries. Few poets can be bothered with the scholar's pedantry, however, and many have lost all recollection of the trivialities of their mundane existence.

Throughout the book, al-Ma'arri deploys the excessive rhetoric of sensory overload so typical of Paradise narratives to a devastating and destabilising effect. The reader is left wondering what al-Ma'arri's own notions of the afterlife might be.

A century ago, Miguel Asín Palacios, scholar of Islam and Roman Catholic priest, published his *La Escatología musulmana en la Divina Comedia* (1919), a work that appeared in English in 1926 as *Islam and the Divine Comedy*, abridged and translated by Harold L. Sutherland. Asín Palacios argued that Dante imitated Islamic narratives of Muhammad's night journey and celestial ascension. The *Epistle of Forgiveness* was one of the texts included in his erudite survey.

The Book of Muhammad's Ladder (*Liber Scale Machometi*), has not survived in its original Arabic, but exists in Latin, in two manuscripts, and in an old French version. It was one of a series of translations of Arabic and Hebrew works commissioned by Alfonso of Castille (r. 1252-1284). The work tells us that the Arabic was rendered into Spanish by Abraham, a Jewish physician (Ibrahim al-Hakim), at the behest of the King. The Spanish version was then rendered into Latin, again at the King's behest, by Bonaventure of Sienna, royal notary and amanuensis. Abraham was one of five Jews active at the court of Alfonso, during the years 1260-1280, while Bonaventure was a Tuscan, one of a number of Italians maintained by the King in his employ.

Unfortunately, both the Arabic original of the *Liber* and its Castilian version have been lost. It is clear from even a cursory reading of the *Liber* in Latin that the Arabic original was a compound work, an amalgamation of several accounts of Muhammad's ascension through the heavens available in the classical period. What we have then is a composite text in Arabic, translated into Castilian by a Spanish Jew, and then re-translated into Latin by an Italian notary, which was further rendered at a later stage into old French.

Did the *Liber* inspire Dante Alighieri to compose the *Divine Comedy*? Prior to the publication in 1949 of the Latin and Old French versions of the *Liber*, the scholarly world was divided into those who assented to the Islamic sources of Dante, and those who proclaimed dissent, principally Europeanists outraged by the notion that one of their crowning (Christian) masterpieces might be in any way indebted to the Islamic heritage. It is now clear from what we know of the *Liber* that the extreme formulations of either thesis are untenable, though we are left to ponder the implications of whether this little book travelled to Florence and provoked Dante.

Espionage?

Ibn Jubayr (d. 1217), a native of Valencia, performed the pilgrimage three times in the course of his life. Throughout his career he enjoyed close connections with the Berber Almohad Court: his first appointment was as secretary to the Almohad governor of Ceuta, Abu Sa'id 'Uthman, son of the caliph 'Abd al-Mu'min (r. 1130-63), and he later formed part of the entourage of advisers to caliph Abu Yusuf Ya'qub al-Mansur (r. 1184-99).

Ibn Jubayr's second visit to Mecca was intended to thank God for Saladin's re-conquest of Jerusalem in 1187, whilst his third followed on the death of his wife in 1206/7. We do not know exactly why Ibn Jubayr decided to perform his first pilgrimage. A later account explains it as an act of atonement: the governor of Ceuta is said to have compelled him to drink seven beakers of wine. Be that as it may, the first pilgrimage formed the substance of the treatise for which Ibn Jubayr became famous: his *Rihla* ('Travelogue').

The work includes a list of the scholars in the East with whom Ibn Jubayr studied, attesting to how his pilgrimage fulfilled the injunction of the 'Seek Knowledge' hadith. The eloquent descriptions of Mecca and the pilgrimage ceremonies were intended through their author's rhetorical surfeits to encourage other members of the Almohad caliphate to perform Hajj, thus contributing to the controversy raging in the Islamic West about whether the Hajj was compulsory or not.

Ibn Jubayr's text is also informed by political propaganda, confirming caliph al-Mansur's claim to universal rule and his projected return to Damascus, the capital abandoned by the Umayyad dynasty in 749–50 when they fled to the Iberian Peninsula. It was also, I think, a work of espionage. Ibn Jubayr's description of Norman Sicily, of Norman ports and resources, of the fragility of Norman power in the island, suggests that at least this part of the work originated in an information gathering exercise, a preliminary to an invasion of the island by the mighty Almohad fleet.

Parody

A scintillating and subversive exploration of the 'Seek Knowledge' imperative, written in the tradition of the 'travelogue' (*rihla*), is the nineteenth century work *Leg over Leg* by Ahmad Faris al-Shidyaq (d. 1887). In this rambling and rambunctious book, al-Shidyaq describes how his alter-ego 'the Fariyaq' roves through the world of the Ottoman Mediterranean, from his native Lebanon, to Egypt, Malta and North Africa, and includes accounts of his visit to England and France. The full title of the work is eloquent testimony to its generic contiguity with both the voyages of the hadith scholars in search of knowledge, and the travelogue: *Leg over Leg, or: The Turtle in the Tree Concerning the Fariyaq, What Manner of Creature Might He Be. Otherwise entitled: Days, Months, and Years Spent in Critical Examination of the Arabs and their Non-Arab Peers.*

Empire and Patronage

Scientist, mathematician, astronomer, astrologer, historian, controversialist, and diplomat, Abu Rayhan al-Biruni was a true polymath: he is even said to have performed a caesarean section. Born in 973 in Khwarazm, modern Uzbekistan, he learned Arabic and Persian and was given a thorough grounding in the Islamic sciences, i.e. Qur'an, grammar, jurisprudence and theology; and in the non-Arab sciences: astronomy, mathematics, and medicine, predominantly in the Greek tradition.

Al-Biruni's life is marked by the quest for patronage, and he held various positions at the scintillating but tumultuous courts east of the Caspian. Of his political career he wryly remarked: 'I was driven into worldly affairs and became the envy of fools, the pity of the wise.' His political fortunes took a turn for the worse in 1017 when he secured the worst form of patronage imaginable: a position from which he was not free to seek release. An Afghan warlord, Mahmud of Ghazna demanded that the ruler of Kath in Khwarazm, al-Biruni's patron, transfer his entire court, lock, stock and barrel, to Ghazna. The Khwarazmian dynasty was toppled.

Al-Biruni's life in the service of Mahmud of Ghazna from 1017 to 1030 is obscure. He was probably detained against his will. A later history notes that he incurred Mahmud's displeasure for a horoscope he had cast as court astrologer. He accompanied Mahmud's raids on northern India, in present-day Pakistan. Mahmud took many Brahmins as prisoners of war. These Brahmins became al-Biruni's authorities for his study of India and Indian religion. With his (albeit limited) knowledge of Sanskrit, al-Biruni translated into Arabic the Yoga-Sutras of Patançali. His magnum opus, known today as *The Book of India* (*Kitab al-Hind*), is a work in 80 chapters which include discussions of the Hindu concept of God and His creation, causality and the soul, reincarnation, eschatology, religious and civil law, ritual and worship, Sanskrit grammar and Indian poetic meters, geography, astrology and astronomy.

The Book of India may not strictly be a travel book as such, and al-Biruni may not have penetrated further south into the sub-continent than the Punjab, but it is an impressively sustained work of intellectual exploration, a remarkable piece of ethnography, an ambitious and bold text unlike few others I know.

Tales of Mystery and Exploration

The story of Moses and his mysterious companion in verses 60-82 of Qur'an 18 (*Kahf*), provides a model for exploration and discovery, even though the Qur'anic narrative of this set of events seems to deny the value and the worth of exploration and discovery. Moses and his servant discover the water of life and encounter there one of God's pious servants. Moses asks his permission to accompany him on his journeys and is only allowed to do so on condition that he does not question the mysterious stranger about the reasons for his actions. Three baffling and morally inscrutable actions ensue: the scuttling of a ship, the killing of a boy and the rebuilding of a wall. On each occasion Moses breaks his promise and, when the stranger ventures to explain his actions, he rebukes Moses for his lack of self-control and acceptance.

This Qur'anic narrative is highly elliptical and allusive: it is not intended to be easily understood but rather to capture the impenetrable mysteriousness of God's unfolding of His designs for mankind. As a model for exploration, the narrative is hardly, at first blush, a powerful endorsement of the kind of exploration which in European civilisations is so closely associated with discovery. Discovery in the European context is often portrayed as a successful human achievement (think of Columbus and 1492), while the Qur'an allocates all knowledge and discovery to God and His elusive servant but it does not do so in order to prevent mankind from inquiring and exploring. Rather, it counsels recognition of the likelihood of failure. This exhortation to acceptance and the consolations of acceptance for man's limited powers of discovery proved strong incentives for several early Abbasid Caliphs.

In 832, caliph al-Ma'amun visited the pyramids of Egypt. He would have been familiar with several explanations for the construction of the Pyramids: that they were Joseph's grain silos; that they were the towers which, according to the Qur'an (Ghafir 40:36-37), Pharaoh had built in order to climb to the heavens and gaze on the God of Moses; or that they were the temples of Hermes the Egyptian, the father of alchemy and astrology, built by him to protect his writings and secrets from the Flood with which God drowned the world of Noah.

The early 'Abbasid caliphs were keen on alchemy and astrology. For example, the Round City of Baghdad was constructed by al-Mansur in 762, upon the casting of a favourable horoscope, and alchemy was sponsored by the caliphs in the hope of ensuring a steady supply of gold for their building projects and wars. Al-Ma'amun was a devotee of esoteric knowledge. Many esoteric texts in Arabic describe how an initiate has the good fortune to discover a cache of manuscripts and books hidden under the altar of a temple or the statue of a god. Al-Ma'amun may have hoped for this same piece of good fortune. He instructed a sage to decipher the Egyptian hieroglyphs, so that he could add their wisdom to that of the Greeks, Persians and Indians which his scholars were busily translating into Arabic.

The sage collated as many inscriptions as he could find but could only translate the Greek and the Coptic. He conjectured that the hieroglyphs were of astrological significance, formed after the shapes of the stars and the planets.

The sage's conclusion seems to have whetted al-Ma'amun's appetite and he decided to break into the Great Pyramid of Cheops. First his soldiers battered it with a catapult, but that did not work. Then they decided to work on a blocked tunnel in the north face of the pyramid. They forced open the blockage with fire, having used vinegar to loosen the mortar of the bricks. They followed the tunnel deeper into the pyramid, and discovered a marble box inside, containing nothing but decayed human remains. At that point al-Ma'amun called an end to the expedition.

The Caliph had reached Pharaoh's burial chamber but it had already been plundered and he came away empty handed. He may have been disappointed but he would surely have been comforted by the realisation that he was conforming with the parallel of Moses in the Qur'an in not delving too deeply into what God wished to keep hidden.

If the Caliph al-Ma'amun was obsessed with esotericism, his next but one successor al-Wathiq (r. 842–847) was a chiliast. This caliph was not interested in secret knowledge as much as in trying to ascertain whether the end of the world and the collapse of civilisation was nigh. To do this, he decided to find out the status of the people of Yajuj wa-Majuj, Gog and Magog, whose onslaught the Qur'an says will herald the coming of the End Time.

In verses 83-98 of Qur'an 18 (Kahf), we are told the tale of a ruler called Dhu al-Qarnayn, The Lord of the Two Horns. Many Muslim scholars identified him as Alexander the Great, though equally he seems to be related to the horned Moses (as sculpted, for example, by Michelangelo). Made powerful by God, he travels to the setting of the sun, and discovers a people there, whom he treats in accordance with God's law. He then travels to the rising sun where he encounters a second race who have no shelter from the glare of the sun. He next travels to a place vaguely referred to as 'between the two barriers' where he encounters a race of people who 'almost do not understand speech' (93). This people do manage to communicate, however, and they enlist Dhu al-Qarnayn's aid against Gog and Magog. He builds a wall made of iron bricks, encased in molten brass, impenetrable by man. Dhu al-Qarnayn notes that the wall will be destroyed when the End Time comes and God describes how on that day, Gog and Magog will become His army.

The Caliph has a dream in which Dhu al-Qarnayn's wall has been breached. Salim the Translator is nominated as the man for the mission 'because he speaks thirty languages.' He is given a troop of fifty warriors, is handsomely remunerated, and they are equipped with the best weapons and with two hundred mules to carry provisions. This is an elite force of crack troops for a dangerous mission. They set off from Samarra on their journey through the Kingdom of the Khazars. Salim narrates his account to the Spy Master General and Director of the Imperial Postal Service, Ibn Khurradadhbih (d. 912), who recorded the story in his *Treatise on the Highways and the Kingdoms*. Salim describes the construction of the barrier wall and its gates in minute detail. He even presses his ear to the iron and seems to hear a tumult of cries and shrieks on the other side. He informs Ibn Khurradadhbih that when he returned to Samarra, he told the caliph his tale and showed him the iron which he had scraped from the wall.

Salim was not an armchair traveller. Neither was al-Masudi (d. 956) who travelled around the Caspian Sea in an attempt to determine its riverine topography, nor was al-Muqaddasi (d. c. 991) who declares that he could not compose his geography without first travelling throughout the lands of Islam, checking distances, determining the value of taxes, tasting water, assessing the air quality, and conversing with the locals.

Merchantly Marvels

Pilgrimage and trade were often inseparable. Trade and dissemination of the faith were often inseparable too. More Muslims presumably travelled for mercantile than they did for religious reasons, though the merchants have left behind few textual records. But the distinction between travel for trade and travel for religion is illusory: the prominence in the Qur'an of an ethical vocabulary of a mercantile provenance and the tradition that Muhammad was himself a merchant made for a cultural and intellectual ambience in which trade could be considered an integral expression of faith.

Probably more than any other class of Muslim traveller, merchants confronted the unknown but their experiences remain largely unknown to us because they were not regularly written down but passed on by word of mouth. However, when they were recorded in writing, they are fascinating.

In 921 the Caliph al-Muqtadir sent an embassy from Baghdad to the King of the Volga Bulgharians. One of the participants on this embassy, Ibn Fadlan, wrote an account that is the earliest extant, sustained first-person prose narrative in Arabic. On the journey from Baghdad across modern Iran and north via the eastern Caspian shoreline through the Turkish nomads past the Ust-Yurt plateau to the encampment of the King of the Bulgharians on the confluence of the Volga and Kama rivers, Ibn Fadlan and the embassy join a caravan of massive size (some 5,000 travellers) which is held hostage by a solitary Turk. The Turk demands a ransom of bread and deigns to allow the caravan to pass on its way. Mercantile narratives tend to blur the familiar with the marvellous, the known with the unknown: and some have seen the size of this caravan as an exaggerated marvel. Of course, the fabulous and the fantastic find a place in all Arabic geographical writings: they are not the exclusive monopoly of merchants.

Another marvel, though it is not a marvel that Ibn Fadlan designates as marvellous in his eyes, is the detail that the king's retinue included a tailor from Baghdad. During the period he was held hostage by the King of the Bulgharians, Ibn Fadlan encountered this tailor and they have a conversation about the exigencies and practicalities of performing the ritual prayer during the white nights of northern Europe (the rites, dependent on the position of the sun and the hours of daylight and darkness, are thrown into complete disarray so far north).

The *Accounts of China and India* is a composite work, incorporating an apparently authentic, anonymous, compilation of oral accounts from 851, supplemented by material written by the seafarer, Abu Zayd al-Sirafi (d. 915/16). The topography of the text stretches from Somalia to the eastern shores of China and Korea and it heralds the appearance of an Arabic human, as opposed to an imperial or astronomical, geography, a human geography that was to achieve its apogee in al-Mas'udi's *Meadows of Gold*. Al-Sirafi's *Accounts* and comparable works of mercantile travel were clearly intended to be a sort of 'Rough Guide' for merchants, equipping them with basic knowledge of customs, laws, foodstuffs and routes.

The garrulous sailor Buzurg ibn Shahriyar, resident of Ramhormuz in the Persian Gulf, composed in 985 a curious work known as *The Wonders of India*, teeming with tall stories and sailors' yarns. It has little, however, to do with India, and most of its action seems to belong to trade routes further east. The heroes of these tales, purportedly the experiences of a certain Captain

'Allama, are sailors, and shipwrecks occur on every other page. After one shipwreck, Captain 'Allama tells Buzurg how in a mangrove swamp, where the ground was littered with the trunks of ancient trees, piled on top of one another, he chose a fine tree-trunk to serve as a mast for his ship, straight, supple, and of the right thickness. Taking a saw to cut off some fifty cubits, his first incision caused the tree to move and crawl away – it was a snake.

Snakes mistaken for tree-trunks are a stock feature of Arabic travel narratives and signal that the author and his audience, as well as the protagonists of the anecdote, were on the edges of the known world. Ibn Fadlan encounters a snake mistaken for a tree in the realm of the King of the Bulgharians.

But what about Buzurg's tale of the female elephant trained to do the shopping, making its purchases with cowries and bartering with the grocer? Upon the elephant's return, we learn, it is beaten if the shop-keeper has cheated it, whereat the elephant goes back to the grocer, and turns the shop upside down, until it has been given what is missing or gets the cowries back. A researcher at Tokyo University conducted a study that concluded that Asian elephants can perform addition using single digits. One thirty-year-old female elephant had an 87 per cent success rate in the tests.

One of the commonest of all maritime tales is of the island that turns out to be a sea-monster. It occurs in *The Accounts of China and India*, the Voyages of Sindbad the Sailor and in many other traditions, from fourth century Greek Bible commentaries to the Voyages of St Brendan the Navigator. Buzurg's version involves a giant turtle sleeping on the surface of the sea.

Another common mishap was capture at the hands of a giant (usually a cannibal), sometimes even by a tribe of giants. One of my favourites is the Old Man of the Sea who fastens himself on to the back of an unfortunate sailor. And lest anyone think that these marvels somehow transgress the ideologies of travel outlined thus far, consider the case of al-Sindbad the Sailor. On one voyage, Sindbad becomes a cannibal, having been buried alive with a group of merchants, but generally the scope of the imagination of these tales is, as with similar works in Arabic such as *One Hundred and One Nights*, disappointing and predictable. This is doubtless because the version as we have it is largely the work of a fifteenth century Cairene scribe who sought to turn it into a morality play, warning Muslims against greed and cupidity, and promoting the values of the traditional Islamic sciences as opposed to the natural sciences. In other words, he has constrained these voyages within the 'seek knowledge' paradigm.

The Perils of Travel

The majority of the travel writing surveyed thus far is basically optimistic about both benefits and hazards of the voyage. However, there exists in Arabic a body of writings left by those who hated travel or who wanted to subvert the cultural hegemony of travel as an Islamic ideology.

By the end of the ninth and the start of the tenth century, most poets earned their living through the composition of praise poems. These poems had acquired a familiar pattern. Central to the pattern was a passage where the poet (almost always an urbanite) describes how, in the manner of the pre-Islamic heroes, he had braved terrifying wildernesses and crossed frightful deserts to reach his patron. This imaginary journey had become a poetic reality.

In a long poem, Ibn al-Rumi (d. 896) described how he hated travelling and was terrified of it, inveighing against its misfortunes, and the risk to life and limb it involved. His poem tells of how he once went on a rain-soaked journey, wading through mud like a drunkard, spending the night in a dilapidated inn under a leaking roof. Travelling by land in the wind and the rain may be bad, Ibn al-Rumi's poem tells us, but it pales into insignificance when compared with travelling by sea and the risks of shipwreck and drowning.

Ibn al-Rumi declares that he has exhausted himself by thinking up novel lines of poetry rather than by braving the tiresome dangers of a heroic journey. He then throws himself upon the mercy of his noble patron. To be sure, the irony is that the unknown into which the poet refuses to travel is not geographical, but fiscal – i.e. whether his patron, his known destination, will reward him for the cultural and social risk he has taken – Ibn al-Rumi still hoped to be paid for his refusal to travel! We do not know whether he was successful or not.

Al-Jahiz (d. 868/9), an older contemporary of Ibn al-Rumi, was a theologian who was also a very acute observer of life in Baghdad and Basra. By the time he came to write the *Book of Misers* some time during the 850s-870s, the hadith movement, the movement to collect the sayings and deeds of Prophet Muhammad, was well underway. As we saw earlier, the hadith scholars liked to celebrate their peregrinatory exploits in heroic tales of endurance and devotion to the amassing of knowledge, even on occasion to the point of death through starvation. It is not uncommon to read of student travellers selling their clothes in order to survive and living in conditions of unimaginable frugality, whilst they await deliverance from God, say in the form of a caravan perhaps bringing some money from home.

Al-Jahiz's *Book of Misers* parodied the lifestyles of the hadith movement, their techniques of legal reasoning and misuses of Arabic to justify such parsimoniousness. In one of his bravura caricatures of misers, al-Jahiz created out of an individual named Khalid ibn Yazid a figure to whom he gave the name Khalawayh the Mendicant. As Khalid, the pious miser, this character delivers a death-bed testament to his son and heir, berates and abuses him for not living up to his high standards of morality; as Khalawayh the Mendicant, he boasts to his son of his high status in the criminal underworld. The humour arises out of the confusing of these different registers: pious death-bed farewell, moral exhortation to unimaginable stinginess, and the obscure argot of the criminal.

The genius of al-Jahiz's parody is to latch on to the fear of the shame of begging which the narratives of the hadith-folk exhibit (to beg would be to imply that you did not put enough reliance on God to look after you) and to apply their moral values to the life of an out and out scoundrel. Al-Jahiz transforms Khalid into the leader of the Banu Sasan, the criminal classes who referred to themselves ironically as the Sons of the Persian monarch Sasan. Was Khalid a real person? We do not know. Al-Jahiz introduces him as if he were. As Khalawayh, his travels are obviously fabulous and imaginary but entirely plausible.

The uses and abuses of rhetoric to persuade and deceive an audience by a peripatetic preacher are a central feature of another type of virtuosic composition in Arabic: the *Maqamat*.

The *Maqamat* of al-Hariri (d. 1122), written in an Arabic of the highest quality and utmost complexity, enjoyed enormous popularity. The basic point of departure of these virtuoso exercises is almost always the same: the hero Abu Zayd al-Saruji, a man in command of the most bewitching Arabic, has assumed a false identity; the narrator al-Harith b. Hammam is part of the audience and like them is duped by the hero's assumed identity and his linguistic fireworks; the plot always hinges on a confidence trick of some sort; it is foiled, and the hero's identity is revealed – precisely because of his linguistic virtuosity.

In the first of al-Hariri's *Maqamat*, hero and narrator meet for the first time when al-Harith arrives in Yemen, in a state of abject poverty. This singles him out as a pious student on a journey in the quest for knowledge.

He meets a crowd gathered around a preacher fulminating against self-indulgence, exhorting the Muslims to repent from their sybaritic habits. Al-Harith, bewitched by the power of the preacher's words, follows him to a cave, desirous to learn who he is and perhaps even to derive some knowledge from him. When he finds the preacher scoffing a lavish banquet and washing it down with wine, al-Harith piously and pompously upbraids the preacher, who is enraged at his cover being blown. When the preacher's anger abates, he invites al-Harith to partake of his meal but al-Harith decides to leave, in a state of stupefaction at uncovering the truth behind the preacher. Al-Hariri thus leaves open the question of whether al-Harith has in fact acquired any knowledge from Abu Zayd.

These impostures take place all over the central Muslim world (Yemen, Iraq, Egypt, Azerbaijan, to name but a few) but travel to and from each destination is not really a focus of attention. The unfolding of the plot may be unknown to the characters but it is familiar to us and we relish listening to a drama unfold in which the Arabic language – the real hero of the performances – seems to be put on trial. These compositions subvert cultural equivalences, between Islam and its ideology of travel, and between the Qur'an and the truth-value of its privileged language, Arabic, but because normal moral order seems to be restored in the end they ostensibly affirm the rightness of these equivalences. Like travellers on a journey, however, we the audience have been given to taste the fruit of the tree of knowledge, and nothing can ever remain quite so simple.

Travel as (After)Life

In the eras in which the texts of my survey originated, many Muslims travelled in order to be Muslim. When they moved through the realms of Islam, they were conscious of being Muslim, despite the dangers they may have been exposed to on the pilgrimage, from bandits or shipwreck for example. When they ventured into the unknown, they became even more conscious of being Muslim and often relied on the Qur'an to orient their experiences of the unfamiliar. In death, they would be free from the temptations of this world and languish in Paradise. And yet despite these certainties of identity, travel writing in Arabic is like travel itself: a process that is inherently ambiguous, one which often destabilises the individual's taken-for-granted certainties. We can thus say, with some confidence even, that travel writing is a highly culture-specific type of writing that is also universal, for in these respects travel writings in Arabic resemble travel writings produced in Europe.

The North African Ibn Battuta (d. 1377) is reputed to have covered more than 73,000 miles between the years of 1325–1349 and 1353–1355, visiting some forty-four countries in the process. It is clear that he was skilled neither as a scholar nor an author, and so upon his return in 1356 the Sultan of Morocco commissioned Ibn Juzayy, an Andalusi scholar, to compose a travelogue (*rihla*) in which Ibn Battuta's experiences, as well as his observations about the Islamic world of his day, would be recorded.

Most modern scholars are extremely sceptical about Ibn Battuta's visits to China and the Kingdom of the Bulghars. No one has succeeded in developing a viable itinerary from the information given in the book, even though it is not clear that the provision of viable itineraries was the aim of its authors. This is not an assertion that Ibn Battuta was an imaginary traveller or a monstrous fibber. It was the end product, the book, and not the traveller, which was important for its patron, its narrator, its ghost writer and presumably its audience, for this book is a testimony to a triumphant Islam, reigning supreme over a vast area of the globe. The *umma*, the community thus traversed and circumscribed, is a religious utopia and Ibn Battuta's book succumbs to the temptations of delusion characteristic of other utopic visions. As I read his book, I find myself intrigued by its cryptic fascination with the after-world. The book metamorphoses and transmutes space into lived experience, in a utopian gesture that emphasises the transience and ephemerality of this world in order to celebrate the inexorable pull of the after-world.

BIG, BAD TRUMP

Brad Bullock

Here's a story about how the United States elected Donald Trump. For many educated, thinking US citizens, Trump's victory wasn't just stunning, it was unthinkable, and it remains somewhat incomprehensible. Going on two years of rule under the Trump administration, conversations with friends at home and abroad are still punctuated by reactions to the daily outrage and chaos that define this presidency. And we all struggle, desperately, to find satisfactory narratives for understanding how the US could deliver such a person into the White House.

There's no lack for explanations from commentators and political pundits, but the very nature of modern news media, and indeed of Trump himself, make the telling of a comprehensive story about the arrival of this president unlikely. Or better, we have important pieces of a story, but we aren't looking back far enough for its context or looking in the right place for the storyline.

Before we start, this is not actually a story about Donald Trump. Overwhelming evidence confirms that, if not certifiably unhinged, he is genuinely brash, rude, and narcissistic, an inveterate liar who prefers to live in his own parallel universe. A political hack who doesn't like politics, much of what Trump says and does is noise. His position on real issues is typically, embarrassingly, uninformed and changes with his moods. It's a mistake, however, to write him off as stupid or to minimise his power to influence real policies – consider his various attempts to vilify immigrants generally, and Muslims specifically, as in his 'Muslim bans' seeking to forbid or restrict travel into the US. Nor is this a story that centres on his 'base.' Apparently, the frequency or severity of Trump's inept crudities, inconsistencies, and outright lies have no bearing on their approval ratings. It's not accurate to claim that most of his supporters are actively racist or xenophobic, but

Trump has unquestionably encouraged and emboldened those who are, and his insistence on building a wall along the border of Mexico continues to animate his followers. Trump and his base are not the story – they are, instead, the result of it.

Finally, though the press necessarily features in this story, it's not about the news industry's failure to provide an adequate narrative. That ability was weakened long before Trump came to power. Within the structure of a 24/7 news cycle and soundbites with little context, where sensationalism and spectacle are constantly, instantly delivered by web outlets, there's little room for sustained investigative journalism, much less a consistent story that strives for objectivity. A successful, decades-long campaign from the right to impugn 'mainstream media' predicts the unprecedented antagonism heaped against the press by Trump's administration and his followers (who anyway have their own eclipsed version of 'the news' to follow, just like the rest of us). This reality locks Trump and the news media into a weird, dysfunctional relationship: the more outlandish Mr Trump behaves, the more he must become the story itself. Worse, his antics supplant discussions of serious mischief being carried out by the ruling party.

The story to tell is one about what's happened to the whole US electorate over time. Yes, we are now a deeply divided nation of progressives and conservatives, of 'blue' and 'red' states. Today, people lack even basic knowledge of civics. Corporate influence and partisan politics prevent even sensible compromise. Those currently running the Republican party slide further towards embracing a strategy that denies inconvenient facts delivered by scientists and journalists and scholars, to the point that we've begun to circulate the toxic term 'post-truth era'. But none of this explains how we got here. For that, we need to explore an historical arc of political participation that bends towards apathy and indifference. Too many US citizens have been lulled into a state of sleep or suspended animation, one where we either take our democratic institutions for granted or distrust and devalue the government itself.

Something has gone terribly wrong in a democracy historically held up as a 'beacon to the world.' But this is larger than our extreme political divide: self-identified Republicans and Democrats alike decry the political state of things and are embarrassed, disturbed – even horrified – regarding the character of this administration. From what we witness, many of us have trouble recognising our country.

We must consider that a primary reason for our situation is that we, the people, have been changed dramatically by broad and powerful social forces, shaping us towards losing a sense of value, trust, and ownership in our own democratic institutions. It's not just that we've been convinced that politics and who's in power doesn't matter much. We've been encouraged to prioritise other activities: among them, averaging more hours at work, consuming things, and entertaining ourselves. Or, once upon a time we really were more politically engaged and we expected our government to deliver solutions to problems.

Here's the storyline: declining political participation and a shallower sense of civic responsibility are both cause and effect of our increasingly contentious political climate in the US. Powerful forces have operated on us. Yet, we still live in a functioning democracy. We, ourselves, are ultimately responsible for the political polarisation, unbridled partisanship, and disaffection. This is not a new narrative, but it rarely appears in public discourse even as new chapters are added. Self-implication is never pleasant. Yet, in a very real sense, we are reaping what we have sown, wittingly or not.

Providing a comprehensive tale about our electorate would produce a massive tome, so highlighting some important turns along the path will have to suffice. Dividing modern history into decades is an imperfect but useful analytical device for this task. Where to start? The 1930s and the period of the New Deal mark the establishment of the welfare state in the US and follows a decade of capitalist profit-taking and the onset of America's Great Depression. The federal government began a series of programmes aimed at the security of common people, and the people began to see government as their advocate.

To the claim about US political participation: has it really declined? Yes, but it's complicated. Of all the ways to measure political participation (e.g., activism, protests, letters to the editor), voting behaviour is the sensible choice. Scholars associate it with faith in government, democracy, and its institutions generally. Voting is our most basic civic action. Plus, we have good data for it. Voting rates go up and down by election year, but aggregating data by decades reveals a definite trend. We'll focus on evidence from national elections since they tend to garner more interest than state and local elections (where decline in participation has been generally more pronounced).

Starting with participation in presidential elections as a percentage of voting age population, we find that voting rates averaged 54.8 per cent in the 1930s. They steadily increase in the '40s and '50s, peaking in the 1960s at 61.6 per cent. Since then, there's a steady decline from the '70s through the 1990s, where they stood at 52.1 per cent. Rates have increased slightly in this century, bolstered largely by interest in the Obama elections, and are now comparable to where they were in the '30s and '40s.

Voter participation is considerably lower for national midterm elections (miserably so when measured against comparable democracies). In the 1930s they averaged 45.6 per cent. Aggregating them in a similar way we find that the trend is basically the same. After a downturn in the '40s, partly due to World War II (WWII), they climb to peak again in the 1960s at 48.2 per cent, and have effectively been going down ever since. It's worthy to note that for a worse voter turnout than the 2014 midterms (38.5 per cent) we'd need to go back 72 years to 1942. Pundits mostly cite apathy, anger, and negative campaigning for the poor 2014 turnout. But again, we didn't get there overnight.

Into the woods

So, we have solid evidence that US political participation has declined. Constructing a rough timeline by decade, with some general observations about what issues or groups dominated each, reveals another important pattern. Observers have noted that periods of significant change or disruption are often followed by a 'backlash' period when, pendulum-style, we head back towards the dominant, traditional social order that was originally challenged (as in the 1950s and 1980s). Consider that except for gay rights, however, the pendulum has failed to 'swing left' since Reaganism in the 1980s.

In their book *Authoritarianism & Polarisation in American Politics*, Hetherington and Weiler think they know why: New Deal issues and policy choices stemming from them (issues that generally elected Democrats) have been gradually replaced by disparate 'world views' that revolve around clusters of symbolic positions largely explained by one's location on scales of

1930s	New Deal, faith in government, welfare state
1940s	WWII, start of Cold War
1950s	suburbanism, communism/Red Scare (race, homosexuality, nationalism, traditionalism: white, Christian, straight, male, authoritarian)
1960s	racial injustice, poverty, 'white flight'
1970s	Watergate, feminism, decline of unionism
1980s	Reaganism, Moral Majority (communism, individual accountability, law and order, nationalism, traditionalism: white, fundamentalist, Christian, straight, male, authoritarian)
1990s	end of Cold War, global capitalism, terrorism (Muslim)
2000s	social media, climate change, terrorism (Muslim), immigration, gay rights
2010s	Obama & 'hope over fear,' gay marriage
	Trump & anti-government nationalism (anti-immigration, anti-press, selective traditionalism: white, fundamentalist Christian, male, authoritarian)

authoritarianism. They present persuasive evidence that this evolution principally results from an intentional Republican strategy called positive polarisation: using divisive issues that turn on abstract notions of impending threats, either to personal or national security, or to the existing or traditional social order (e.g., the Red Scare and 'the Southern strategy'). Key issues that play to authoritarian voters are: 1) racial and ethnic differences; 2) crime/law and order (security at the expense of civil liberties); 3) ERA/feminism versus traditional family structure; and 4) militarism (over diplomacy). Fear, anger, and tests of religious or national loyalty replace nuanced policy debates grounded in complex issues. Americans who already lean authoritarian develop an authoritarian worldview that reflexively calls for 'strong,' decisive leadership (i.e., action over negotiation) and demonises the left. Those low on authoritarian scales have gravitated to a diametrically opposed worldview that likewise demonises opponents, leaving no room for dialogue or finding common ground.

If they're right, then a climate of political polarisation, partisanship, and disaffection is, at least for now, the permanent state of things – an environment hard to alter, with all the predictable dysfunction.

Since the 1980s, we seem to operate in an arena of constant or impending threats, a 'tyranny of the urgent' scenario that can effectively shift towards Republican candidates even those voters who score only in the middle on authoritarianism.

Notice that we've devolved into this democratic dysfunction during a period characterised by expansion of the franchise and ever-increasing levels of education and access to information – the Jeffersonian ideal. These factors would predict an increase in more politically involved citizens, ones highly invested in their democracy and suitably armed against tyrants. This hasn't happened.

So, we must look elsewhere to explain our disaffection and shallower sense of civic responsibility: namely, larger social and cultural forces, technological change, and their long-term effects on ideology.

Only through an examination of such major shifts can we understand why our path necessarily leads to more apathy or anger at real or perceived others, and why people here are so easily swayed by negative campaigning and misinformation.

Intentionally or by default, we've arrived at this place by steady process. The timeline may be useful since it does provide context for the journey we've been on, but we've got to expand upon why the political pendulum has not yet already shifted back to the left, as predicted. Social scientists have provided scholarly signposts all along the way, but unfortunately their contributions rarely make it into common discussions about a bigger picture. I'll use a few of their insights that have proven particularly relevant. Often, their observations draw our attention away from more popular storylines or predict what's coming long before we reach a turn in the road.

After WWII, a victorious US enters the 1950s as the world's primary economic, military, and political powerhouse. Faith in government and civic participation have never been higher. Histories typically describe a time of stability and economic prosperity, but complete histories make note that the Cold War begins almost immediately after Yalta and that domestic prosperity was due largely to labour unionism and extraordinary investments in general welfare programmes collectively known as the GI Bill. Within that security, and riding a wave of patriotism, conservatives mount the Red Scare, which included curtailing the freedoms and opportunities of numerous minorities or marginalised groups. Communism as a perpetual threat is successfully utilised, notably by the Republican Party, as political strategy (one that carries the day for four decades until the collapse of the USSR).

Yet there's an important twist in the story that has received scant attention: a new form of corporate power that creates profound changes in the attitudes and behaviours of American workers and their sense of civic responsibility. The most prescient analyst here is certainly C.W. Mills, whose seminal *White Collar* (1951) emphasised the expansion of a new, salaried middle-managerial class. Their status derives from their connection and loyalty to a corporate brand. Their success has less to do with skill or performance than with posturing within a corporate structure, devoid of labour ideology. Not only did Mills correctly predict that their ascendance would cause the coming decline in unionism, but also the increase in an ideological aloofness that blows with the political winds. Salaried workers settled for many more hours of relatively meaningless work to prop up an image fuelled by consuming status items. Such preoccupation, and the time it requires, helps to explain why so many Americans since claim that they don't have time for politics. Post-war, corporate capitalism also created, according to W.F. Whyte, an *Organisation Man* whose necessary 'commitment' and 'loyalty' to corporations encouraged cynicism in Americans who, having won World War II, quickly settled into an 'empty suburban life, conformity, and the pursuit of the dollar.'

We've already noted that voting rates peak in the 1960s. The usual narrative stresses how concerns about the civil rights of minorities and women, and America's ongoing involvement in the Vietnam War, took root in social movements that encouraged direct activism and protest marches. These movements successfully reimagined and rearranged American life; they left in their wake a sustained ideological and political energy that carried us into the next decade. It's true that the results were profound: the US government had effectively brought redress to millions of its citizens and had closed economic and cultural gaps constructed around race and gender. The pendulum had swung fully left. But already in 1981, during his first inaugural address, President Ronald Reagan famously quips that 'government is not the solution to our problem; government is the problem,' to great applause. How best to explain this rapid transition? Political historians rightly cite widespread disillusionment stemming from the Vietnam War and the Watergate Scandal – still considered a watershed that left more people cynical and less trusting of government and politicians.

By then, however, social scientists were drawing attention to another, corresponding narrative: US citizens were expressing increasing personal feelings of alienation and general social disaffection. The hollowness and isolation of suburban life, with its poor social networks and lack of shared values (beyond achieving money and status), is the stronger current, one pushing attitudes and behaviours that weaken civic identity and political participation. *Habits of the Heart* (1985) is an exemplary work for explaining this part of our story. It credits a worsening form of radical individualism for the loss of practices that lift political activities beyond one's personal preferences and lifestyle choices, practices that tie citizens securely to the welfare of neighbourhood and nation. This, it claims, left civic participation mostly devoid of meaning. In a sense, if it didn't work for *you* right now, why bother? About the same time, US citizens fully embrace what sociologist Amatai Etzioni identifies as moral relativism – the notion that consensual standards impose values onto individuals, that each person is responsible for their own moral code. That explains an ideological shift away from community and civic-mindedness, one that nurtures a culture and politics free from obligations to a greater whole but at the cost of shared values and experiences that bond and motivate groups to act. The loss of that structural underpinning causes not just a sense of isolation among common citizens, but also a sense of individual helplessness to initiate any substantial change.

Returning to the political strategy of staying in power by using impending threats, finding in Muslims a new enemy is essential after the demise of the Soviet Union (and after China is established as a trading partner). The 1990s is notable for Samuel Huntington's controversial article, embraced by many conservatives, entitled 'The Clash of Civilisations?' It asserts that 'future wars would be fought not between countries, but between cultures,' and that Islamic extremism would become the greatest threat to world peace. Critics argued this helped solidify an oversimplified and unimpeachable 'us vs. them' worldview fixated on Muslim terrorism. Yet, in the same year, George Ritzer's *The McDonaldisation of Society* (1993) emphasised something else completely: that an increasingly standardised, predictable consumer society – one overwhelmed by advertising and television – was producing citizens with short attention spans (thus, the rise of 60 second political ads, and then 5-6 second sound bites devoid of context or subtlety). No wonder, said Ritzer, that the only perceived civic responsibility left was to consume. Consider, in this context, the memorable message by President George W. Bush after 9/11: to help combat Islamic terrorism, citizens should continue to shop. The American people then comfortably settled in to watch edited episodes of the Iraq invasion on their televisions. Later, in *Civic Engagement in American Democracy*, Skocpol and Fiorina draw attention to yet another formative change affecting political behavior: the rise of organisational specialists who do your civic work for you. At a time when, on average, Americans were already working well over 50 hours a week, and people 'didn't have time' to figure out political complexities or actively protest, they started limiting their participation to giving money to full-time 'experts'. Having done their part by pocketbook, other traditional forms of civic responsibility, including voting, began to seem less necessary.

Transformative social forces in the new century include our tendency to move more frequently, the rise of social media, resulting forms of self-referential habits, and, lately, the impact of 'fake news.' But familiar themes continue to dominate our narrative about how the voting public has lost touch with its democracy. Robert Putnam's *Bowling Alone* is a landmark for recording how US political life goes from one of deep group ties – with neighbours and through membership in civic organisations – to one of political detachment. Effectively, social isolation feeds political disaffection. His statistical model identifies television-watching as a significant contributor to this worrisome trend (people start admitting that they use television not just for entertainment but for company). His analysis is still often cited in critiques of newer social media. It doesn't help that by now Americans have accepted historically high levels of mobility for career advancement – about one in six people in the US changes address every year – so 'putting down roots' or investing time in neighbours, neighbourhoods, and political activities takes a hit. The lives of a whole new class of rootless, 'serial relocators' – roughly 10 million strong – is recorded by Peter Kilborn. Such 'economic nomad' families thoroughly prioritise seeking transfers to new jobs that afford them a bigger house in the next suburb. They don't see the point of putting down roots or getting to know neighbours since soon they expect to move to another place just like the one they leave.

Recent, impressive forms of social media have so quickly and thoroughly altered how politics is played that it deserves special attention. We'll keep our eye on the US electorate. First, extensive studies by the Pew Foundation chart the rapid rise of both internet and smartphone use. US adults connected to the internet went from just over half in 2000 to 84 per cent in 2015 (it's now closer to 9 in 10 adults). The rate in 2015 was already 96 per cent for 18 to 29-year-olds. More remarkably, the share of Americans with smartphones went from 35 per cent in 2011 to 77 per cent today. In comparison to earlier forms of mass media (television, personal computers), opportunities to feel connected or escape into entertainment have increased exponentially. The obvious result is a society where 'normal' interaction is now virtual and thoroughly machine-mediated, and where all activities – political or otherwise – compete with our growing social media involvement. Some social critics predicted that these media trends would revive civic identity and political activism, especially among younger people. But initial expectations that these technologies would increase political involvement have been greatly revised. Of particular note are studies by Sherry Turkle. In *Alone Together*, she suggests that not only are users – particularly young people – distracted by their need to be 'constantly connected' but that the structure of that connection leads to a potent kind of self-referential isolation, one that discourages both reflection about larger issues and independent decision-making. Terms like 'clicktivism' and 'slacktivism' are in circulation to describe net-based political activities that, simply put, require very little effort (e.g., 'liking,' reposting, or commenting on posts). Whatever the cause, 'millennials' associated with these trends now constitute the same proportion of the electorate as do Baby Boomers (about 31 per cent), but they register and vote at significantly lower levels (e.g., in the 2012 election, 69 per cent of Boomers reported voting compared to only 19 per cent of 18 to 29-year-olds).

Then there is the disturbing loss in the impact of actual facts towards shaping opinion and action. The most compelling response to the phenomenon now called 'fake news' comes from Hochschild and Einstein in *Do Facts Matter?* They argue that social media has encouraged political activism, but mostly by expanding a political class they call the 'active misinformed.' Not only does real information fail to enlighten their decisions, but their lack or distrust of facts (from scientists, for example) makes them easy to manipulate politically. America's 'Tea Party' movement comes to mind. Russia used the same social media to create cyberbots and fake profiles to influence the outcome of the 2016 US presidential election. Connections between those same Russians and the Trump campaign continue to dog the Trump administration. And, his supporters don't care. After years of Republican-led efforts to sow fear and distrust of government and in its institutions responsible for public welfare, they are true believers. Trump and his ilk assure them they don't need 'facts.' What is true is dictated by entrenched beliefs, and those beliefs are daily affirmed by rather recently-established, traditional forms of right-wing news outlets (print, radio, and television). Those on the right and the left have come to fully understand that 'news' is not something reported, but rather created. Once journalism drops all pretence of objectivity, it becomes propaganda.

Without really meaning to, we've arrived in new and uncharted territory, a place where the US could elect an inexperienced, preening bully to the highest political office in the land. So, who's afraid of the big, bad Trump? Clearly not his base, who appear unreachable. But all the rest of us should be afraid of him, or at least of what he represents. What's happened to civic-mindedness and political participation in the US matters to everyone. It's obvious by now that who's in the White House still has enormous implications – not just nationally, but globally. The apotheosis of Mr Trump, a would-be autocrat and false populist, has emboldened other, actual autocrats and fuelled the political ascendance of leaders who openly disparage democratic institutions, the press, transparency and diversity.

If this isn't the political system we now deserve, it is the one we have allowed. In the face of sweeping social and technological changes, political apathy and disdain for our political system, entrenched partisanship, the seeming need of successful campaigns to appeal to symbolic issues that largely instil a sense of threat, fear, or anger, and with a resulting preference for authoritarian leaders, what to do? We already know. History teaches us that to maintain or reclaim a healthy democracy, *we, the people*, must start tending the garden. Democratic practices and institutions wither and die without us.

Important lessons recently appear in *How Democracies Die*. Levitsky and Ziblatt claim that it isn't by military coup, but typically through a lack of care for democratic institutions and practices, that democracies slide into autocracy. As they put it, 'Democratic backsliding today begins at the ballot box.' This leads us back to authoritarianism. They list four historically-established warning signs of dangerous authoritarian leaders: they show a weak commitment to democratic rules, deny the legitimacy of opponents, tolerate violence, and demonstrate willingness to curb civil liberties or the press. They further contend that (except for Richard Nixon) no previous US president in the last century has met even one of these four criteria, whereas Donald Trump meets all of them.

Social scientists and others provide substantial advice for restoring community, civic participation and a thriving democracy, but the common theme is that it takes some real effort. Ordinary people need to organise effectively at the grassroots level, and then they must (physically) show up. When virtual community-building efforts and political organising via the internet are combined with *real* meetings – off-line and in real time – social ties and political activism are strengthened. The Indivisible Movement, organised at the local level of towns and cities, is a prime example. Likewise, there are plenty of good examples of people bonding over political volunteerism that takes the form of physical activism: protests, marches, and door-to-door campaigns. These habits also combat feelings of meaninglessness and isolation.

I remain cautiously optimistic that the US can recapture some of the democratic spirit from the protest years of the '60s and '70s and return to a civilised discussion of actual issues (rather than shout at the other camp from across a symbolic divide). Already some suggest that ridding ourselves of Mr Trump and his cronies could provide a catalyst for a political reawakening. Whatever the case, it's up to us, and US citizens need a new playbook. The transformation we need will take the combined efforts of our many heads, and different ways to use our hands and feet. In brief, it will take more of us, and much more from us.

TRANSLATIONS

Burçin K. Mustafa

My motivation to study language and eventually translation began one winter morning in 2006. I was watching the BBC morning news at my London home while preparing to leave for university. With a cup of Nescafé in my hand and the distant whistle of a winter wind in the background, I attentively listened to the presenter announce that the security level had been raised to 'SEVERE' due to an increase in *chatter*. Despite the fear and paranoia that accompanies warnings of a potentially imminent terrorist attack, my thoughts were consumed with that one word: *chatter*. I assumed it referred to an increase in communication between terrorist cells through the internet and via phone calls, indicating they were discussing plans for an attack. But what really unsettled me was how a simple word had the power to justify an attitude of fear and paranoia, despite its ambiguity. I wondered if anyone else had also questioned the justification for the spread of panic on the basis of one word, a word I had yet to define.

The image that was to be routinely triggered in my mind by the word *chatter* is of a group of young Arab men in an untidy apartment littered with pizza boxes, sending emails and making phones calls as they prepared to stage an atrocity. I questioned the source of this imagery and was eventually able to locate it. This visualisation embedded in my memory stemmed from the Hollywood blockbuster *The Siege* (1998). My visual reference was one of fiction and in a sense functioned like a surrogate, filling a gap in my own personal experience to understand a set of otherwise incomprehensible propositions. In short I had tapped into a fictional narrative to give meaning to 'real events'. Hollywood's chaotic image of terrorists portrayed in *The Siege* was later reinforced by stories surrounding the 9/11 attackers, especially the FBI's claim that Muhammad Atta frequently visited strip bars. However, a critical mind would ask: did the fictitious image of the terrorists presented in *The Siege* and similar films influence the description of the 9/11 attackers? Was it a case of fiction influencing reality? In fact this reference to fiction to understand reality in relation to the 9/11 attacks is not an isolated or unique occurrence. While watching the televised scenes of the 9/11 attacks many viewers made a visual reference to the film *Independence Day (1996)*. Similarities were not just limited to the images of destruction; also present in both narratives are themes of annihilation by an inhuman and menacing enemy. It is these very themes that would become necessary components of the official 9/11 narrative and a justification for a relentless war on terror.

The experience prompted me to question the imposition of meaning given to certain Arabic words appearing in the British lexicon, such as *fatwa*, *jihad* and *mujahid*. Even though the word *fatwa* in Arabic means 'a legal opinion', in British culture the imposed meaning is different and carries highly negative connotations which emerged in 1989 during the reporting of the Rushdie affair. *Fatwa* is not defined according to the source culture's usage of it but rather through the British observer's cultural and ideological gaze, which reduces its meaning to one event: Khomeini's call for the death penalty. The early names used to describe Muslims and Islam also demonstrate this form of cultural and ideological imposition. Through a Christian gaze, specifically the ascription of godhead to Jesus, Muslims were referred to as Mohammedans and their religion Mohammedanism. Edward Said asserts that the way foreign subjects (e.g. the words *fatwa*, Muslims and Islam) were understood and explained was dominated by the observer's colonial world view. This form of cultural and ideological imposition gives credence to Gayatri Chakravorty Spivak's claim that the subaltern (the cultural and ideological other) cannot speak, because what they have to say about themselves is silenced by the observer's voice. This form of cultural and ideological imposition related to words used to describe Muslims continues not just with titles such as Islamists, Extremists, Moderates and Reformers but also in regard to the word Mohammedans, which was used in 2018 by Gerard Batten, the leader of the UK Independence Party, to describe Muslims while discussing the imprisonment of former leader of the English Defence League, Tommy Robinson.

Through the choice of words, language is often used to mark a distinction from what is considered normal and acceptable and what is deemed abnormal and hence unacceptable. A case in point is the use of the word regime to describe governments that are considered illegitimate by Western authorities – for example, the Iranian regime in contrast to the Israeli government. A more recent example is provided by Jordan Peterson, a professor of psychology whose YouTube videos are enjoying a degree of notoriety. Peterson argues Islam is fundamentally different from other religions and describes Islam's prophet as 'a warlord', which carries a pejorative sense, as opposed to more neutral terms such as military commander or military leader. Besides the reductionism and essentialism – both tools of Orientalism – this characterisation contains, the use of the word warlord functions to trigger and simultaneously draw from negative narratives about Islam, namely that it is a religion of violence. What is particularly fascinating is, through a manipulative use of language, Peterson uses this word to clandestinely insert a subjective and biased premise from which he starts a discussion; a premise he does not qualify nor justify. To engage his discussion without firstly challenging this cultural and ideological imposition is to succumb to a premise that was given no grounding.

A parallel that can be drawn is the use of the word terrorism as opposed to war. Predominantly when violence is committed by a Western democracy it signifies humanity (e.g. civilising missions), whereas violence committed by others pursuing ideological causes even in cases of resisting invasion and occupation is considered to signify savagery (e.g. terrorism). Terrorism is not a new phenomenon, but what is unique is the manner in which we are drawn to a socially accepted position that 'we do war; they do terror' through a manipulative use of language. In the most extreme demonstration of this standard, while the 9/11 attacks against the World Trade Centres and the Pentagon are classified as illegitimate acts of terrorism, the bombing of Hiroshima and Nagasaki as well as the firebombing of Dresden and Hamburg are considered to be legal and justifiable acts of war. On this point a critical mind may ask Jordan Peterson if he also considers President Truman and Prime Minister Churchill to be warlords?

These and similar observations led me to an uncomfortable realisation that certain underlying assumptions remained hidden from me, yet were able to affect the meaning I inferred from language and the narratives I was surrounded by. This deepening awareness was enough to trigger my research interests. First, I had to understand how we derive meaning from language. There are many factors beyond linguistic norms that affect the sense we infer from a text. For example, personal bias is one of those factors, but not necessarily the most important. According to the theory of cognitive dissonance, people hold a variety of cognitions (perceptions) of the world and themselves and when they clash with observable phenomena this creates a dissonance (discord) between the beliefs they carry and what they have observed. The anxiety this produces is referred to as cognitive dissonance and to resolve it there is a habitual tendency in people to eliminate their anxiety by altering their observations to achieve consonance with their beliefs. As an example, consider this:

> A single parent who suffered intense emotional turmoil after their only child was killed fighting in the 2003 Iraq war, and who holds a belief that their child was fighting for freedom and equality, will have a tendency, according to the theory, to be dismissive of information which indicates their child in fact fought for oppression and exploitation.

In addition to cognitive dissonance, there are other factors that may have unconsciously formulated a meaning of the above text in a reader's mind. For example, was there an assumption that the single parent was a woman of Western origin? When I present the above example most people assume the single parent is an American woman and likewise, when I ask them to translate it into languages which use feminine and masculine markers they mainly use the feminine form for the word parent. Our reliance on assumptions is based on personal experience or in its absence a surrogate (borrowed experiences) to formulate a meaning from a text. Some of these assumptions are based on subjective beliefs and specific narratives and an overall biased experience of the world. This is the reason why people can produce a different meaning of the same statement or text. In his *From Necessity to Infinity: Interpretation in Language and Translation*, Omar Sheikh Al-Shabab argues that meaning inferred from language is through an interpretive frame, which consists of six elements: Being, Environment, Understanding, Experience (Knowledge), Assertion and Identity. Al-Shabab not only contends that an interpretive frame influences the meaning we derive but also suggests that without it the span of possible meanings is infinite and thus it is the interpretive frame that limits these variables and gives a definitive meaning to a specific text. A text can be viewed like a jigsaw puzzle which has missing pieces and the reader brings their own pieces to complete the puzzle and therefore the meaning. Some texts will have more missing pieces than others and rely more heavily on the reader's own interpretive frame so the variances in meaning inferred from the same text by several readers can be a manifestation of their differing and unique interpretive frames.

Ideology contributes to the way in which we decipher the world and the meaning we derive from a text. Consider how certain beliefs may affect the meaning inferred from the following text:

> When the British first engaged the Taliban on the battlefield they found their tactics much more resourceful then they had first assumed. This resulted in a long and hard battle, but eventually the terrorists were defeated, and the heroes were victorious.

The description of the two groups as either terrorists or heroes, is reflective of notions such as 'freedom', 'equality', and 'democracy', which are appropriated according to certain beliefs. Thus the meaning that is inferred is heavily dependent on ideology which consists of several unified beliefs, quantifiable or speculative, that affect the way adherents of those beliefs derive meaning and interact with the world. An ideology can be compared to an internet search engine because different search engines use different sets of rules (beliefs) and thus produce different results (meanings). Without using a search engine, it is not possible to produce any search results and by the same logic, inferring meaning in varying degrees is dependent on ideology. An ideology is a necessary veil between humans and the world that surrounds them and human agency independent of an ideology becomes negated. Not only is our perception of information and events influenced, but also our reactions to what we have perceived. People do not act on their own individualism, but rather on an imaginary perceived individualism formed through an ideology.

Beyond the scope of how different people understand the same text and even the manifestation of ideology can also be seen in the differing moral values that exist between societies. Morals and core values stem from ideologies and are an intrinsic part of not only creating an identity for one's own self and society, but also in producing a point of separation from the ideological other and their society. Purported positions on gender, race, equality and freedom not only define the self, but also act as a set of criteria to differentiate from adherents who have different ideological assumptions and thus different social positions.

Where there exists a plurality of ideologies within society and there are no apparent coercive elements to accept one particular way of thought, people no longer identify themselves and their allegiances in terms of nationalism or on fixed ideological grounds. What is prevalent instead are fluid notions of freedom, equality, justice and democracy, which are claimed by the various dominant political parties. What does have dominance and to an extent alleviates the lack of a cohesive ideology is unity based on a mutual rejection of what is perceived to be wrong, immoral and barbaric. However, opposition to one thing does not tidily equate to the championing of something else. The world cannot always be reduced to this binary caricature, for example being opposed to terrorism does not equate to a specific ideal or even being opposed to war. Nevertheless, in contemporary Western liberal democracies the role of tangible and fixed ideals is replaced, in varying degrees, with the rejection of what is feared, and demonised. This object of fear is not left in the abstract sense but rather is personified through assigning it to specific 'foreign' ideologies and entities such as Al-Qaeda and ISIS. These groups are used to draw focus to what society is not and what it despises, and thus allows for the creation of a defined image of fear through which a degree of social cohesion and commonality is achieved.

In our current social context fear not only creates unity within society, but it also produces a separation from other societies, real or imagined. This is because even though the object of fear is specific, such as Al-Qaeda and ISIS, there is slippage in that it is extended to Muslims and Islam in general. Unfortunately, the association with Islam and terrorism continually projected in the news media and Hollywood fiction function as a surrogate in the absence of personal experience. Just as I referenced *The Siege* to comprehend the word *chatter*, people who lack personal experience of Islam and Muslims may also resort to a fictitious surrogate to understand an otherwise incomprehensible set of propositions. The planting of this association between Muslims and terrorism proved a useful component to justify military action against a dehumanised enemy and was crucial in the official explanation of why the 9/11 attacks occurred. The motive of the attackers was not ascribed to a political goal, according to George Bush. It was because 'they hate our freedoms'. A motive only applicable when it is assumed the attackers are irrational to the extent they would attack the world's superpower based on an emotion.

To further explore the relationship narratives have to ideology and their ability to influence how we infer meaning, consider the following case. If you were telling the story of a tragic car crash that happened in the winter of 1975, would you start your narration from when the driver left their house on a snow-covered morning at 8 a.m. or an hour later when they turned onto the road the crash happened? Would you feel it necessary to mention that the crash took place in Southeast London and on that morning the roads were covered with ice? Would you mention the driver's claim that the crash was the result of mechanical failure caused by a mechanic who forgot to tighten a brake cable the day before? Also, would you expect the judge's verdict to be more balanced than the competing accounts of those directly involved in the accident? Lastly, how would your own narration of the entire event be affected if the mechanic claimed racial discrimination and the judge only believed the driver because he was a 'rich man working in the city'? These variables illustrate how narratives of the same event can differ due to available information, personal bias and agenda. Even the images and the meaning generated while reading the above questions would have been affected by personal experiences and biases. Many readers of the text will have assumed the mechanic to be a man even though gender is not specified. Likewise, a person's attitude to the judge's verdict and the mechanic's claim of racial discrimination will be affected by their own experiences and knowledge of London's judiciary in the 1970s. It's possible the reader may have assigned racial profiles to the characters even though they were never specified. The telling of the story, the information that is included and the account that is given priority will have been influenced by an individual's biases. What is profound is that the biases which shape narration will remain hidden, yet will be able to clandestinely impact the listener's reaction to the event through the given account.

The opening scenes of *Hostiles* (2017) well illustrate the importance of how a narrative is structured. It depicts a violent and graphic attack by

Native Americans against a family of white European settlers. The dynamics of the scene immediately position the Comanches as being the antagonists (the barbarians), and the white settlers as the protagonists (the victims). American cultural theorists, Robert Stam and Louse Spence, argue that 'the besieged wagon train or fort is the focus of our attention and sympathy, and from this centre our familiars rally against unknown attackers characterised by inexplicable customs and irrational hostility'. What such accounts negate are the horrific events which provoked a barbaric response. These same conventions of narrative framing and the response they elicit also apply to much grander narratives which are embedded in social and political orders. When Mona Baker, Professor of Translation Studies and Director of Centre for Translations and Intercultural Studies at Manchester University, introduced narrative theory to translation studies, she suggested that a narrative has a social manipulative effect in that 'it socialises individuals into an established social and political order and it encourages them to interpret present events in terms of sanctioned narratives of the past'. The way a narrative is told affects the social reaction to an observable event. Let us consider the western media's representation of Muammar Gaddafi's violent execution and their grisly display of his battered corpse. This is because an act routinely considered to be inhumane, a public lynching, was given a positive notion of liberation and justice through a specific narrative gaze. The British tabloid *The Sun* went so far as to feature a full-size graphic picture of Gaddafi's bloodied head on its front page with the title 'That's for Lockerbie, and for Yvonne Fletcher and IRA Semtex victims'.

We know that a narrative is composed of a protagonist, an antagonist, a disruption caused by the antagonist, a journey in which the protagonist struggles to rectify the effects of the disruption, and a resolution where the effects of the disruption are resolved. Within this structure and according to the dominant Western narrative of the 2011 Libyan crisis, Gaddafi was the antagonist while NATO and the Libyan opposition to Gaddafi were the protagonists. The disruption was Gaddafi's authorisation to kill legitimate protestors, the journey was the NATO aided military mission to overthrow him and the resolution was his death; hence the positivity ascribed to his lynching. Narratives work in concert with the use of fear to unify society and achieve political goals by comparing their function to what is referred to as Plato's noble lie. Here, grand lies shield society from the true horror and complexity of politics, but through the lie social unity is achieved and the ruling elite can strive for their political goals, albeit on a false premise.

Translation is an interesting part of the narrative equation for several reasons. What really drew my attention to translation theory is how, unlike other language acts, the reader of a translation is unable to verify its accuracy. This results in greater reliance on the narrator of the message rather than its actual author. Yet, despite the reliance on a third party, translation has and continues to play an important role in our lives either directly or indirectly. Consider, for example, the many electronic items that rely on translated manuals, the number of spiritual and political beliefs informed by translations. Despite its importance, translation is poorly understood, regarded as little more than the transference of a message from one language into another. Like a photocopy machine, many believe, translation requires the text to be scanned, and its equivalent produced in another language. This mechanised explanation of translation is problematic because it relies on the existence of equivalent words between languages and that the message is entirely contained in the original text itself. In reality, the meaning of a text is partially inferred from the assumptions the reader brings to it from their interpretive frame, so translation is not merely an act of replacing signs. Rather, a translation is a rendering of the translator's own interpretation of the original text. It is an imitation of the original, but ultimately could convey a radically different message from the one the source author had intended. Despite this potentiality it is the message of the translation that is ascribed to the original author.

The alien from John Carpenter's science fiction film *The Thing* (1982) epitomises this aspect of translation. The 'Thing' is an organism able to imitate humans through absorbing and reproducing their cells. However, it is never completely identical to the human it has imitated and more importantly, its appearance allows it to clandestinely pursue an agenda different from the human it has replicated. Likewise, a translation has the ability to influence people on the perception it is a rendering of the original text rather than the translator's subjective interpretation, which may have a different agenda and as a consequence may produce a very different meaning.

Due to these factors, translation presents an intersection, in time and space, through which the original text can be adapted to suit differing local ideological agendas that form the translator's interpretative frame. The Athenian concept of democracy was altered via translations to propagate specific doctrines in England during the late eighteenth and early nineteenth centuries. In his essay, 'Translation and Democracy in the Nineteenth-Century England', Alexandra Lianeri asserts that the translations of texts relating to democracy were, 'far from being an impoverished reproduction of the "real" original meaning of democracy, translation contributed to the constitution of a new political order and its stabilisation as a social political unity'.

Similarly, translations of the Bible has been influenced by ideological forces and those who follow any particular translation have, often unknowingly, had their morality shaped by forces they may have otherwise opposed. The shift in almost all Bible translations, during the middle of the twentieth century, from the use of the word 'kill' in the translation of the sixth commandment to 'murder' was ideologically driven to legitimise war. According to the Christian scholar, Wilma Ann Bailey, 'when "You shall not kill" became "You shall not murder," translators set a new ethical direction and sanctioned all kinds of killing that fall outside of the narrow definition of murder'.

Translation can more accurately be defined as the representation of a message derived from a specific language and ideologically affected locality and presented in a different language and ideologically affected locality. The notion of translation being a mechanised value-free transference becomes redundant. It more accurately belongs in the same realm as other mediums of subjective cultural representation such as film, literature, photography, historiography and theatre. However, just as in *The Thing*, translation's power to influence is in its ability to hide the assumptions and agendas which produced it through the perception it is a bias-free imitation of the original.

A speech delivered in 2015 by then Home Secretary Theresa May, entitled 'A Stronger Britain, Built On Our Values', in which she propagated the reformist approach to Islam by imposing an ideologically contrived meaning on a Qura'nic verse illustrates this. May declared:

> Islamist extremists believe in a clash of civilisations. They promote a fundamental incompatibility between Islamic and Western values, an inevitable divide between 'them and us'. They demand a caliphate, or a new Islamic state, governed by a harsh interpretation of shari'a law.

Even though May's allusion to the binary divide presented by those she refers to as 'Islamist extremists' has descriptive merit, she essentialises the notion of an 'incompatibility' between 'Islamic' and 'Western values' to be uniquely part of an 'Islamist extremist' discourse. Not only does this create a narrow paradigm in defining what amounts to extremism, but also assumes that transitive Western social norms are universalising and should be taken as an idealised model for others to replicate. Based on this assumption May goes on:

> Some say we are picking on religion or religious beliefs, but to them I say – as a practising Anglican myself – we are doing no such thing. Islamist extremists may say they are acting in the name of Islam, but there is no legitimate basis for extremism in Islam or in any major religion. The Qur'an says 'do not go to extremes in your religion' and 'let there be no compulsion in religion'.

The translation of 'do not go to extremes in your religion', which May uses to support her assumptions is lexically ambiguous in that the definition of 'extremes' is based on a divergence from specific norms. To determine exactly which 'extremes' are being censured in the Qur'an, it is necessary to locate the verse's textual and historical context. Conversely, reflective of the cultural and ideological impositions previously discussed, 'extremes' is not defined according to the source culture's understanding, but rather through a meaning imposed by the then home secretary. It is the case May's speech already defined extremism, which included the promotion of an 'incompatibility between Islamic and western values', and thus, the imposed meaning, according to May's interpretive frame, is that the Qur'an has censured people from promoting an 'incompatibility between Islamic and western values'. However, the verse in context presents a very different meaning than the one advocated in Theresa May's speech. In actuality the quote appears in two different verses (Q. 4:171 and 5:77), and, as translated by Mohammad Abdel Haleem, reads:

> People of the Book, do not go to excess in your religion, and do not say anything about God except the truth... (Haleem 2005, 66)

> Say, 'People of the Book, do not overstep the bounds of truth in your religion and do not follow the whims of those who went astray before you… (Haleem 2005, 75)

What is immediately apparent is that the direct addressees are not Muslims because the verse begins with the phrase, *Ya ahlal Kitabi* (People of the Book) which is a Qur'anic designation for Jews and Christians. Moreover, according to several Qur'anic exegeses the 'extremes' (using May's translation) which are being censured is the evaluation of any human to the status of deserving worship.

Narrative related translation has played an essential role in shaping the political discourse, maintaining the rhetoric and legitimising state objectives along a specific trajectory. The narrative of the war on terror, where translation is used at each juncture, illustrates this very well. The disruption element (the 9/11 attacks) were supported by a translation referred to as the Bin Laden confession tape. The journey element (the war on terror proper) was legitimised by a string of translations confirming the continual threat Al-Qaeda posed to the West. And finally, the resolution (the killing of Bin Laden) was authenticated by a translation of a communique reputed to be from Al-Qaeda confirming Bin Laden had been killed by American Special Forces. I consider the Bin Laden confession tape to be the most important of these translations because it was the first piece of evidence presented to the public that linked Bin Laden to the attacks and thus authenticated the official narrative. A BBC report, broadcast on 12 December 2001, stated:

> Vice-President Dick Cheney and other American officials have described the amateurish video believed to have been filmed at a dinner last month as a 'smoking gun' that leaves 'no doubt' about the al-Qaeda leader's guilt.

The following day, 13 December 2001, the US Department of Defence (USDOD) released the translation of the video tape reputed to have been found in Afghanistan and which apparently shows Bin Laden confessing to the 9/11 attacks. It is worth noting that even though the translation of the dialogue contained in the video footage was prepared and released by the USDOD, claims of neutrality were supported by professional non-partisan translators who identified no inconsistencies. However, there are two important points to note regarding the manner the translation was undertaken. Firstly, the introduction informs the reader, 'due to the quality of the original tape, it is NOT a verbatim transcript of every word spoken during the meeting, but does convey the messages and information flow'. Secondly, it is also stated in the introduction that the chronology of the transcript was changed to conform to the order of events assumed by the USDOD. These initial acknowledgments are crucial because from the onset they indicate the meaning which is presented in the translation relies on a specific interpretive frame.

In my own analysis of the tape I focused on those segments suggestive of Bin Laden's guilt of the 9/11 attacks and found several irregularities. The main one I will present here stems from the following USDOD translation of Bin Laden himself:

> The brothers, who conducted the operation, all they knew was that they have a martyrdom operation and we asked each of them to go to America but they didn't know anything about the operation, not even one letter.

The incriminating part here is 'we asked each of them'. Without this phrase the rest of the recording could be dismissed as Bin Laden's conjecture of what happened based on widely available media reports at the time. According to the translation Bin Laden is admitting guilt by using the first-person pronoun 'we'. However, after analysing the video's original audio it is clear the Arabic phrase is طُلِبَ مِنهم (tu-li-ba minhum) which uses the Arabic passive verb and means 'they were asked'.

My transcription of the source for this segment is as follows:

> All that we know that there... [Inaudible] and they were asked to work in America and Europe and leaving their countries so that they did not know one letter (My translation).

Even though aspects of this part of the tape are inaudible, what is clear is that Bin Laden uses the Arabic passive rather than the active verb which could have been used as either طَلَبْتُ (ta-lab-tu), that is, 'I asked', or طَلَبْنا (ta-lab-na), 'we asked'. Thus, according to the source audio, the use of the Arabic passive is not a clear indicator of guilt and at the very least is an ambiguous statement that does neither confirm nor negate guilt. If the translation had used the English passive and presented the text as 'they were asked', a clear conclusion of guilt could not have been claimed based on the translation of this statement. The video was also used as a prosecution trial exhibit in the 2006 criminal case of The United States verses Zacarias Moussaoui. What is intriguing is that the accompanying translation prepared by the US government of the dialogue for the trial also used the passive, 'they were asked'. The exact causes of this change are unclear; however, it is evident that the decision to replace the Arabic passive verb with the English 'we asked' gave the 2001 USDOD translation a definitive meaning of guilt during a crucial time in the propagation of the official narrative. Moreover, from the perspective of interpretive frames, it can be reasoned that the translators of the USDOD's 2001 version translated what made sense according to the official 9/11 narrative and this superseded Arabic language norms. In the simplest terms the assumptions which underpinned the official 9/11 narrative influenced the source text meaning. In a circular manner this produced a translation that supports the very assumptions that produced it. Crucially, all these influential assumptions remained hidden from the readers of the 2001 translation who were led to believe Bin Laden had confessed to asking the attackers to go America.

Our reliance on assumptions to draw meaning from the texts we read and the events we experience, and our recourse to surrogates in the absence of personal experience to understand something that otherwise would be incomprehensible is indisputable. These assumptions can hide in narratives and translations, clandestinely altering the trajectory of our own interpretive frame. Considering the potential ramifications of this subtle but powerful form of manipulation, assumptions which one may not be aware of or even agree with are able to influence dominant narratives through translation. It should be our aim to unearth and expose such underlying assumptions, which remain hidden in the forms they have imitated. Only then can we test their validity before using them as criteria to interpret texts and events. In the words of the character MacReady, who uncovers the existence of The Thing:

> I know I'm human. And if you were all these things, then you'd just attack me right now, so some of you are still human. This thing doesn't want to show itself, it wants to hide inside an imitation. It'll fight if it has to, but it's vulnerable out in the open. If it takes us over, then it has no more enemies, nobody left to kill it. And then it's won.

HALWA HISTORIES

Irna Qureshi

Every week, when my maternal grandmother completed an entire recitation of the Qur'an, she petitioned that the reward for her effort be passed to her deceased forefathers. Before the sun goes down on a Thursday, she said, the souls of our departed loved ones perch on the ledge of the family home to see if they've been remembered. Since they can no longer earn credits for themselves, it is incumbent on the living to contribute. Although a glass of milk would do, Nani Jee liked to cook something special, perhaps a favourite curry of the relative she was remembering. The food would be laid out on a tray, ready to be donated to someone in need, just as soon as grandma had finished reciting prayers over the offering. She would plead from her prayer mat by including the names of her forefathers, remembering the toddler she lost four years earlier, the mother she grew up without; and always as per Muslim etiquette starting with the Holy Prophet and his family, and finally for the sake of equity remembering all Muslims already settled in their graves.

My grandfather, whom everyone called Babu Jee on account of his literacy, said it was good practice to bank blessings for those in the present world so the rewards await their arrival in the next. 'Isn't it enough that I cook for you in this life? You want me to start cooking for you in the next one too?'

Grandma would mock as her husband implored her to offer God's blessing only with the best possible halwa: wholesome and sweet, a delicate beige in colour, glistening with ghee to the point of being translucent, and so soft and smooth in texture that it melts in the mouth and glides down the throat without so much as a bite. Since his beloved dessert was usually reserved for special occasions, Babu Jee hoped to satisfy his craving in the afterlife.

My grandparents hailed from Nila, a village bordering the River Soan in the north western tip of undivided Punjab. The ancestors, as they perched on the ledge of the family home, would know that from time out of mind this region has known mourning and men at arms. It is close to the Salt Range, a rocky offshoot of the Himalayas thrusting out between the valleys of the Indus and Jhelum rivers. On the banks of the Jhelum Alexander the Great defeated Porus in 326 BC. In the foothills stands the ancient Katas Raj Temple whose pond, according to the *Puranas,* was created from the teardrops of Lord Shiva mourning the death of his wife. In 1519, near the scenic lake at *Kallar Kahar* Babar, the first Mughal Emperor, had a platform. The *Takht-e-Babri* carved out of the living rock from which he addressed his army that marched from Kabul in his quest for Delhi. Nor was that the end of the procession of the men at arms or the mourning they leave in their wake.

Like most Punjabis, my grandparents were halwa connoisseurs – Nani Jee in cooking and Babu Jee in eating the rich dessert. So iconic is the sweetmeat that the Punjabi word for confectioner, halwai, derives from it. Halwa's popularity lies in the region's renown as the bread basket of India. Wheat, the primary ingredient, is integral to Punjabi identity and strong landowning tradition where social prestige is determined by the ability to grow one's own wheat. Each household has its own distinct halwa recipe, each with its own taste and texture.

As *Karah Prasad*, halwa holds deep significance for Sikhs, for whom preparing *Karah* is, in itself, a religious act requiring prior purification and recitation of scriptures during the process. Thought to be initiated by the Gurus to be served at the close of communal worship, the simple recipe – equal parts whole wheat flour, sweetener and clarified butter, cooked with water equal to their combined weight, and served from the same bowl – promotes humility, eliminates class distinctions and reminds the congregation of the abundance, sustenance and sweetness of life which the Gurus have bestowed upon them.

Grandma was an only child, born just after the turn of the twentieth century and raised lovingly by her maternal grandparents, after the plague 'with the rats falling from the roofs' claimed her mother when she was barely ten years old. She wasn't allowed near the tandoor in case it darkened her fair complexion, so it was only upon marriage that she learned to manage her own kitchen. She may not have been the best cook, but Nani Jee understood that a good halwa required practice, patience, physical effort and the purest home-grown ingredients. In order to make the most of the abundance and flexibility of wheat, in frugal times, she also needed ingenuity and a mastery of the breadth of preparation techniques in her culinary repertoire passed down by previous generations.

On the occasion of Eid, Nani Jee went to great lengths to ensure her halwa was the centre of attention. Her benchmark every year was to produce the finest, softest and whitest flour resulting in a far superior dessert, its sheen and luxurious richness a subtle marker of the cook's class and affluence. Having cleaned the wheat of stones, straw and other debris, she left it to soak overnight to soften and lighten, before straining and setting it in the afternoon sun to dry. Long before sunrise the following morning, Nani Jee would set to work at the quern from her dowry to produce flour of the finest degree of smoothness. Having adjusted the space between the two stones, she poured the swollen grain through the cavity in the upper disk with one hand, clasping the upright handle with the other to rotate the stone, changing positions as her arm grew tired. She shunned the village automated mill believing it produced a flour inferior in quality and nutrition. In any case, it was cheaper to grind her own. For relief from the monotony and loneliness of labouring at the quern, and to give thanks for the bounty before her, she would recite extracts from the Qur'an; her soothing, melodious tone accompanying the measured, rhythmic whirring of the revolving stone lulling her youngsters back to sleep. Drenched from the grind, she now passed the milled flour through a fine sieve to remove the abrasive brown husk until she was satisfied with its fineness.

Grandma could barely read anything other than the Qur'an when she married Babu Jee in the mid 1920s. Theirs was a formidable partnership, with respect for each other's values at its core. Given her devout nature, grandma asked her husband to recite Sura Yasin, such a commanding chapter with benefits manifold that it's often referred to as the 'heart of the Qur'an'. It is said to be particularly valuable in easing the path that lies ahead and is therefore recited to the dying. They say my grandfather was unable to recite so his bride insisted he commit the verse to memory. It would be enriching for him, she reasoned. A *havaldar* in the army, he was often posted out of town – Ambala first, then Abbottabad and Razmak – so he'd have the benefit of carrying the verse with him, being able to call upon it at a moment's notice.

Returning on leave just a couple of times a year, Babu Jee brought with him accoutrements like English soap and toothpaste. He was one of the first men in Nila to wear a wristwatch and the Raleigh bicycle that he rode forty-five kilometres to Chakwal was so rare that his kinsmen called it an iron horse. When the family slept on the flat-roof on hot summer nights, he would ceremoniously set up his prized gramophone on a table, laying out a cloth underneath. As the songs of Iqbal Bano and Noor Jahan travelled across the rooftops, villagers would congregate to marvel at this new contraption.

Babu Jee insisted that his wife learn to write Urdu. What he conveyed in letters to his wife, he didn't want to share with a third party. Accepting this challenge, Nani Jee would hide the chalkboard she practised on, lest the womenfolk mock her for writing love letters, training her eye just enough to read only her husband's handwriting.

It had been more than two years since his last letter arrived in Nila, written from the ship that was transferring troops to Malaya. With uncertainty ahead, his wife would now receive his pay. He also entrusted to her the responsibility for the future of their first born, a girl named Shehzad. Since she was approaching marriageable age, he would accept whatever decision his wife took in his absence.

Nani Jee sat by the stove of her neat outdoor kitchen in the freshly swept courtyard, exchanging cooking updates with her *bhabi* who was occupied on the other side of the mud wall. Bibi Khatoon was the wife of Nani Jee's half-brother with whom she shared a special bond; Bibi Khatoon also happened to be Babu Jee's half-sister. This sort of brother-sister pair marriage exchange was common in Nila and made for some convoluted interrelationships, although it was always the matrilineal or patrilineal relationships rather than bonds created through marriage that took precedence. While the main gate from Nani Jee's courtyard opened onto the road, for ease and security she'd had another gate installed beside her outdoor kitchen which opened directly into her brother's courtyard.

Nani Jee began to soften the sifted flour by soaking it in milk, making it lighter still and easier to digest. Sturdy yet radiant, thrifty and resourceful, she bought nothing she could produce herself. Even though it was a few years since the cow from her dowry was reluctantly sold, it still irked my grandmother that the ghee for the household had to be paid for. Unwilling to compromise on quality, she sent a labourer to source the purest homemade ghee – from its appearance alone Nani Jee's trained eye had to be satisfied that every last trace of buttermilk had been evaporated. Now, with her largest, heavy bottomed *karah* on the lowest heat, Nani Jee poured in the ghee and sugar in equal parts, then she added two parts water, and brought the *chaash* (syrup) to a boil. If the syrup didn't cook for long enough, it would taste raw. Overcooking would leave the halwa with an unappealingly dark hue, or worst still, a brittle texture. Some dedication and elbow grease were now needed to push the wooden spoon continuously back and forth through the dense, sticky mass – the finer the flour, the greater the risk of the mixture catching or becoming lumpy. Nani Jee stopped only when she saw that the oil was separating, the dessert was starting to come away from the side of the *karah,* and pushing the spoon through the mixture was no longer a struggle. She timed it perfectly, making sure the *halwa* was ready and a serving set aside for *darood*, just as the men returned from Eid prayers, ready to sweeten their mouths.

When Eid fell in winter, Nani Jee's halwa preparations began up to a month beforehand. She used a complex, time-consuming and labour-intensive process to make *nishasta,* a very fine and nutritious flour with a pleasantly sour tinge which had to be creatively balanced in combination with other flours. She began by covering the wheat with water in a *doli* (wide mouthed clay pot), leaving enough room for the kernels to swell up. The *doli* was left in the sun for a couple of weeks, changing the frothy water every two or three days. As the kernels began to ferment, the pungent smell drew complaints from the children. Once the grains were plump, the water was filtered out and the process of crushing could begin.

Next, she painstakingly pounded the plump brewed grains in her pestle and mortar, a few at a time until the grain cracked to expose the starchy endosperm. Having placed beside her a couple of clay dishes filled with water, Nani Jee would transfer the contents from the mortar after a bit of pounding. As the pounding separated the components, the undisturbed water bath made the leftover husk rise to the top and the key ingredient

– the clear white pulpy starch – seep out from the kernel and settle at the bottom of the dish. Tilting the vessel carefully washed away the husk and left the undisturbed crystal clear, pure white starch at the bottom.

To dry out the *nishasta*, Nani Jee covered it with a piece of cotton fabric and spread on it ash from wood fire she'd retained from the cooking stove. Left overnight, the ash acted as a sponge, absorbing the remaining moisture without adding any smell or colour. When the cotton fabric was removed, what was left was a clean white powder – of the consistency and colour of corn starch. This, grandma would spread out on a mat to dry completely before scraping off the pieces and rubbing them between her fingers. Once the *nishasta* resembled a lump free powder, it could be stored away.

Of the fifty or so houses packed into enclosed ancestral land measuring some thirteen acres, Nani Jee's house was one of the few that fronted onto the main road. Passed down by forefathers of Nani Jee's maternal grandfather, the same clan occupied the simple one or two-roomed dwellings, separated on either side by a narrow path. The clan's women were able to move freely since the path was completely private and any male, non-family member was immediately identified and strictly forbidden entry. Grandma's location at the head of the ancestral land made her the envy of her half-brothers and cousins since she now controlled one of the entrances to the 'sector'. Much to her consternation, her courtyard became an informal thoroughfare for the extended family to reach the main road. And much to everyone else's chagrin, every time she fell out with her neighbouring brother's wife, Nani Jee padlocked the adjoining gate and closed off the short cut to the entire clan.

To have inherited land in her own right was a source of great pride for Nani Jee. In a bid to give her economic independence, her grandfather also allotted her some scraps of land by the River Soan on which she could grow her own wheat and lentils on a sharecropping basis. To get construction under way, Nani Jee pooled the saving from her husband's army income and sold her wedding gifts – the notably hefty bracelets from her in-laws weighing the equivalent of 250 grams, as well as the cow from her grandparents. When the funds ran out, she paid the labourers the equivalent of their fee in grain. To save on cost, Nani Jee herself set to work with the builder and labourers. Wearing her husband's discarded khaki drill uniform shirt over her traditional *kameez,* she would spend the day fetching water for cement. Help was at hand too – on occasion, up to eight aunts and cousins would return with her from the Persian wheel, each gracefully balancing two pots on her head.

Compared with the size of the courtyard, the two rooms were small, but it was usual to build only what was needed. Nani Jee referred to the rooms as *'maals'* (from *'mahal'*, meaning palace), the main chamber being the primary indicator of Nani Jee's aesthetic and status. Commanding immediate attention was an intricately decorated timber shelf strategically placed directly opposite the entrance. Here, Nani Jee displayed her favourite possessions – the larger brass vessels along the wall at the back and the smaller dainty bone china pieces along the front. She painstakingly removed each item daily, attentively dusting and meticulously replacing it in the designated spot. The room also housed Nani Jee's precious dowry pieces – two *palangs* (bed cots) and *peerhas* (low seated, high backed wedding stools) with exquisitely lacquered feet – one each from her own dowry and the other from her mother's. When a girl was born, Nani Jee would say, a deodar tree ('timber of the gods' in Sanskrit) was felled and left by the well to be weathered. When the girl matured, the timber was used to produce durable furniture for her matrimonial home.

The smaller *maal* was sparse in décor and furnishing. The adjoining store featured a small brick shaped hole which opened into the courtyard of a notorious dacoit. Rumoured to have murdered two men in a duel, Bheru Badmash fiercely guarded his own neighbourhood and in the event of a threat – snake, scorpion, intruder – it was reassuring to have him nearby.

Four houses separated Nani Jee's home from her aunt, Maa Arshan, whose halwa-making was even more punctilious resulting in a crystalline sweetmeat with a barely perceptible bite. It was also considered excellent for a cold or stomach ailment. '*Dodhi wala halwa*' she called it, after the milky pulp or '*doodh*' she painstakingly mined from the kernel. Maa Arshan's technique involved scrupulously rinsing out the wheat starch by kneading ball after ball of dough in a warm water bath, patiently straining the emerging milky white liquid through a lightweight muslin *dupatta* into a strategically placed wide, flat bottomed earthenware vessel. Once all the precious starch had been extracted, the remaining dough, now wholly glutinous and springy, was deemed a waste product and fed to the goats. As the starch settled in a thick white pulpy layer at the bottom, the clear water at the top was gently drained. The freshly prepared moist extract was then roasted gently with sugar and ghee in an earthen cooking vessel.

Given the effort involved, it was only possible to make this sort of decadent halwa in small quantities, just enough for the immediate and extended family. So Nani Jee always made a second batch on Eid, this time in a much larger quantity, specifically for distribution to the menial workers known as *kami*. The *kami*, which literally means 'lesser', were a distinct social group of craftsmen who did not have land and couldn't therefore grow their own wheat. Through birth-ascribed occupations that were vital for village life – among them barbers, cobblers, carpenters, potters, blacksmiths, washermen, tailors, musicians – the *kami* depended on the agricultural community for their livelihood. Under the cashless system, each family of menial workers provided year-round labour, based on their craft, to one specific *zamindar* (land-owning) clan, in exchange for a fixed proportion of the harvest, paid in sheaves of grain, through a longstanding agreement going back many generations. Just as the agreement could not be broken, a *kami* could not shed his caste and the title – be it *nai* (barber) or *darzi* (tailor) – and remained attached from one generation to another.

Thus, on the auspicious day of Eid, much like their parents and grandparents before them, the *kami* visited each of the *zamindar* households with which they were associated to offer their greetings. In return, by way of an Eid tip for their ongoing labour, each *kami* received a generous portion of halwa to take back to his family. The visiting *kami* presented his own bowl into which each household tipped the kami's share of the dessert.

Nani Jee prepared a less laborious halwa for the *kami* using shop bought semolina, even though for such a special occasion, its crude texture rendered it below par for the immediate family. Nevertheless, roasting semolina made light work – Nani Jee waited just long enough for the grain to emit its fragrant aroma. Any less and the semolina would taste raw; over roasting would darken the grain unnecessarily. The process was relatively quick and since one cup absorbed four times the water, it was also economical. Since white sugar was precious and, in any case rationed, Nani Jee sweetened the halwa with the cheaper jaggery, made from concentrated sugar-cane juice. Although she used jaggery routinely in her kitchen, for instance to sweeten the tea which soldiers returning from the Great War had introduced to the region, it was no longer a fashionable halwa ingredient since its dark colour and grainy texture would negate the effort of soaking the kernels to soften and lighten the end result. Nani Jee skimped on the ghee too – the trick was to add a dollop at the end for a shiny finish. Given the lower grade ingredients, the *kami halwa* was inevitably grainy, chewy, dark and dense.

Considering the number of households they visited on Eid, the *kami* inevitably collected more halwa than it was possible to eat. Enterprisingly, they recycled the leftovers by adding flour to make a dough, shaping it into flat cakes and baking these in the tandoor. The cookie-like treat extended the halwa's shelf life in the days following Eid. It also proved to be a popular, portable treat among children of the neighbourhood including Nani Jee's boy, who would bring a small measure of wheat to the *kami* house to exchange for a couple of halwa rotis on his way to school.

Although Nani Jee's grandfather, who had assumed responsibility for her decisions, wasn't averse to boys having a formal education, he was of the view that studying beyond matriculation was harmful – scientific knowledge, he believed, could result in abandoned faith. Nani Jee's only son was growing up fast and preparing for matriculation at the prestigious Mota Singh Khalsa High School. Most of Ahmed's classmates were Hindu or Sikh for whom life in Nila was prosperous – some belonged to trading families, others ran businesses in the thriving bazaar, others still had large landholdings.

The five Muslim boys in Ahmed's class knew from experience that agricultural wealth in Nila was the preserve of the few since most holdings were meagre and fragmented. The area was entirely dependent on rainfall so every season farmers waited for nature to dampen the soil before seeds could be sown. So much so that once the soil was wet, even the dead waited to be buried because seeding took precedence. Again, farmers looked to the sky to water the sowed land. Come harvest time in April, the sharecropper took his allocation and the various *kami* labourers collected their share. Nani Jee kept a sharp eye on the remainder, making sure she stored enough to see the family through until the following year, reserving what she could for barter. Falling short before the end of the year was a matter of much embarrassment, and if you had to borrow grain, you did so discreetly. Anyone fortunate enough to have a bountiful harvest kept it out of sight to ward off the dreaded evil eye. Those unable to get through the year without the fatal facility of credit now faced the wrath of the Hindu moneylender, with repayment at the highest rates of interest, in the form of equivalent measure of grain.

For a village like Nila with no industry other than agriculture, where men were mostly unskilled and illiterate, and where it was considered degrading for anyone other than the subordinate *kami* caste to perform any sort of paid labour, joining the army was a blessing, thus men at arms became a permanent part of local life. The tradition of serial recruitment was the norm. How many ancestors perched around how many houses knew the drill? As long as you had good lineage, were fit and healthy, and educated to matriculation, you could command a regular salary as well as respect. The Punjab became renowned for recruitment of martial races after the 1857 Indian Rebellion, when British officers deemed the region's men, along with Gurkhas and Pathans, to be fierce, brave and loyal fighters. The area consequently produced some of the best soldiers in British India. In fact, the nearby village of Dulmial, commonly known as 'the village with the gun' was famed for sending 460 soldiers out of a population of 878 males as part of the massive volunteer army raised to serve in the British forces during World War 1, the largest participation of any village in South Asia. Nine lost their lives, whether on the Western Front or in the debacle of Mesopotamia (Iraq) I know not. In recognition of this service and sacrifice, in 1925 the British government presented Dulmial with a cannon, now located at the entrance of the village.

The soldier life was on the one hand stable, secure and honourable. On the other hand, it was inevitably insecure as the conflicts of empires and would-be empires increasingly resounded around the world over the course of the twentieth century. Unsure of what the future held and perhaps in need of some hope, Nani Jee arranged Shehzad's wedding with the son of her favourite step-brother. Her daughter would be moving two doors away. By now war was much more than rumour. Hitler was on the offensive and Japan was on the march. This time an even larger volunteer army was raised to serve the British war effort. Despite war time austerity curtailing the scale with which weddings were celebrated, Nani Jee was determined her daughter's nuptials should be a fitting occasion for a family of her social standing. With provisions scarce and restrictions abundant,

Nani Jee's brother (also the groom's father) accompanied her on foot to the government depot in Dudial, with pooled coupons from the extended family to draw the permissible quantity of essentials like bales of fabric, all of which were transported back to Nila on camels.

The *kami* labourers were on standby, with the head of each caste supervising a specific task. Several hundred guests were expected since, as well as clan members residing in neighbouring villages, every member of the fifty or so households located within Nani Jee's residential sector had been invited. While catering for any gathering traditionally fell to the *nai* (barber), the preparation of halwa for a joyous event was always the *darzi's* (tailor) duty. A memorable wedding dinner featured two courses – a meat curry served with rotis, followed of course by halwa, which on this occasion would be richer for the addition of *khoa* (dried whole milk solids), '*cho cho paunda*' (dripping with ghee) as Babu Jee would say, and topped with scant slivers of dried fruit for a touch of luxury.

Ten days before the wedding, Nani Jee began to host nightly song circles in her courtyard. With daily chores complete, women from the extended family joined the bride's girlfriends to sing an assortment of familiar songs centred on Shehzad's impending send-off. These were folk songs or *tappay* about rites and relationships as well as dreams, desires and domesticity; some sung solo, others with a choral response, with enthusiastic collective hand-clapping, accompanied all the time by the *mirasan* (the wife of the *kami* bard) on a small barrel drum. As the song session heated up, one of the girls would embellish the drum beat with the rap of a spoon. Leading the singing was Ami Jee's cousin, Garaan. Known for her exuberant personality and excellent repertoire of folk songs for every occasion, her melodious voice at any gathering was a crowd-puller. She was known to also craft her own lyrics, making them all the more relatable by adding a name here, some other detail there.

Like many women in Nila, she had witnessed the harsh reality of war. The news that both her sons were officially recorded 'missing in action' had left her in a state of limbo. With no remains to bury, she was unable to accept her loss – and without closure, she clung to the hope that they might still be alive. She articulated her pain through song with such heart-wrenching sincerity that no mourning gathering was complete without her.

Now, on the bittersweet occasion of Shehzad's marriage, night after night for the duration of the festivities, Garaan sang one wedding song after another, the lyrics poignantly capturing the contempt which Nani Jee and her daughter must have felt at this hour towards the perpetrators of a war that was keeping Babu Jee from them.

Hitler tera bacha marray
Kyon lama laayan nee
Hattian te mehndi aye
Babu Shehzad da Japan tay kaidi aye

Hitler, may your son die
Why did you start the war?
The shops are selling mehndi
But Shehzad's father is captured in Japan

GOD KNOWS BEST

Leyla Jagiella

I want to begin with a story. And, I have to admit, this is not my story. It was originally composed in the year 1627 by the Ottoman poet Nevizade 'Atayi. Translated and partly retold in much more elaborate and eloquent form by Mehmet Kalpakli and Walter G. Andrews in *The Age of Beloveds*, it has also made a beautiful appearance in Joseph Allen Boone's *The Homoerotics Of Orientalism*. The titles of these two publications may already provide you with a hint at the direction in which this story will go. There will, unsurprisingly, be some mention of beloveds and homoeroticism. And the reader will most likely expect that I will write on what is by now an almost clichéd narrative that the Muslim past was tolerant and diverse and embracing of many sexualities, unlike a large part of our post-colonial Muslim present. Much has indeed already been written and published on this narrative already. So much that even I – allegedly somewhat of a stakeholder in current Muslim Queer debates – am getting quite tired, not to say bored, of it. So, don't worry dear reader: Homoerotics and tolerance will play a certain role in this essay. But I actually want to go somewhere else with all of this.

The story that I refer to proved to be a huge hit with the Ottoman readership of the seventeenth century. You could call it an early modern Ottoman bestseller. Atayi presented it in the form of a poem, as part of his 'Heft han' (Seven Stories). I shall give you a short prose retelling by heart:

Once upon a time in Istanbul there used to live two adventurous young friends. Their names were Tayyib and Tahir. Coming from well-to-do families, they did not have any existential worries to care about. All they needed to think about was how to best enjoy their time. By that, they wasted their youth with much pleasure and merrymaking. But, in the end, also quickly wasted a lot of their money while doing so. And one day they had to come to the sad realisation that they only had each other in this world. Because all other friends that had been with them in their best days had now left them in their worst days. Apparently, they had been more in love with Tayyib and Tahir's money and the comfort that their company offered to them than with Tayyib and Tahir themselves.

Tayyib and Tahir had barely reached twenty years old at that point and had already realised that the delights of this world were not the best to chase after. They decided to become dervishes. And they embarked on a ship to Egypt to join a famous Sufi order where they would dedicate their lives to the remembrance of Allah. Unfortunately, their ship was caught by infidel Frankish pirates. And Tayyib and Tahir were separated and sold into slavery in Europe. Tayyib ended up with an English master called Sir John, while Tahir became the slave of an Italian called Gianno.

Let us discard all modern concerns regarding consent and the possibilities of true love in settings of slavery for a while. And let us, for the moment, simply believe what Atayi has to tell us: that Sir John and Gianno were good masters to their slaves and that they were genuinely worried about the wellbeing of the young men in their possession. And Tayyib and Tahir were likewise attracted to their two kind and equally handsome older masters. And after a while, Sir John and Tayyib passionately fell in love with each other, as did Gianno and Tahir.

The two couples were almost as happy as one could be in this world. But Tahir and Tayyib were still distraught that they had been separated from each other. One day Tayyib poured out his heart to Sir John and told him about his yearning for his friend Tahir. Sir John was deeply moved by Tayyib's feelings for his best friend and made sure to contact Gianno as soon as possible. Finally the two couples were able to unite. They spent happy days together, each couple reveling in the love of the other couple. Tahir and Tayyib were back to pleasure and merrymaking but this time, even better, in the company of two older men who loved them dearly. At this point Atayi could almost have ended this story with, and 'they lived happily ever after'. Alas!

A zealous Christian troublemaker – 'who believed the love of beauties a crime', as Atayi tells us - discovered the love between the two Frankish noblemen and the two Turkish young men. He denounced them to the police commander of the town. The Frankish authorities, alarmed by the scandalous claims made by the zealous Christian, separated the young lovers. Tahir and Tayyib were chained to the oars of a galley, while Sir John and Gianno were thrown into prison.

It was at this point that a miracle occurred. In prison, Sir John and Gianno contemplated the possibility of converting to the Muslim faith of their beloveds. During the following night, they both had a dream in which the Prophet Muhammad appeared to them, removed their shackles, opened the door of their carcer and told them that 'the gates of all of their desires had been thrown open'. When they woke up, indeed, all their shackles and chains were gone and the prison doors were wide open. Meanwhile, the galley on which Tahir and Tayyib were enslaved was captured by Ottomans enabling Tahir and Tayyib to be set free. By further miraculous twists and turns, the two young men were able to reunite with the likewise miraculously liberated Sir John and Gianno. Sir John took the name Mahmud and Gianno took the name Mesud. They returned to Istanbul with Tahir and Tayyib where the four lovers lived together - happily ever after.

We can read this story now in the apologetic setting of proving the tolerance that existed within Islamic traditions. I have done so myself a number of times, during talks and workshops on such issues such as sexuality in Islamicate societies. It is almost inevitable that by reading this story in our times we immediately politicise it. We give it some significance in a discourse that we build to confront the narrative of a repressive and oppressive shari'a-centric Islam that is so prevalent in our world. The narrative that we try to confront is a reductive one, without any nuance. But by confronting it we find that what we have done is created just another narrative that is equally as reductive. Worse still, both narratives are far away from the message that Atayi wanted to convey with this story, and with why it became such a bestseller in its time.

Atayi did not consider it to be particularly remarkable to tell a story of two homoerotic couples. He was following a well-established convention that had also been cultivated by such illustrious names as Hafez and Sa'adi before him. Again, much has been written on the topos of homoeroticism in Islamicate culture already. It would be too simple to claim that there were no people in previous Muslim societies who did not object to such idealisations of same-gender love. There have always been some. Although, interestingly, when seeking an embodiment for religious sexual repression,

'Atayi chose the persona of the Christian zealot who blew the whistle on Tahir and Tayyib. A very conscious statement on the righteousness of 'love of beauties'. What is even more revealing is the fact that a sacred vision finally comes to the aid of the lovers to defeat the plot of the zealot and to even lead Sir John and Gianno into the blessed arms of Islam. In the end, everything is fine. Everybody has become a Muslim. Everybody is free. Everybody is in love.

The curious combination of elements in this Ottoman bestseller shock even some of us who have been quite used to the trope of homoeroticism in Islamicate literature. There is a modern tendency to set up such literature as a 'world of its own'. We know that there were respected scholars of Muslim law who wrote homoerotic poetry on the side and saw nothing bad in that. Thomas Bauer has written on the inherent 'tolerance of ambiguity' that was a typical feature of classic Islamicate civilisation: People were able to access and negotiate seemingly contradictory sources of knowledge (such as for example the Qur'an, Greek philosophy and Persian *savoir vivre*) without feeling conflicted. But usually we get the impression that the majority of people knew the difference between the Qur'an and Persian *savoir vivre* and would keep them apart, they did not confuse the one with the other. In 'Atayi's story, however, there is not any ambiguity left: The Divine Will, most probably in the form of the Prophet himself, approves of the love described and aids it against the bigoted.

We have a theoretical knowledge of the cultural ambiguities of a past Islam and those of us defending inclusive approaches to our faith nowadays – whether in the face of Western Islamophobia or of repressive approaches within Muslim societies – often resort to literary sources such as 'Atayi, Sa'adi and Hafez to make this knowledge tangible to readers and listeners. But the truth is that despite our theoretical knowledge we still far too often find it difficult to feel the spirit of these sources. We understand intellectually that for 'Atayi and for the society in which he lived, his work, a bestseller in homoerotic relationships, and a spiritual journey are not necessarily opposites. But in our obsession to constantly dig out such sources to make a point regarding Islam we demonstrate how far away many of us are from the Islam that 'Atayi breathed and lived. We cannot wrap our heads around the Islam of Nevizade 'Atayi. Something has been lost in translation over the centuries. Forever and irretrievably, it seems. I will come back to the role that Colonialism did or did not play in this (after all, was 'Atayi's Turkey ever properly colonised, in the strict sense of the word). However, just for the sake of making another more tangible statement: we can never become pre-colonial again in a post-colonial world.

Was it only Muslims' relationship with sexuality and eroticism that had been lost in translation over the centuries? Given that the worship of beauty and the expression of a *millat-i 'ishq* (a confession of love) in literature formed a central focus of Islamicate cultures for centuries of its existence, we may realise that this changed relationship with eroticism is just a symptom of a larger wound of the heart that Islam has suffered. When there is a wound of the heart, how can the whole being recover? After all, we know a great deal about the importance of the heart in Islam. In the twelfth century the Anatolian Turkish poet Yunus Emre wrote: 'you may perform the Hajj a hundred times. But it won't help you if you break a single human heart'. Curiously, the seventeenth century Punjabi poet Bullhe Shah wrote almost exactly the same: 'tear down the mosque and temple. But do not break a human heart. It is there where God resides'. How interesting, a twelfth century Anatolian and a seventeenth century Punjabi expressing the exact same idea in almost the same words.

The idea that breaking a human heart is worse than neglecting one's ritual duties towards God cuts across ages and geographies in Islam. Muslims have known this from medieval times until today and from the Balkans up to Southeast Asia. It also cuts across social classes and strata. Atayi's story was literature for the Ottoman elites. The poetry of a Yunus Emre or a Bullhe Shah has been sung by illiterate bards for ages and is known to almost everybody within their respective cultural contexts. As such, we can call it a central idea of global Islam. Almost as widespread as, say, fasting in Ramadan or praying five times a day.

The issue here is strongly connected to the spirit that has been lost in translation in our modern perception of 'Atayi's story. Beyond circles of a slightly New-Age-y Sufism, the idea that the human heart is more sacrosanct than ritual performance has become decentralised within our modern discourses. Even the more established Sufi tariqas admit that 'yes, the heart is important'. But then to prove their shari'a-conformity in the face of modern conceptions of Islam, relegate it. This despite the fact that such a 'but' would be totally alien to Yunus Emre and Bullhe Shah. Bullhe

Shah is someone who is quoted by Pakistani Communists as much as by Pakistani Sunni Extremists. But his philosophy, and the philosophy of many other like-minded poets and thinkers of Islam, has become largely inconsequential with regards to how we relate to Islam. This is not to say that rays and sparks of his ideas do not light up here and there. But as far as the evolving religious and social forces of our current Islamic world are concerned, the words of a Yunus Emre or a Bullhe Shah have become as much strangers to us as the stories of a Nevizade 'Atayi. And when quoted, they are more often than not subjected to modern sensibilities. I have mentioned Pakistani communist appropriations of Bullhe Shah. Something similar has happened with Yunus Emre in political discourse in Turkey. But such embrace of classical Islamic poetry are as modern as they are misappropriations.

The renowned Maulana Jalaluddin Rumi once wrote:

Millat-é 'ishq az hama dîn-hâ jodâ-st 'âshiq-ân-râ millat-o mazhab khodâ-st.

The sect of love is distinct from all religions; the sect and doctrine of the lovers is God himself.

New Agers love this *shêr* (couplet) and read it as a confirmation of their ideas. Salafis and Wahhabis denounce it as *shirk*. The modern tariqa Sufis say 'yes, but the language of poetry should not be confused with its spiritual message and only the initiated can understand Rumi properly after years of study.' The Maulana of Rum, whose secret may be sanctified, was neither of these. He was not a modern man. He was a poet, a lover, a mystic, and an esteemed and respected scholar of *fiqh*. He was a Muslim in a way that we are unable to be Muslim today.

Many of the intellectual struggles we face in modern Islam could be solved by simply relying on the knowledge that 'the heart is more sacrosanct than any ritual performance'. It could all be pretty simple and easy, no? But somehow it isn't. And even when we have a theoretical knowledge of principles such as these, we cannot get our head around how Muslims of the past were able to negotiate similar struggles without seeing a need to dissolve such perceived contradictions.

I referred earlier to Thomas Bauer, who has written on how much a 'tolerance of ambiguity' was central to classical Islamicate thought but has been lost in modernity. Shahab Ahmed has described the historical situation and the change that has occurred in modernity in his *What is Islam?* While Bauer still seems to see a need to somehow extract a secular and non-religious 'Islamicity' from actual 'religion', Ahmed demonstrates very well how such a bifurcation would have made no sense to the pre-modern Muslims. The so-called ambiguity that is 'tolerated' exists, in the end, only in the eyes of modernity itself. A civilisational discourse that had made the heart the centre of *adab* (good manners – again, something is lost in translation) is not ambiguous. It just has its priorities right.

Both Bauer and Ahmed blame modernity for the break that we have experienced in our Muslim traditions. Since modernity came and conquered the world, the heart has become a symbol of irrational emotionality. Not a good guide on the path towards progress. A plurality of knowledges could not be tolerated anymore. People needed truth; rational, demonstratable, unambiguous truth. Colonialism certainly played a big part in that development. Not only in those regions, where good old-fashioned imperial Colonialism proper had direct rule over populations. Colonialism, as the global dominance of the West, was felt everywhere.

There is a great deal to be learned from authors such as Bauer and Ahmed on the larger historical and political games that have alienated us from the spirit of pre-modern Islam. The large corpus of post-colonial studies also has much to add to that. As such, our break with the spirit of classical Islam is a political problem. Extensive analysis has been done on this political problem, but I would also like to look at it as a spiritual problem. Not denying the wound that both modernity and colonialism have inflicted on Islam and on our ability to relate to our Muslim heritage, I also feel that – at least as believers – we need to talk about our own spiritual complicity with maintaining this wound and not letting it heal.

A well-known hadith – one that is very much in the tradition of the 'sect of love' – says that God will appear to each believer in the way that the believer thinks of Him. The most obvious message that people are likely to draw from this hadith is the necessity of believing in a merciful God. Which is also very much in the spirit of the Qur'anic verse that teaches us to 'never despair of the mercy of God' (39:53). Again, this is a teaching that almost every Muslim has heard but which has become largely inconsequential in practice when we try to negotiate *halal* and *haram* (and the erroneously forgotten stages in-between) in our lives. But there is another message in this hadith; one that I consider more profound: One on the absolute nature of the Divine and its actual transcendence of all human viewpoints of the Divine.

Here, as well, most Muslims will say that they know about this very well. We are all taught that no human being can fully comprehend Allah and that all our human knowledge of religion is by nature limited and imperfect. The Qur'an assures that 'above every knowledgeable one there is one who is more knowledgeable' (12:76). And even the most dogmatic fundamentalist (or, actually, especially the most dogmatic fundamentalist) will add an *Allahu a'lam* to his pronouncements – 'I cannot say anything with absolute knowledge, God knows best'.

Allahu a'lam has, as well, become one of those ritualised elements of our modern Muslim existence that has become absolutely inconsequential in our lives. We find the most essentialising discourses being uttered by Muslims, in angry and emotionally agitated voices and then an *Allahu a'lam* is added to it all, as if the speaker had not just basically condemned everybody else to hell with a quiet and somewhat passive aggressive conviction. What if we would actually approach matters of faith and religion with a constant reminder of *Allahu a'lam* in our hearts? What if we would actually make that 'knowledge of not knowing anything' an actual practical reality in all our dealings with others?

There is no reason to romanticise our Muslim past too much. There has been devastating repression and oppression in the Muslim past as well. Each society creates normativities and they will always be painful and problematic for those who seek to negate them. The Muslim past was no paradise on earth. But the different attitude that the pre-modern Muslim had towards so many issues that as modern Muslims we find hard to wrap our heads around does have a lot to do with our alienation from the profound wisdom that the statement 'God knows best' carries. The early Muslim debates between the Mut'azila and their opponents were essentially debates on the question 'what can we actually know?'. The arguments thrashed out later in the debates between Ibn Rushd and al-Ghazali focussed on the same subject. And the concerns of the Persian transcendentalist school founded by Mulla Sadra in the seventeenth century, strictly opposed by the Sheikhs in the eighteenth century, were focused on exactly this. Again and again the intellectual tradition of Islam raises the question: 'what can we actually know?'

In the modern age, Muslims have sought to champion the idea that Islam is an especially 'rational' religion. The idea has bred the notorious 'engineers' Islam' that became so prevalent in educated circles in the Middle East in the course of the twentieth century. It has also bred a whole range of books expounding on the scientific character of the Qur'an. The Qur'an certainly urges us to think and reflect again and again, ruminating over and over and introspecting as well as analysing our contemporary context. It is due to its adoption of Greek philosophy that Islamic tradition certainly gives a high value to human reason. But pre-modern Muslim ideas of this version of rationality were actually quite different from the modern conception of a scientific rationalism. Qur'an and hadith urge us to listen to our hearts at least as much as to our minds. In fact, Muslim tradition can be discerned as viewing the heart as the actual seat of the mind while emotional and rational intelligence are not always disentangled fully. In fact, they may actually be the same.

In our current social and political climate, the idea of mixing rationalism with emotion may seem dangerous. Wouldn't that eventually justify the reign of that dismissive retort of 'alternative facts' that we see rising in our day and age? When what we feel to be true becomes what we know to be true. But that is not what previous Muslim debates on the question of what we can actually know implied. Because, after all, these debates never denied that there was something that was without doubt true. God is the Truth (al-Haqq).

But what much of pre-modern Muslim tradition emphasised was, in many ways, what in our times Chimamanda Ngozi Adichie has called the 'danger of a single story' or an overarching and dominant narrative that drowns out all other voices. If God is the Truth, but at the same time beyond full human knowledge and comprehension, and if He meets each and every single believer according to the image that the believer has of the Divine, then there simply cannot be only one true story, or only one true narrative of Islam. Certainly, many pre-modern Muslims argued that there existed many narratives of Islam, some that are better than others. But that argument would at some point sooner or later always arrive at its limits.

When we come to a true realisation that 'God knows best' then we also come to an understanding that knows that each single human being carries his or her own story. A story that has as much of a history, as much of a rationality, as much of an emotionality as our own story. We can grasp that each and every human being longs as much for love and recognition as we do, and that it is that longing which moves each human being's story, their own personal narrative. It is only then that we may actually begin to understand why breaking a human heart is worse than neglecting one's ritual duties.

EMPIRE AND FREEDOM

Giles Goddard

'But history, real solemn history, I cannot be interested in. Can you?'
'Yes, I am fond of history.'
'I wish I were too. I read it a little as a duty, but it tells me nothing that does not either vex or weary me. The quarrels of popes and kings, with wars or pestilences, in every page; the men all so good for nothing, and hardly any women at all – it is very tiresome.'

Jane Austen, *Northanger Abbey*

There is a book, published in 1892, written by the Hon. Lady Inglis, entitled *The Siege of Lucknow*. It is a first-hand account of the defence of the Indian town of Lucknow, written by the wife of the general in command of the Residency when the fort was attacked. She speaks of the sterling defence by the tiny white force, supported by Indian soldiers of the British Army, against the mutinous rebels who had the temerity to attack the British Empire. On several occasions Lady Inglis' life was saved by her loyal servants. In the end the siege was lifted when reinforcements arrived from Calcutta.

It is not a good book. But it has a place in the Goddard canon; the book was given to me by my father, who had it because Lady Inglis was his grandmother. My father had a deep and passionate interest in his family history, tracing his line and that of my mother back as far as he could in every direction.

I was ordained a priest in the Church of England in September 1995, and on my ordination, he made a gift for me: a photo montage of all my illustrious ancestors on both sides, back to the beginning of the nineteenth century. They were: the first Bishop of Barbados; the Rector of Holy Trinity Wall Street who went on to become the first Colonial Bishop of Nova Scotia; the second Bishop of Perth, Western Australia; Sir William

Pepperell, first Governor of New England (who came back to England after the Unpleasantness of 1776); the aforementioned Major-General Sir John Inglis; a couple of mid-ranking clergy in this country; and my grandfather, Air Marshal Sir Victor Goddard.

'Let us now praise famous men,' runs the inscription in the centre of the montage, and around it stand stern looking bearded men in clerical garb or military uniform, and their wives, elegantly overdressed for the temperatures in which they must have had to survive. Louisa Hutton, the wife of the Bishop of Barbados, is particularly beautiful, her black hair in ringlets setting off a fine bone structure and deep dark eyes.

I did not know my father well. He was kept very much in the shadow of my mother, and when he died, in 1998, I was surprised by the warmth and richness of the tributes we received. He was a businessman whose career was marked by a lack of success. My parents' marriage was also not happy. My father sought solace in his family history. He was proud of his origins, claiming only partly in jest that we were descended from John of Gaunt (1340-99), the First Duke of Lancaster, and he hoped to make me proud too.

My mother came at it from a different angle. Her life had been marked by sadness. Her father died of tuberculosis when she was six. He was a Lieutenant in the Royal Navy and the widow's pension was tiny, so her childhood was spent in genteel poverty. My grandmother married a second time when my mother was twelve; her new stepfather was an oppressive and difficult man. The marriage to my father had been unhappy from the start, and was marked by tragedy when my brother, aged three, drowned in a pond in my grandmother's garden.

My mother took refuge in her family history as well. Born Susan de Lacy Bacon, descended from baronets, she constructed a narrative of class which dovetailed with, but, she thought, outshone her husband's. 'I married beneath myself,' she said to me once, in a moment of candour.

So I grew up in a middle class English family in the 1960s and 1970s, for whom the dominant story was of imperial worth. Not grandeur – even in the nineteenth century bishops were not especially grand, and colonial bishops even less so. And what wealth there had been was long gone. ('When I grew up,' said my mother recently, 'my grandparents had a kitchen like Downton Abbey's.' Her memory had expanded their house as well as its kitchen.)

I grew up being inculcated with a narrative about the families of which I am part and about the nation of which I am a member. The narrative was one of Purpose. Of Doing Right. Of going out and helping the natives by preserving them from the consequences of their own foolishness or by instilling in them the virtues of the Church of England. My parents embraced, in all its fullness, the White Man's Burden. It was something to be proud of in a world which seemed to be failing them. It was something to celebrate.

I had a classical education. I won a scholarship to a public school in Sussex founded originally for the sons of the clergy. As punishment, sometimes, I had to write out lines. I remember one in particular: 'Lancing College was founded in 1848, the year of revolutions.' But even though Lancing prided itself on being liberal, the curriculum was solidly conventional. British history lessons covered the key events. We learnt Dates. And Treaties. And Battles. We learnt, particularly, about the nineteenth century. The Age of Empire. The Great Reform Acts. The Mother of Democracy extending suffrage – but never to the colonies. The coronation of the Empress of India. Cecil Rhodes. Of course, sometimes, there were hints that not everything was quite as it should have been: but international history was expressed mostly in terms of the struggle with the French for global colonial dominance.

From the Indians and the Africans, we never heard. On a visit to India in 2001, I visited the town museum in every place we stopped. I looked especially at the presentation of the history of the nineteenth and early twentieth centuries. I was perplexed, initially, by an event which seemed to have taken place in 1857 – the first War of Independence, or the Indian Rebellion, in which many people were apparently martyred for the cause of liberating India from its oppressors. When I realised that the exhibits were referring to what we had always called the Indian Mutiny, I was taken aback.

I think the history curriculum has changed now. It seems to focus mainly on the Holocaust and the Second World War, but I have no doubt that when nineteenth-century history is taught, there are nods towards the ethical questions around the behaviour of the British in their colonies – not least because many teachers and many of those being taught are from families which originated on the 'wrong' side of Imperial control. Activist students are demanding change – the Rhodes Must Fall campaign in Oxford has had an effect on the University's approach to the Historical Tripos, although Rhodes' statue remains high above Oriel College. And the call for diversity in English literature is being heard with an increasing number of works by non-white and non-English authors being included as set texts.

But the overall narrative has not changed. Commenting on the Rhodes controversy, and a similar demand to remove the Royal Navy hero Lord Nelson's column due to his support for slavery, Sir Roy Strong, the former director of the Victorian and Albert Museum said: 'once you start rewriting history on that scale, there won't be a statue or a historic house standing.... the past is the past. You can't rewrite history.'

A list of key events in British history in the 'popular mind' would be likely to include, at least: the Norman Conquest, the Magna Carta, Henry VIII's split from Rome, the defeat of the Spanish Armada, Shakespeare, the expansion of the Empire and the First and Second World Wars. Some might include the Glorious Revolution and the scientific progress made in the nineteenth century.

With the exception of the Norman Conquest they are all events which reflect a story of plucky little England against the world. The Magna Carta is understood as an early manifestation of the profound English virtue of fair play, and the rest are victorious results of British skills and stratagems – a long march of triumph over a hostile world.

I am referring specifically to an English understanding of our national story. Scotland, Wales and Ireland all have their own narratives, which include an unavoidable awareness of the fact that they have each become part of the British imperial story, either as de facto colonies or as junior partners in the scramble for territory. Or a combination of the two.

As we rehearse the familiar story, inconvenient parts of our history are quietly forgotten. The treatment of Ireland, Wales and Scotland. The loss of the United States. The rape of India and the shameful division of Africa. The Suez Crisis. The active encouragement of the slave trade – the campaign to ban it took forty years to achieve success. Britain's imperial past is what makes us great, and no amount of agitation by ex-colonials will change that.

For evidence, see for example the increasing emphasis on the observation of Remembrance Sunday despite the fact that no one living remembers the First World War and very few the Second; the ritual has become a way to remind ourselves, as well as of those who died, of the most recent significant victories achieved by our armed forces. Or see the furious reactions to suggestions of further revision of school history curricula to make them more representative of the stories of people from the Indian subcontinent or Africa, and to make them more reflective of the policies and practices of the imperial civil service.

I grew up with a very clear sense that the British Empire at heart behaved well towards its subjects. We were taught to be amazed that a single Representative, on his own, far out in the bush and away from 'civilisation', could exercise responsibility over hundreds of thousands of Indians – proof, if proof were needed, that our rule was just and fair. We were taught that the introduction of railways and administration had laid the ground for the successes which post-independent countries could claim. If it wasn't for the British, who knows what might have happened? Other Empires were, we were told, much worse. It was only necessary to glance at the post-imperial history of Angola (colonised by the Portuguese) or the Democratic Republic of Congo (colonised by the Belgians) to see what unhappy fates the lucky beneficiaries of the British Empire avoided.

History, runs the well-known phrase, is told by the victors. The French philosopher Voltaire once said, 'the first foundations of all history are the recitals of the fathers to the children, transmitted afterward from one generation to another; at their origin they are at the very most probable, when they do not shock common sense, and they lose one degree of probability in each generation.'

But has the narrative of Empire really lost one degree of probability each time it is repeated, from one generation to another? It has had, in England, remarkable resilience. The story of the other side of empire is only now being heard. *Inglorious Empire* by Shashi Tharoor is a retelling of imperial Indian history from the point of view of India. One statistic will suffice. In 1700 India had a 27 per cent share of the world's economy. When Britain left in 1947, India and Pakistan combined had three per cent.

I have no doubt that Lancing College was funded, directly or indirectly, by the proceeds of imperial taxes and tariffs, and by the plunder brought back when white people's tours of duty came to an end. The baleful effects of the empire – and of course, of the French, Belgian, Dutch and American empires – on the colonised is now acknowledged, widely although insufficiently. But none of this seems to have affected the overarching English take on Empire, as understood by nationalist commentators and politicians; I still hear with sad regularity the recounting of the benefits of the Empire to those who were colonised. The myth of the beneficial legacy of the Empire seems to be becoming more, rather than less, entrenched.

But there is another part of the story, too. I need to tread carefully here and be very clear: I am not in any sense claiming that there is any equivalence between the experiences of the people of England and the people we colonised. Yet whereas countries which achieved independence in the mid to late twentieth centuries have had the opportunity to confront their history of colonisation and to seek to move on from it, with greater or less success, the same can't be said of the English.

Reni Eddo-Lodge's seismic book, *Why I Am No Longer Talking to White People About Race*, examines this phenomenon from a black perspective. I read it with stab after stab of recognition: the assumption of unexamined privilege; the reality of unconscious bias; the depth of intravenous racism in the world in which I tried to become an adult. England the un-invaded nation (since 1066, at least) where the influential class, the establishment, has perpetuated its graceless arrogance since before the arrival of the Normans. The children of the royal family smirking at the black preacher at the wedding of one of their senior scions. England, where the Brexiteers perpetuate a faded stereotype of un-regenerated nostalgia because nothing has occurred to encourage them to question their antique identities.

There is a cost to people of colour of this seam of fear masquerading as power; there is a cost to white people too. For in refusing to allow the past to be reconstructed, the present remains disturbingly static. I wrote the first draft of this article overlooking the Plaza Merdeka in Kuching, Borneo – Independence Square. When Kuching was the capital city of the Kingdom of Sarawak, ruled over by the English Raja Brookes for a hundred years, the square was known as MacDougall Place after the first bishop. It was renamed after Sarawak's independence and incorporation into the Federation of Malaysia in 1963. Across the world streets, squares, buildings, cities and countries have been renamed to symbolise a new beginning, and Independence Day is a day for celebration in every former colony.

But there has been no similar cathartic event in England. We have not re-told our history now that we are no longer the victors. There has been no Independence Day or, more accurately, End of Empire Day, no renaming of streets and parks to create a new national story. Instead, there has been the relinquishing of one colony after another, either quietly or after decades of violent struggle; leaving Britain, as has often been observed, without an empire and still looking for a role.

TS Eliot, the quintessential American Anglophile, could have had British imperial history in mind when he wrote *Gerontion*:

> After such knowledge, what forgiveness? Think now
> History has many cunning passages, contrived corridors
> And issues, deceives with whispering ambitions,
> Guides us by vanities. Think now
> She gives when our attention is distracted
> And what she gives, gives with such supple confusions
> That the giving famishes the craving … Gives too soon
> Into weak hands, what's thought can be dispensed with
> Till the refusal propagates a fear. Think
> Neither fear nor courage saves us. Unnatural vices
> Are fathered by our heroism.

Nationhood and narrative are deeply intertwined. Every nation has a founding story, whether it be recent, following a colonial past, or ancient. Romulus and Remus, Alfred burning the cakes, Zimbabwe's struggle for freedom, Malaysia's carefully negotiated journey out of colonisation towards independence. Every nation has a shared story which it gives to its young people. But that story can change. Germany radically redefined itself after the Second World War, and although we are seeing a rise in far-right politics in Germany as we are across the world, the depth of consensus is noteworthy. Spain overcame Franco's dictatorship and has developed a new narrative. But Britain has remained trapped in an understanding of its past which it has not seriously sought to escape, and as a result the country is imprisoned by its history. The story of global dominance, of British tolerance and generosity towards our subject peoples, of past glory and wealth, is a story which is nourished by insecurity and fear. Unnatural vices are fathered by our heroism.

The country has been slowly declining in relation to the rest of the world for the last hundred years. Other countries have become richer, and we have, at best, stagnated. International events have masked the decline. The most obvious are the two World Wars and the steady pomp of the monarchy. There have been times when it seemed that we might be able to develop a new, better story. The first Blair administration before the disastrous invasion of Iraq offered a real sense of hope, and Margaret Thatcher's innovations, like them or hate them, began to tell an alternative tale. But Thatcherism collapsed into neoconservative exploitation, and Blair and by extension the New Labour project are forever tainted by Iraq; and so the defining moment in British imperial history since the second world war is the Suez crisis.

But the Suez crisis has been forgotten, and the Victorian triumphs remembered. The more inadequate as a nation we become, the more we want to retell stories of past grandeur. This is what I mean when I say that the dominant narrative is nourished by insecurity and fear. Nationally and individually, we seek to bolster our inadequate present by referring to a glorious past. 'We've done it before,' runs the undercurrent, 'and we can do it again.'

My personal story is not unique. Reference to a classical past, with family histories of imperial triumph and derring-do, colonial splendour and just and goodly rule, is found everywhere, and not only in the Conservative Party (although it is among the Tories where this is most visible). The former Foreign Secretary Boris Johnson's casual assumptions that he could say whatever he liked because he's British, or the absurd posturing of the pro-Brexit Tory backbencher Jacob Rees-Mogg, are manifestations of the story, an expression of wilful denial and blindness in the hope that, somehow, Britain will be great again. My own story of vulnerable parents seeking affirmation in the past as they had so little in the present, is repeated with variations in shires and county towns up and down England – but also in left-wing and centrist assumptions, that it is right that we have a permanent seat on the UN security council and it is right that our international development aid comes with economic strings attached. We have become a desiccated nation living in a historical desert, surrounded by the dry bones and fallen trees of imperial splendour.

I sometimes think of history as being like sedimentary rock. It builds up, moment by moment, over the years; animals and plants and people fight, and starve, and die, and fall to the ground, and are covered by other animals and plants and people; and gradually the story hardens to rock, and within the rock there are some particular individuals who are preserved – fossils – to be brought out into the light and examined and re-examined. This is history as archaeology.

But there is no single history; indeed, we need to be critical of the very idea of history. Whose history are we telling? Which facts are we adducing? What is a fact, anyway, and what is knowledge? What constitutes, in this context, knowledge? The historian Arnold J Toynbee warned in 1955: 'History not used is nothing, for all intellectual life is action, like practical life, and if you don't use the stuff well, it might as well be dead.'

It doesn't have to be like this. If we accept that history is a construct – a palimpsest – then it can be reconstructed. The fossil evidence could be re-examined. There could be an alternative story, a better narrative. We'd have to work it out, collectively and personally, but it would not be impossible to develop a new story.

Let's imagine for a minute what that story might be. Let's start by thinking what might need to change for a new story to have coherence.

First, the assumption of superiority needs to go. Britain needs to develop a new kind of honesty about its past, learning from the work being done by many historians at the moment. It needs to acknowledge the destruction, the ravaging of peoples and states as a result of the imperial project. This is not to say that other states and rulers have not caused destruction – of course they have – but we need to scotch the notion, still there in many quarters, that the British Empire was, on balance, beneficial for the people it conquered.

Second, conflict has to be replaced by collaboration and healthy competition. Implicit in the notion of supremacy is the notion of hierarchy – in particular racial hierarchy. The Swedish botanist and zoologist Carl Linnaeus, 'the father of modern taxonomy', has a lot to answer for (although in fact he was more nuanced than many people assume). The rationale behind his classification of living organisms also drove the categorisation of people by 'race' in the eighteenth century as part of the fever to label, number and define, with whiteness always at the top of the pile. Recently we've seen the resurgence of white supremacy across the North Atlantic hegemony. It was always there, just below the surface, but now it's become explicit again. A new and genuine understanding of our global humanity would enable a new focus on solving, together, the problems which face us. India, Pakistan, Malaysia, everywhere; all are seeking solutions to similar issues. Why can't we collaborate?

Third, Britain needs to lose the sense of its own exceptionalism. We are a medium sized European country which behaved in the nineteenth century similar to other medium sized European countries. We had a few lucky breaks – in particular, an abundance of coal to power the Industrial Revolution, and a convenient relationship between ships and the slave trade – and made the most of them. That's it. End of story. So why do we persist in thinking that we are in some way special?

The flip side of that is, fourth, a realistic understanding of who we are as individuals. There is nothing which is more poisonous than the sense that we have failed to live up to our glorious past, either individually as members of families, or as a nation. This sense of falling short of a misconceived past is insidious, and it leads us to overcompensate by privileging Englishness and our colonial roots.

And fifth, the notion of forgiveness needs to be somewhere in the mix. Which also involves saying sorry. Some people wonder about the value of retrospective apologies; but they have been used, effectively, many times – for example in Canada about the treatment of indigenous people. But forgiveness works both ways; we need, perhaps, to think about forgiving ourselves for what happened in the past as well as seeking forgiveness from the descendants of those we harmed. This is not about letting the privileged amongst us off the hook, but to allow us to get on with making *actual* changes to our behaviour instead of constantly feigning paralysis because of our supposedly liberal guilt and shame.

If we manage to do all that, what would the new story sound like? And what would it require of us?

To speak first of the particular before moving to the general – I was brought up in a household that proudly perceived itself as liberal. My parents saw themselves as firmly on the progressive end of the political spectrum, underpinned by their belief that their colonial forebears had been forces for good in the benighted world beyond Europe's shores. We had black people at school – mainly the children of princes or ambassadors, some of them were my friends – and my work in social housing before ordination as a priest included being Development Director for an Asian housing association. I read Hans Küng's magisterial book on Islam as soon as it was published (well, some of it) and was quietly proud of the connections I made between the dynamic of exclusion for lesbian, gay, bisexual and transgender (LGBT) people and for people of colour. But how shallow and unreflective I was became apparent as I began to question more profoundly my own narrative. Twenty-three years as a parish priest in South London have helped, including befriending and engaging at a close level with communities from Nigeria, Uganda, and Sierra Leone. Having a Muslim partner has helped.

But I have been helped not only by the friendships and relationships which I have built up over the years. I have tried to work, from my position as an establishment insider of sorts, for social justice over most of my working life – battling with the Church Commissioners over their investments, working across faith traditions on climate change, struggling for LGBT+ rights in the Church of England – trying to ensure that different voices are heard.

In June of this year, I invited Jamaican-born Rose Hudson-Wilkin, Chaplain to the Speaker of the House of Commons, to preach at the Waterloo Festival. She gave us a call to arms. 'Usually,' she said, 'I am the only person who looks like me, apart from the staff at the City functions and dinners I am called to attend – why?' She spoke with power and passion to the young women, especially women of colour, in the congregation: 'Don't let anyone tell you that you aren't good enough. Don't listen to them: you have the power, if you are willing to take it.'

Beyond doubt the awareness, the richness of cultural interchange, at the ground level, from the inside out, is transformative. By becoming more open to the narratives of others, my own has been profoundly changed. The process has required a questioning of my own unacknowledged sense of entitlement, and a willingness to listen and change, which is not always easy. But the results have been startling, and the more I discover about the world out there, the more I am convinced that the English imperialist narrative is deeply destructive not just for those we have dominated but for ourselves as the erstwhile dominators.

In that context, to return to my question: if we manage to do all that, what would the new story sound like? And what would it require of us?

It would not require any of us to deny our history – merely to acknowledge that for most of us, history is, at best, ambivalent. In some ways, it has created some extraordinary things – in particular, a connectedness and a richness in diversity which is fundamentally part of the UK's experience now. It is much to be regretted that the Commonwealth has become dysfunctional; it should be an opportunity for celebration, a way to move on from the darkness of our imperial past.

It would not require us to take a step back from trying to improve our own lot and the lot of humanity. Collaboration, genuine and creative collaboration, could solve untold problems. Starting with climate change and food poverty – remember that we throw away one third of the food we produce – and moving on to solutions to the challenges created by the power of technology. A collective understanding of shared humanity would lead to a re-focused and authoritative sense of shared endeavour. Who knows what the future might hold?

It would not require us to lose our individualism. For privileged white Britons, overcoming our fetishisation of the past would, on the contrary, enable us to understand what is good in our private and family histories. My grandfather, for example, is far more notable for his eccentric but exciting thinking about time and space than he is for anything he did in the war. There may well be other examples among my ancestors of real contributions to the human struggle – I don't know. It would be worth investigating, if we could see past the false glorification.

Such an approach would enable all of us to begin to taste a new kind of freedom, a freedom which has escaped us until now. A freedom based on shared respect and shared values, on celebration of our shared past and a belief in a collaborative future. It would enable us to enjoy the fullness of global culture, not because we think we ought to but because it's there, it's available, and it's good. World music, world literature, world art, world science, world culture.

It doesn't imply a narrowing down – on the contrary, it would mean a radical opening up of resources and experience which could lead to unimagined discoveries – a profound appreciation of the varieties and depths of different cultures across the world. And even if it didn't, it would create a new sense of personhood based not on fear but on love, not on disrespect but on celebration.

Each of us is a palimpsest. Each of us has a unique and extraordinary personhood which has been built up not just over years or decades but over centuries. We aren't like sedimentary rock, gradually and slowly being created out of the skeletons and detritus of the past which eventually solidifies into the element known as Giles, or Halima, or Wai Ling, or Ntsike. There is death in our past, yes, but there is also life, and both must be acknowledged.

The great spiritual traditions all manifest a shared understanding of shared humanity; at the top of the mountain we are one. So, can we move to a new narrative, in Britain; and can I move to a new narrative, as Giles Goddard? Can I become a delta, not a desert, not a rock?

There is a place of richness and diversity and fertility, a liminal place between the known land and the unknown ocean – a place, yes, sometimes subject to flooding and storms, but a place which offers nourishment beyond imagination to anyone who works out how to live there, how to put down roots and let the abundance of water flowing from the hills provide all that we need for life.

Do we have the courage to leave the desert and move to the delta?

BUILDING CHRONICLES

Nicholas Masterton

In 2012, 259 people died inside a garment factory in Karachi, Pakistan. It was a day when workers were collecting their salaries, so the building was massively over-occupied. There should have been a maximum of 260 people working at the site but there were actually approximately 800 to 900 people in the building at the time. When the fire broke out, the only staircase in the building quickly became unusable due to the intense heat and smoke so people were unable to evacuate. There was no emergency or external staircase. There were doors that led onto the adjacent building that formed another part of the factory complex, but those doors had been locked by the management, leaving people trapped on the floor they were on. Deficiencies in the cargo lift meant there were cavities on the ground level, which is where the fire started, enabling smoke from the fire to travel up the elevator shaft much faster than it should have done.

In April 2017, in collaboration with the European Centre for Constitutional Human Rights (ECCHR), Forensic Architecture (FA) worked on a project to gather evidence for a court case against the German clothing manufacturer KiK, based in Dortmund, to win compensation for family members of those who died in the KiK garment building fire in Karachi five years earlier. Using testimony, photographs, a few videos and drawings of the building to construct a 3D model of it, we looked at building regulations from Pakistani Law, Karachi Town and Planning Law, and Social Accountability International SA8000 guidelines, which are a social certification standard for factories, and we scrutinised the building to see if it was in compliance with these building codes. We identified the exact clauses that proved the building was in violation of building codes, and produced a video of evidence for the court in Dortmund, enumerating the ways the clothing company had failed to meet guidelines and protect its workers. Working with Edmund Ang, a specialist from Imperial

College, we created two smoke simulations. One recreated the exact conditions of that night and the level of permeation of the smoke and the rate of the spread of the fire. In the other simulation, Ang reconstructed the main and only staircase serving all floors going through the building and the elevator shaft to demonstrate the smoke egress through the doors. 0.5 square metres for the whole building was a reasonable estimation of egress for the surface area and he was able to run that simulation to see how the smoke would have spread had the shaft been fire safe. Working with a crowd simulation expert, Dr Virginia Alonso-Gutierrez, we were able to run a series of simulations where the configuration of the building was no longer in violation of the codes. So for example, in the real-life scenario the fire alarm failed and people were only alerted to the danger via word of mouth and by hearing shouts and screams of others and seeing people running through the building. According to the simulation, had a properly functioning fire alarm gone off it would have dramatically reduced the response time and massively increased the number of people who could have escaped. We ran a scenario with basic fire precautions being adhered to such as doors open, exits unlocked and an accessible stairway, to demonstrate the extent of deaths that could have been avoided. The factory owners were sentenced to prison terms but although KiK has provided some compensation to families they have refused to apologise and accept responsibility for the fatalities. From our perspective they were negligent in the way they sourced their clothing. In the pursuit for cheap clothing and in an attempt to push the bottom line in terms of costs they outsourced the risk of the process of the supply chain to this factory in Karachi and the result was an appalling fire and devastating loss of life.

We worked with Nasir Mansoor who is the Deputy General Secretary of the National Trade Union Federation (NTUF) of Pakistan and Zehra Khan, a local architect who is also a member of the NTUF throughout the process. Crucially, this allowed us to show our findings to survivors of the fire. It was important to us that those who had been affected felt that this was their story that was being told and the narrative was one that they felt they had ownership over. They provided constructive critical feedback about our understanding of the configuration of the staircase providing valuable architectural insight into one of the key areas of the building. They were very much on board in terms of the overall message of the findings and it was a perfect example of local knowledge and knowledge on the ground, informing the accuracy of the project.

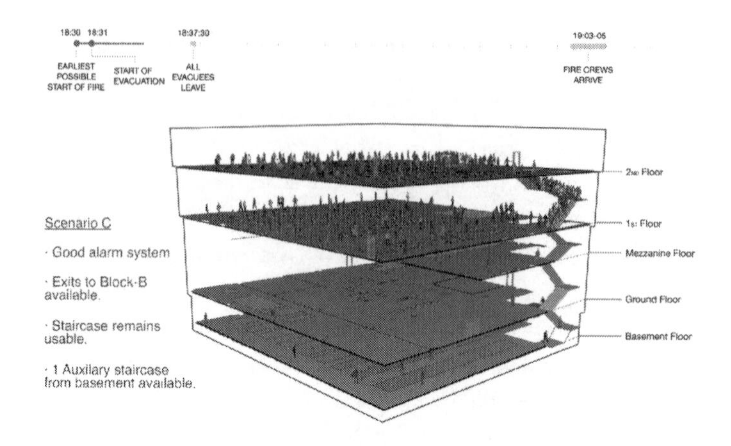

Ali Enterprises Factory Fire: Crowd simulation showing how the evacuation of the building could have taken place if several safety features had been in place such as an alarm system and a usable staircase.

Ali Enterprises Factory Fire: Cross section through the building showing all floors and the occupation of the building at the time of the fire.

The origin of the word forensic, *forensis*, is to bring something to the forum. What we are introducing is the idea that a building is a witness to an event. The trouble with a building, however, is it is unable to speak in the way that you and I speak, so it becomes necessary to interrogate the architecture to let it tell the story of what it has seen. Frequently, war and injustice occur in the urban context so architecture transforms into a space of inscription of violence. Simultaneously, it is a medium of investigating violations of human rights and state oppression through the reconstruction of sites and scenes. By meticulously collecting and analysing data via traditional methods as well as utilising innovative and cutting-edge technologies, official narratives are challenged in the quest to ascertain public truth.

Forensic Architecture was developed by British-Israeli architect Eyal Weizman, emerging out of his research into town planning in the Palestinian Occupied Territories and the way it is used to sanction state oppression. Growing up in the shadow of the Israel/Palestine conflict he was made aware of architecture's use as a political tool in the fight against injustice and decided architects needed to be held to account for their actions on this built stage. The earliest projects started around 2010, focusing on Israel/Palestine, and before long Forensic Architecture evolved from an extension of Weizman's research, into a Turner prize nominated, independent research agency, established alongside its sister project, Forensic Oceanography, also based at Goldsmiths, University of London.

Due to the nature of Forensic Architecture – often critiquing narratives the state has put forward and casting doubt on 'official' versions of events – the organisation is not devoid of detractors, many of whom come from a place of anxiety and suspicion. The establishment within both architecture and the art world have also, at times, been unsure where and how to place this unconventional field of research. We are not just architects and artists; we are individuals trained in a variety of different backgrounds brought together as a collaborative interdisciplinary team. We are investigative journalists, film-makers, programmers. As a RIBA part 2 qualified architect my specialism is computer graphics and 3D animation, as is typical of a recent architecture graduate. Emphasis on skills in time-based media, whether that be film, animation, performance or audio-visual, anything that has a durational quality to it, has enabled the upcoming generation of architects to use technology to operate within virtual space *in lieu* of real buildings. The tools acquired through the process of using time dependent media can be employed by forensic architecture to carry out analysis that has a sequential element and demands a high degree of precision.

The projects we take on are unified by apparent violations of human rights and the involvement of a spatial element. Space and time are critical to our investigations because there is normally a time factor in any situation that unfolds as violations tend to have a durational quality. We also endeavour to take on projects that introduce a component we haven't explored before, so we continuously develop new investigatory techniques. We are frequently approached by NGOs and other bodies to undertake projects but would be very unlikely to ever take on a commission for a government or a corporation. Our aim is to serve the interests of civil society. It feels important to refrain from defining our field too much but more often than not I am asked to explain what it is that we do. My reply is that we are doing cases, carrying out investigations and employing new investigatory techniques to look at violations of human rights and bring purveyors of injustice to account. We are supporting the forces of civil society as opposed to established state systems, and see ourselves more at home in the field of human rights than pure architecture. What we are bringing to the field in which we operate is new techniques and original thinking and highlighting ways in which different mediums cross over and overlap. This is in the make-up of the people who I work with, and is intrinsic to our approach to how narratives are framed.

Architecture is the medium in which we can encapsulate spoken testimony, witness sketches, photography and videos. These pieces of evidence are often presented granularly before courts in temporally and spatially disparate documents and reports. By contrast we aspire to create readings of architectural space which include all these types of evidence in a cohesive and understandable manner. So we contribute to legal and political forums but instead of presenting evidence in the form of pages and readings we have spaces and video installations. Our work involves three stages. It starts with the field in which the injustice occurred and that may involve visiting the site and certainly capturing data. This data is collated in the laboratory or studio, which is the office in which we work, and it is here that we process, analyse, interpret, corroborate and check the information. Finally, we take the conclusion of our analysis and distribute it to the public via the chosen forum. This may be a legal courtroom, social media proliferation, or part of a report. The output forms the advocacy and it is here that the work takes on a life of its own, generating criticism and feedback. A huge part of the project, this convergence of technologies and abilities, is how it lives outside the laboratory and continues to inform narratives relating to the crime scene.

Images are fundamental to what we do but we all know that images can be distorted and do not always convey truth. This is why we do not work with visuals alone. Instead we use a multiplicity of data and sources to corroborate the images. By creating an intersection of all the visuals and sources, we are able to find what we have been looking for because it is in this small intersection that the closest thing to truth is most probably located. Once the work is released into the forum, the feedback engages the system of corroboration. If three articles are published in response to a project's findings, and each has a slightly different interpretation, we seek out areas of intersection and commonalities. There are degrees of precision and accuracy, but there are also many sliders. To arrive at an absolute truth requires an absence of constraints but in reality these can never be negated, for example because of the necessity to act within constraints of time and money. There is always some path that we must tread, perhaps it is the agenda of the NGO that has partnered with us, or commissioned the project. A limit to how much bandwidth exists in the projects means constantly negotiating with uncertainty and qualifying every statement with the fact that we know this to 'this' degree of accuracy. Dealing with a multiplicity of scenarios requires seeking out the overlap to establish the possible truth.

Ideology can never fail to permeate an emerging narrative. Every single action that you take in how to approach a problem, what button to press, how to ask for help, how to consult, all are influenced by ideology. Our strength lies in the fact that the FA office is diverse, with people from various backgrounds and different parts of the world represented. Crucially, the team comprises experts with completely different ways of doing things so every stage of a project necessitates a discussion. At times it's a difference in opinion about the best way to set about addressing the issue. Arguments can be healthy. We always try and step back and consider each situation objectively. At our weekly meetings we will talk through all our current projects and think critically about progress so far and the best way to move forward. It can get heated. My favoured tools of analysis come from my experience of understanding the production of technical data. I think software is a very important factor in how we work. If you ask other people in the office they may prioritise an entirely different medium. We all have our own preferred investigative techniques and we will come up with different angles, but crucially we share our ideas. Every project involves ongoing discussion and that is how we keep things critical, by remaining open to a spectrum of perspectives and listening to all the possibilities.

As a team we rarely end up at diverging conclusions, although what we may have are different methodologies. Discrepancies are few and far between. If you find evidence that excludes the evidence of someone else, perhaps visual proof that questions audio proof, then it becomes necessary to take a step back and re-trace both methodologies. It would be impossible to move forward with conflicting conclusions without closely inspecting each person's working. Findings are very closely tied to the apparatus we use, but, there is more to it than saying this is confirmed or this is denied or this is refuted. It would be a case of stating that this is something we have a low degree of certainty for, rather than it being true or false. Here we have something where you don't have a conclusion, and then in the production of the output of the work that goes into the world, that piece of un-evidence or un-categorisable aspect has to be declared, provoking, or rather inviting feedback. You cannot pretend that you know something with a degree of uncertainty. Often the complication comes from how to communicate that uncertainty. You have to trust intentions as well as expose the methodological sources. The best projects are where the media and sources are all freely available and can be scrutinised by the public. I believe in open source software for the same reason – transparency. If you use a propriety software that costs thousands of pounds, only you and a select number of people can use that software. However, if you use open source software then anyone can see the raw evidence and has access to the means of production and can therefore interrogate the narrative you have established.

Trusting the intention of partner organisations is paramount because it is impossible for us to do everything alone. We are a relatively small organisation so we regularly work with NGOs and charities sometimes in the field, or on the ground to provide us with local knowledge. Our methodologies are constantly circumnavigating whether you trust or don't trust a source. It comes down to a weirdly granular level of looking at the metadata on an image and asking whether I trust that this was taken at the date and time I am being told it was taken. It's a hierarchical scale, both conceptually and practically, and is something we are constantly negotiating.

Being nominated for the 2018 Turner prize has been an interesting experience for FA. We live in intensely political times and recently that has caused anxiety and even a sense of deficit for the art world. If you look at the nominees for this year's Turner prize there is a political drive to all of them. We are not actually setting out to be artists and you could argue the nomination is a double-edged sword. There is no doubt it gives weight and focus to the projects we are working on and throws a spotlight on the human rights violations we are investigating. On the other hand, it means that we have become part of a process of being assimilated by an institution, codified, institutionalised almost. It's like being put into a category by a large and recognised establishment, which then starts to define, cement, solidify. It becomes easy to lose sight of the nuance of what you were doing originally when a body seeks to define you. A tension is lost and those slightly non-conforming, more complex aspects of what we are inevitably become lost in categorisations. It puts the spotlight on us and forces those that write about us to collapse all their ideas about what they think we are into one piece. The work we do and the way that we aspire to work, which is to be open about our methodology and our findings, means we are comfortable with the scrutiny. The difficulty is that if you are being picked up by an entity that is bigger than you or has a louder voice than you, then you have no choice other than to trust them because you are at the mercy of what they decide you are. The exposure requires us to trust those who talk about us, and at times try to talk for us. The best thing we can do is to be ambassadors for investigative practices and techniques and to convey what the reality of those processes we utilise at FA are.

The workshops we hold are informative because once you get into the detail of it and see it practically you see the problems unfolding and how it reflects on a conceptual basis too. When you have in-depth engagement, as was the case at the ICA exhibition in London, where people could really spend time looking at FA projects, that feels more constructive. The workshops enable people to meaningfully engage with our work, examine our methodologies and see the practical intricacies of what we do. We held five different workshops at the ICA and before each there was a 90-minute talk with invited guests to critique our work and talk about their relationship to FA, which resulted in some vibrant and constructive discussions.

One workshop I convened was on motion-tracking, a technique we used on the Grenfell media project. The Grenfell Tower, located in a block of public housing flats in North Kensington, London, caught fire on 14 June 2017, causing 72 deaths. On the night of the fire, images were captured by a great many people on their smartphones. The most critical footage that was captured was during the early stages of the fire when it was rapidly moving up the facade of the building. We searched the internet and put out a request on social media asking people to submit their videos to us as well as to the inquiry and in the end we had hours and hours of footage. We undertook this large project, considering the size of the team, to motion-track all of the footage. This involved analysing groups of pixels in the video, identifying the relevant areas and seeing how they move across the screen. If you can track for any given time period, 16 of these points, these groups of pixels, and if you can do it with enough accuracy you can reverse-engineer the motion of the camera that took that video. It is then possible to reconstruct the camera movements of that person to a high degree of precision and project that image back onto a model of the surface of the building and what you are left with is a stabilised version of that video. When combined with all the other pieces of footage, synchronised and mapped onto the surface of the model of the building, it provides a reading of the surface of the tower and the progression of the fire. The output of this investigative technique can be used as a tool for other people to conduct their own investigations and to refute or to deny the things that they find. For us, synchronisation is incredibly important because we know roughly the movement of the fire and for some pieces of footage we have very good metadata and can confirm down to the second that it is very accurate, while for other pieces of footage we know it happens roughly at a particular time but we're not quite sure if it's in this 15 minute slot or this other 15 minute slot. That is the broadest range of uncertainty that we have but there are some instances where we are certain to within five minutes and other instances where we are certain to within half a minute. The result is a spectrum of uncertainty and a view of the progression of the fire that combines multiple perspectives and creates a new space that doesn't already exist, as a derivative of the mapping. The best way to illustrate this is if you take a paper cube and unfold all the surfaces. Similarly, you can unwrap the surfaces of the tower and what you read is an unwrapped flattened surface of the facades. That visual reading gives you an even more useful way to analyse the spread because you don't need to rotate to the other side to see what's happening.

Video of Grenfell Tower fire projected onto the surface of a model of the building. The video has been motion tracked so that it appears stable once overlaid onto the model of the tower.

FA worked with Air Wars, an investigative agency who provide statistical analysis for air strikes – casualties and fatalities, also a member of the Centre for Investigative Journalism and Human Rights Watch, on the repeated bombing of a hospital in Aleppo in the second half of 2016. That was a process of showing that what was happening to this hospital was not collateral damage. It wasn't part of the general destruction of Aleppo, it was a targeted strike. You could see from the CCTV footage inside the building that these attacks in Aleppo were targeted. There is plenty of narrative where you'll see stories about faking and staging attacks and actors, which is something that is a criticism levelled against the images captured inside the hospital but what we are able to do is reveal a bit more of the complexity. When you start to unpick architecture and you start to unpick space and you start to look at the traces that are left by the various munitions that hit the hospital you hone in on the detail, the structure, the size of the structure and in this way we are able to paint a much more complex story, through reading the building, of how the violence unfolded. I think that this has the effect of redirecting the conversation away from conjecture and speculation and back towards analysis of the architectural space, where there are real pieces of evidence to be discovered. Through aggregation of all these pieces of evidence we can discover the subtler realities of the chronology of a space.

The interesting thing about M2 Hospital in Aleppo is that we started to read the history of the building going forward as well. During the time we were doing the investigation, we discovered the hospital had started building a defensive structure around the front of the building. They had engineered this extra facade, an extra skin implementing a detail of putting hollow sections of pipe across the structure so if there was an impact the pressure differential could escape through these hollow pipes. It was a heavily engineered defensive skin they were building around the hospital that we uncovered and we haven't had a chance to put the resources into showing that bit in our findings. It's one of those things where once you've looked at enough videos and images and drawings you start to see there really is a history that is being told by the structure itself and that structure is telling you things that nobody else is telling you. Amidst all the Twitter chat, this is the slower story, the long read. The building is completely unemotional because it comprises just walls and ceilings but it is relating a narrative and it's a gradual and thoughtful recounting of its story. The structure tells the story. The architecture has to speak more slowly and has to speak more carefully because architecture is generally heavy and solid and difficult to manipulate. That is where we try to send our gaze – so it settles on something a bit more permanent. Buildings that speak is a beautiful concept. A building is constantly being inscribed on by its users and it's always telling a new story.

In early 2017, I and my FA colleague Omar Ferwati investigated a US drone strike on a Mosque in Al-Jinah province, Syria. What is significant about this project is that after the strike, the Pentagon released a black and white thermal image of the building in a 'mission accomplished' style declaring they had hit an Al Qaeda meeting location. They bragged they had deliberately avoided hitting the mosque nearby as indicated by their intelligence, but actually their intelligence had got it completely wrong. They had missed the old smaller mosque and had instead obliterated the new building, blowing up between thirty and forty people inside the facilities hub, which incorporated *wudu* facilities and the Imam's living quarter. It was just before *maghrib* prayers and most of the people were concentrated there. We looked at all the images of the site we could find and saw that where photographs had been taken from outside you could see the speaker for the call to prayer. This way we managed to identify the location of the old mosque. We contacted someone who was able to travel to the area and film the inside of the bombed structure. One side was completely flattened and resembled a large crater full of rubble. The other side revealed the prayer hall, which was roughly intact so you could see the *mihrab*, prayer mats stacked up in a pile, a small unit where they were stored, carpets on the floor and all these little pieces that were painting the picture of what was a functioning mosque. Later, we discovered a video of someone walking through the mosque and showing the facilities side of it, so we could see the washrooms and kitchen as they walked around, eventually reaching the prayer hall. Then you would see this connecting shot from the facilities side which takes you back into the area that had been bombed. This footage gave us not only a spatial mapping of the mosque but also several moments in time, before and after the bombing, where we could clearly see the details of what it was and the transformation that occurred before and after the strike. There was a bombing on the facilities side of the building, and then an evacuation, some panic, and subsequently 'hellfire' missiles were fired at the people standing outside, and we were able to find visual evidence of this. From the first images that came out we could see pock markings on the road that formed roughly an arc pattern which is consistent with a fragmentation jacket that comes off a 'hellfire' missile, which is a cylindrical parcel which explodes. If the missile is coming at an angle you get a windscreen wiper-type pattern on the ground so we had the person who filmed the interior also film the road and we took a still video of the road and were able to project that onto the surface and bring the camera into a plan view. Looking at it from above you could see this very clear arch, made by the missile exploding just before it hit the ground. When the Pentagon was informed that we had such overwhelming evidence the US military conducted their own internal investigation to establish whether or not they had made a mistake and incredibly they concluded that they had in fact used the correct amount of intelligence and the correct amount of force. This sparked the UN Syria mission investigation into the strike and their conclusion was that, to the contrary, the US military had not carried out their intelligence properly. The confirmation from the UN Syria mission felt monumental for us in terms of advocating what was basically a deadly and negligent strike.

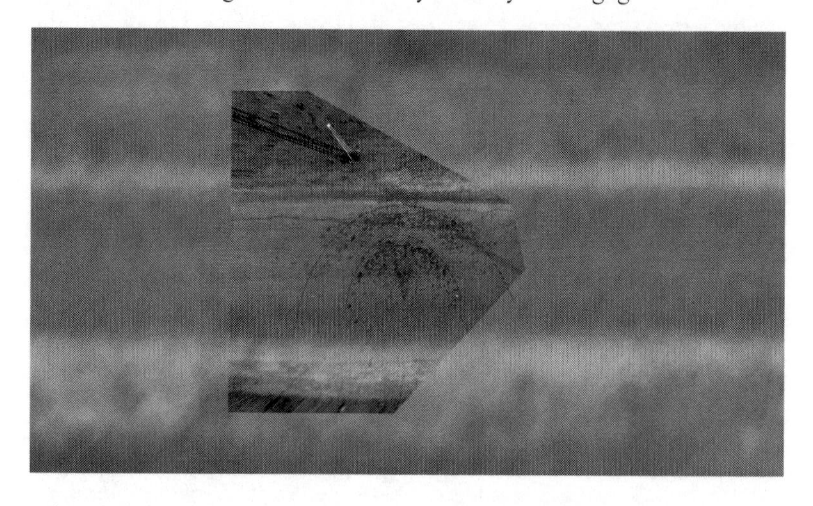

Al Jinah Mosque: Projected image of fragmentation pattern from hellfire missile overlaid onto satellite image showing arc-shaped markings on the road near to the mosque.

The projects we are involved with are often deeply upsetting examples of injustice and it is important to practise self-care. When starting work on a project any really graphic material has usually been flagged and only if it's absolutely vital to the project would it be necessary to view it. Often we are looking at technical architectural detail so most graphic media is not necessarily useful to us. It all comes together sometimes though so at times there is no avoiding it. But you can control it: for example, by not having audio, minimising the size and keeping it small on the screen, not blowing it up into a huge image - so you need to know your software to ensure it doesn't pop up on you. We have quite extensive workshops that provide training but you have to exercise caution and use your own instincts. We are a close-knit team and try to support each other. We're also very focused, each of us harbouring our methodological proclivities which sometimes means it's not always smooth because we're having disagreements about how to do something. But ultimately there is a trust and bond between colleagues, which is very important especially when we're talking about the emotional and psychological impact of our work.

When you are questioning the narrative presented by powerful bodies such as governments and corporations, you expect them to push back. The discrediting of artists or investigative journalists comes very naturally to the state. I think if you are the state, that is your reality. As far as you are concerned you are the maximum authority and you don't expect this level of interrogation of your official narrative. But we feel passionate and secure about the work we are doing. Having ownership over the work and being responsible for the narrative that has been deconstructed and re-created may seem like a huge responsibility. It does, however, engage you with the desire to pursue truth and uphold civil society – regardless of the challenges.

Based on conversations with Nicholas Masterton.
www.forensic-architecture.org

DREAMING

Nur Sobers-Khan

There has been a trend for some time within Islamic Studies, and amongst Muslim diaspora communities, of condemning rationalist narratives of our identities, religion, and history. The attempt to escape from the epistemological world of the Enlightenment has led us down a variety of narrative pathways – to conceptual frameworks of the *ghayb*, the unseen world, the imaginal realm, *'alam al-mithal* of Suhrawardi, to postcolonial yearning for precolonial utopia, to decolonising museum exhibitions, course curricula, our sexualities and understandings of our selves. I list these attempts at escaping from an episteme that we perceive as oppressive not to denigrate but rather to celebrate the diversity of approaches. However, there is always the risk that the more one struggles in the net of rationalism, through a reading of texts, the writing of public apologias, that the more one becomes ensnared in the very trap one is trying to escape. While I cannot claim that dream interpretation narratives allow us a way out, it is a mode of narrativising that allows a respite from the logic of modernity and literal Wahhabism and from falling into the trap of rationalising and psychologising our inner worlds. It permits us some epistemological autonomy.

The existential complaint of Muslim diaspora times, which many of us share, can be summed up in a term coined by Leyla Jagiella (whose work is also featured in this volume): the Wahhabitus. Drawing on the well-established notion of the habitus, originated by the sociologist Pierre Bourdieu in 1977, the concept has been influential in a number of fields. The habitus is the system of generative structures and schemes into which we are inculcated, which determine our thoughts, perceptions, and actions. The notion of the habitus was used more recently by Saba Mahmood in her groundbreaking study of the anthropology of Islam in which she brings the habitus back to its Aristotelian roots in an effort to escape (somewhat) the determinism of Bourdieu's original formulation. Stressing the instructive process by which the habitus is acquired, Mahmood argues that habitus can be attained via a set of conscious bodily and mental practices culminating in an unconscious and embodied conception of the self and set of actions, thoughts, and ways of being.

This idea was developed further in the work of Aisha Beliso-De Jesus, who researches Santeria belief systems and practices in the diaspora, and draws on Mahmood to elaborate a 'spiritual habitus': the 'self-forming capacities for action', which are created through both bodily and spiritual practices with unseen beings who form part of Santeria beliefs. Drawing on these developments, the Wahhabitus is a tongue-in-cheek but also deadly serious concept necessary to understand our predicament. The Wahhabitus, as I have understood it, encompasses the spiritual and bodily practices, thought-worlds and assumptions of the Wahhabo-sphere, which embodies a modernising, austere aesthetic of Protestant text-based reasoning, rationalism, utilitarianism, and also prudery. The Wahhabitus is the ensemble of this matrix, which we have swallowed and embodied, and continue to reproduce, even in our activism and research, which (at times) we believe has to be somehow 'useful' or 'doing good' for 'the community'.

I propose the conscious creation of an alternate habitus, whose ontology is narrated by the living practices of dream interpretation that defy the logic of the Wahhabitus. These practices, with which we are all familiar and go on within families and among friends, can be a method and framework for radical ontology creation. This narrativising of dreams allows us to create possible other worlds and other futures, the inner (and perhaps even outer) autonomy that every diasporic Muslim intellectual seems to desire at this moment, from the late Shahab Ahmed's attempt to create a conceptual framework to allow 'contradictory' ontologies of 'Islam' to co-exist coherently (clearly still a modernist, rationalist project, although a much needed thought experiment that has got the entire diasporic Islamo-intellectual sphere talking) to the imaginative project of the late Intizar Hussain, the prolific Pakistani novelist and short story writer.

Hussain's project of creating an abstract internal civilisational microcosm through engagement with the wider Islamic episteme is expressed through his Urdu-language fiction and echoes in some respects Shahab Ahmed's nostalgia for the premodern world of wonder, perplexity, and richness that we find woven throughout *What Is Islam?* Hussain's translator describes his project of ontology-building and the creation of inner shared geographies: 'For him *watan* (homeland), he insisted, was not merely defined by the territory within which he now claimed his rightful citizenship, it was also the larger civilisational space from which he derived his imaginative strength.' That is to say, lacking a geographically-bound homeland, he expresses the need for a rich ontology of spiritual topographies, symbols, and narratives that defies the reductive rationalism and insistence on 'coherence'. The need for a breaking free from the Wahhabitus, its neuroses, sexual and bodily inhibitions ('wahhabitions', if you will), unimaginative and aesthetically impoverished life worlds, has been felt for some time, and one antidote is the multivalent narrative possibilities of the dream interpretation tradition.

Many of us will be familiar with the 'canonical' texts of dream interpretation in the languages considered to be central to Islamic knowledge production, Arabic and Persian, the manuals of Ibn Sirin, 'Abd al-Ghani al Nabulusi and Imam Ja'far al-Sadiq, which offer a range of symbols with multivalent and relational readings of their meanings. We are also familiar with the chapbooks sold around shrines, in a range of 'vernacular' languages, printed on thin grey paper that sometimes dissolves to the touch, the writing partly illegible through excessive re-printing. Small in format, meant to be carried in a purse or a pocket, these works are meant to be kept on one's person, consulted in the mornings after a particularly vivid dream, or in conversation with family and friends during the narrativising of dreams. Often containing tables of symbols and their meaning, organised alphabetically, or by descending symbological hierarchy of spiritual importance, these works are very accessible to readers. Beyond texts both 'canonical' and 'popular', there are oral traditions existing within communities and families of what symbols in dreams mean, such as the common knowledge that something can mean its opposite, but also not: tears, for instance, can indicate joy; a wedding and its promise of new life can indicate an eminent death.

Whether any of these texts are apocryphal or not, or what the oral traditions of folklore, which will vary widely by culture, region, language, are grounded in, or what their textual genealogy is, and whether the symbology encoded therein is culturally or 'religiously' determined, is irrelevant. The point is not about truth and origins, but about narrative and interpretation. The beauty of these systems of oneiric logic lies in their unselfconscious defiance of rationalisation. A symbol carries a range of meanings, and can be interpreted differently according to context, time of day, the gender of the person who had the dream, their state of ritual purity, their piety. Symbols and their meaning range from the mundane to the surreal, are interpreted relationally, and often in the arc of a single sentence can be narrativised creatively to mean anything. However, the narrative leaps and the meaning they create are not without substance, as true dreams are linked with prophecy. The dream world has an ontology of its own creation, bearing its own ever-shifting meaning.

As a simple illustration of the multivalent arational meanings of the dream world, an entry chosen at random from a dream interpretation text exhibits the range and creativity of meanings that can be derived from a single symbol: eyes. They will do as much as any other for an exploration of oneiric meaning. Taken from one of the many non-scholarly translations (into one of the vernaculars of the Muslim diaspora – English) of an unidentified mythical ur-Text of Ibn Sirin, meant for popular usage and meaning-creation, the entry on eyes begins as follows: 'Eyes in a dream represent one's religion or wealth. If one sees grass growing all over him but does not cover his ears or eyes in a dream, it means prosperity'. So far, so surreal. The set of images becomes more elaborate as the passage progresses: 'Having many eyes throughout one's body in a dream represents one's piety, vigilance and excellence of character. If one sees the eyes of his heart in a dream, it means that he sees with the light of clarity'. This spiritual diagnosis is followed by prognostication and the navigating of social relationships through oneiric side-eye: 'If one sees a man looking at him with a side glance in a dream, it means that he will suffer from an adversity, mistrust, disapproval, suspicion and disdain at the hand of such a man. If such a man opens his eyes and looks at him straight-forward in the dream, it means that he will help him in his business or support his interests.' These gazes are followed by a poetic flood of imagery related to colour symbolism, sexuality, and faith: 'If one looks at someone's eyes in a dream and likes them, it means that he will suffer from an adversity, religious corruption or jealousy. If one sees himself having an extra eye over his shoulder in a dream, it means that he will be named to receive money in absentia. If one sees his eyes transfixed in a dream, it means that he looks suspiciously at a relative or someone else's wife. Black eyes in a dream represent a religious person. A bluish-black eye in a dream denotes opposing one's religion. Blue eyes in a dream mean religious innovations. Green eyes in a dream mean a religion which is different from all religions.' After which the dream narration distributes hope and despair in equal measure: 'If an oppressed person sees weakness in his eyes in a dream, it means that someone will help him overcome his adversities. If a traveller sees that dream, it means that he will never return to his homeland. If one sees that his eyes belong to an unknown person in a dream, it means that he will become blind... If one sees his eyes white, and if the white veil is lifted in the dream, it means that he will be reunited with his beloved and his distress will be dispelled.' A combination of spiritual diagnosis, hope, despair, prognostication is expressed through a set of relational symbolic eyes. Syllogisms abound, but the pathway from protasis to apodosis remains unexplored verbally in the texts, and one's insight into the oneiric syllogism is left to one's own devising or insight, or that of the interpreter or interpretive community.

As the reader may have noticed, from the short exploration of the logic of oneiric texts in the traditions of dream interpretation that can be described as 'Islamic', the underlying understanding of what a dream is, and what it does, is very different from the Freudian-derived discourse on dreams. In the Freudian understanding of dreaming, the dream is an insight into the individual's subconscious, an expression of wish-fulfilment or repressed desires. However, it should be obvious by now that in many of the Islamic traditions of dream interpretation, the dream takes place in another world, with its own ontological status. Its world is not dependent on, or generated by, the dreamer – the dream world exists by itself, and is accessed by the dreamer. However, dreams, although they have an independent ontological status, are contextual – they are relevant to more than the individual, often (as we read above about 'Eyes'), the symbols encountered are relevant to a family, a community, to others in one's life and possible future(s).

Veridical dreams, a subset of the dreams it is possible to narrate, are thought to predict the future, and the symbols appearing in true dreams can be used for divination. The various terms for dreams have been explored in the secondary literature on the topic, and the veridical dream is the *ruya*: the true dream or vision, which is recalled by the dreamer with great clarity and detail, and is a marker of piety. While traditions of dream interpretation existed in pre-Islamic Arabia and the ancient Near East, the centrality of dreams to the spiritual lives of Muslims is the legacy of the dreams and visions ascribed to the Prophet in the hadith literature. Dreams, as we all know, have a relationship to prophecy, and the famous hadith is often cited in oneirological literature, declaring that a true dream is either one forty-sixth or one seventieth of prophecy. The centrality of dreams to the end of time is also mentioned in the hadith situating true dreams in the apocalypse, quite appropriate for our times: 'When the end time draws near, the believer's dream will hardly ever be false.'

Many hadith transmitters of the eight and ninth centuries were also dream interpreters, of whom Ibn Sirin remains the most famous today. Recent academic scholarship has established that many of the texts of dream interpretation attributed to him are apocryphal; however, the 'truth' of his authorship is irrelevant to the project of establishing the narrative arc – or if not arc, then elliptical links, recursive meanings, and multivalent spatiality of dream interpretative techniques. It adds to the charm of dream interpretation texts as a genre that they seem to consist more in the cultural and spiritual accretions of unknown authors, rather than emerging from a pristine textual/intellectual genealogy. It would not be surprising if the mothers, sisters and wives of scholars were not somehow involved in the establishing the corpus of symbology encountered in the many texts ascribed to Ibn Sirin and other writers of dream interpretation texts.

In keeping with the oneiric logic of the texts whose authorship has been attributed to him, Ibn Sirin – who relied on oral transmission as a hadith transmitter – is also said to have been deaf. Regardless of the reality of this claim, it signifies his relationship to the *ghayb*, which surely here must encompass the unheard and unspoken as well as the unseen. Dream interpretation is also a practice of listening to the spiritual state of another human being. If the eponymous dream interpreter was either deaf or mythologised as deaf, then what did he listen to? As the celebrated eighteenth century Urdu poet, Ghalib, notes:

Ate hain ghayb se yih mazamin khayal men
Ghalib sarir-e khamah nava-e surush hain.

They come from the Unseen: these themes to the imagination
Ghalib, the scratching of the pen is the sound of the angel.

The other canonical work of dream interpretation in Arabic is that of 'Abd al-Ghani al-Nabulusi, the seventeenth and eighteenth century scholar and Sufi visionary, who has been studied by Elizabeth Sirriyeh, Senior Lecturer in Religious Studies at Leeds University. She writes about the role of narrating one's dreams to one's spiritual master in a Sufi order, in this case the Naqshabandiyya, and how this practice allows the sheikh to gain insight into the spiritual state of his disciple so that he can diagnose it and guide his progress. Nabulusi's dream narration and interpretation of dreams demonstrate to his students the depth of his understanding of the unseen world, or the *ghayb*. His work on dream interpretation, *The Sprinkling of Perfume on Humankind Through the Interpretation of Dreams* (*Ta'tir al-anam fi ta'bir al-manam*) was completed in 1685, and still enjoys a wide circulation in print today. These canonical texts, written by hadith transmitters and Sufi masters, contain a great deal of material that might be considered troubling, or perhaps contentious.

The reason why dream interpretation is particularly suited to breaking the Wahhabitus is that, in the narrativising of dreams, there are no taboos, sexual, social or others, with the implications of symbols and sequences carrying meanings ranging from pilgrimage and prayer to incest and cannibalism. The act of incest, in Abd al-Ghani al-Nabulusi, is in fact symbolic of pilgrimage, defying the logic of Wahhabo-modernity and linking unspeakable taboo with spiritual experience in a single narrative arc. Dreams of varying symbolism represent incestuous relations, whereas incestuous relationships themselves do not necessarily denote incest. As an example of the oneiric logic that defies the rational, dreaming of sprinkling vinegar onto the vine of an olive tree, or urinating earth onto the ground stands for intercourse with one's mother. However, dreaming of intercourse with one's mother, or other women who are within the degrees of blood relationship in which marriage is forbidden takes on an entirely unexpected meaning [to those entrenched in modernity]: 'Sexual intercourse with a woman of the forbidden degrees means bonds after despair, and gifts, especially in the case of the mother after one has broken with her, because it is a return to the place from which one came, with things to spend (*nafaqa*), turning to her after turning away. But if one (dreams that one) copulates with these women in the months of pilgrimage, or there are indications to that effect in the dream, then it means that one treads with one's feet on the holy ground and one will attain what one desires there.'

In the multivalent oneiric world, incest means many things – a return to one's origins, which can be a prognostication for a return to the town of one's birth, or the ultimate return to origins, the end of life and return to dust: If one dreams of intercourse with one's mother who is deceased, this means the end of his life's term, in view of God's word (Q 20:55), 'From her we created you and we shall make return into her, and from her we shall bring you forth another time.' The reference to 'her', of course is not the mother, but rather the earth, our *watan* or homeland, a site of belonging. But as Geert Jan van Gelder, Emeritus Professor of Arabic at Oxford University, who has written a study of the theme of incest in classical Arabic literature, also observes, it is a not a difficult semiotic shift to make. The variations of incestuous intercourse that the dream interpreters explore (from different family members, to positions, to types of intercourse) and their range of symbolic meanings are too numerous to explore here, and I am of course sensitive to the fact that such a discussion in much graphic detail might prove distasteful or shocking to some readers, especially as the men writing the dream interpretation texts are revered hadith transmitters, Sufi saints, and scholars of *fiqh*. How to understand their detailed and imaginative semiotic explorations of topics that Wahhibitus moderns would consider beyond the pale of acceptable spiritual discourse?

Rather than an exploration of the subconscious, or an appeal to essentialist semiotics that have in the past led to the reinforcement of racial and political hierarchies, perhaps the invitation to the labyrinth and creative logic of the dream world can allow us to access 'the peculiar mimetic powers of the imagination, its expansive capacity to transcend time and distance and to open itself to a selfless and sympathetic connection with the suffering and struggles of others.' Dream interpretation, beyond a political project of re-configuring the habitus of the diaspora Muslim, can also be construed as a project of radical empathy through listening to the unseen and unspeakable state of another person. It can be a liberation theology that avoids the essentialising of tradition and idealising of a precolonial past, as a transcendence of rationalism without falling into amorality, a semiotically chaotic space in which future pasts can be imagined, without being robbed of a connection to the richness of textual, oral and religious traditions; a problem which plagues secular revolutionary discourse in an Islamic context. The creation of narratives through the logic of dream interpretation can be a reimagining of our own traditions on their own terms, rather than a project of reductive and rationalising reform. What is proposed here is accessible to anyone who has ever dreamt the irrational or immoral, or beautiful, inexplicable and miraculous, whoever has wandered in the *Huraqalya*: the dream narrative as historical narrative that evades anti-colonial longing for a past of pre-colonial wholeness, happiness, and agency that never existed; a language to explore the tragedy and incomprehension of the present without resorting to modernist utopia-building, for there are no utopias in dreams, just the illogical semiotic mazes of life that offer infinite modes of interpretation.

In our enthusiasm for the illogic of the dream narrative as a Wahhabitus-antidote and fruitful ground for ontology creation, we run the historic risk of allowing the rich world of myth and symbolism to fall into the service of essentialising traditionalist projects that lead to the elaboration of fascist ideologies grounded in notions of racial superiority and the reinforcement of what are perceived to be archaic and therefore sacrosanct hierarchies, such as in the case of the works of Julius Evola and others. Or, access to the literary and imaginative world of dream interpretation can be seen as a reviving of a classic nineteenth century Orientalism that understood 'the East' as a source of mystical knowledge, irrationality, dreamworlds and visions, a prejudice that much of the scholarship of the last seventy years has worked to eradicate. So, it should be clarified that the idea of universally valid myths and symbols, in the thinking of historian and philosopher of religion, Mircea Eliade, and Swiss psychoanalyst Carl Jung, is to be avoided if we are to evade the trap of essentialising and reducing a complex conceptual tradition to purely 'imagination' and 'myth'.

Dream interpretation texts vary according to their context and the language in which they are written. The different symbols acquire varied, intricate meanings according to where the text was composed, and who composed it; the interpretation differs by context, by the individuals involved. Each symbol, even within a single text, acquires a range of contradictory meanings, and dream narratives cannot be situated in the world of Eliade and Jung's universal symbolism, but rather to a world of ellipsis, exploration, uncertainty and narrative creativity that allows unexpected ontologies to blossom. The meanings of each symbol in a dream interpretation text are deeply personal and intimate, as well as contextual. Dream interpretation allows the creation of possible futures and pasts, through the elliptic time of its narrative recursion.

THE WOMEN OF RAWABI

Sabrina Stallone

In our email exchange, Masa Dawoud gave enthusiastic answers to all of my questions but one. The young Palestinian communications manager flexibly provided me with a range of dates and times for a day-long visit I had shown interest in and accommodated almost all of my curiosities about Rawabi. My guided tour of the newly built city, organised on impulse during a longer fieldwork trip to Israel/Palestine, was fast approaching, and Masa readily replied to my messages about the tour's details. But the one burning query I postulated in as many different formulations as I could think of was avoided with astute public relations (PR) savoir-faire: What is the easiest way to get to Rawabi? The question remained unanswered, in a tactical move to avert my attention from the lack of public transport within a project as prestigious and high-tech as this new city. I took the bus from East Jerusalem to Ramallah, entering the West Bank through the Qalandiya checkpoint, as per usual when travelling to any part of Palestine north of Al-Quds, hoping to find a shared or private taxi willing to take me to a destination as yet frequented considerably less than Nablus, Jericho or Jenin.

Rawabi, the newest municipality in the West Bank, has been the steadfast goal of Palestinian-American entrepreneur Bashar Masri, and is known as the biggest private development project of the Palestinian Territories, and one of its most significant employers. Over the past years, Masri has had to tackle numerous challenges posed by the Israeli occupation and their administrative violence. While the grounds on which Rawabi stands are located in the Oslo Accords' Area A, and are thus under the Palestinian Authorities' control, it is but an island surrounded by zones fully administered by the Israeli military. This means that every resource that has to be brought to Rawabi is subject to a strenuous authorisation process with the Israeli government. As such, running water, cemented roads and working electricity were and still are Rawabi's fragile trophies of a bureaucratic war. Its current reputation as a growing, exciting city has been the merit of a relentless PR and communications machinery, which helped Rawabi through its stretches of infrastructural stagnation and turned it into a darling of the international press. Narrative, in Rawabi, has been key: its builders and believers have been pivotal in creating a story, actively sculpting a script for a future that at times did not seem to realistically be on the cards for this urban utopia.

Things, however, are moving. The private urban development effort, with ground officially breaking in 2009, went from a story told to a town built: as of this year, 4,000 residents have moved into their new homes in this new city, and the planned benchmark of the urban endeavour turned social phenomenon is currently at 40,000 inhabitants in the next few years. Although – or precisely because – its walls and city borders are getting more and more concrete, storytelling remains a big part of what constitutes Rawabi, and people like Masa, driven and communicative, make all the difference.

Rawabi is the first planned city of Palestine, as goes the litany that has accompanied its name since its utopian inception in 2007. In endless iterations, Rawabi has become a project preceded by its narrative – one that not only recounts Bashar Masri's success story in its meticulous details, but also aims to contend what counts as *truly* Palestinian. Critics of Masri's project see Rawabi as both the source and a symptom of the normalisation of occupation, and, ultimately, a whitewashing of the Nakba, the Palestinian displacement and dispossession in the wake of the Israeli state foundation. In an article in the *Washington Post,* Masri responded to the critiques of normalisation: 'We will live like normal people until the situation is normal.' This response and its rhetoric display the attitudinal and narrative tensions between those who live and breathe Rawabi, and those who analyse it from afar.

In her treatise of Rawabi, Tina Grandinetti has deemed the urban project a product of the Palestinian Authorities' 'apolitical economic policy': a political framework in which only elites and institutions profit, while the struggle for a Palestinian nation is neglected. In a critical analysis of the city's recent urban development, Arpan Roy calls the current processes and attitudes towards urban modernisation in Ramallah and now Rawabi a 'laissez faire glitz': a new type of performative national(ist) growth that plays into the hands of the new architects of Palestinian identity, the professional and business elites – of which the Masri clan, originating in Nablus, has been part of for generations. It is precisely these privileged classes that fill the ranks of Rawabi's unconditional supporters, the Palestinian capitalists who see in it the future of Palestine. The words they and their supporters use are 'ambitious', 'innovative', at times even 'revolutionary'. Between scholars and entrepreneurs, there is an evident rift regarding what Rawabi is meant to signify for Palestine.

A day in the now awaking city shows that a radical and essentialist tale of the project will not do it justice – and nothing is as striking a proof for it as the city's women. While a fair amount has been written about the city's planning efforts, the female engineers, architects and inhabitants remain somewhat out of focus; especially the city's female agents, who permeate, structure and shape the spaces of Rawabi and its appearance in complex ways. Their presence in the city's spaces and their active role in shaping its narrative call for a gendered lens through which to approach the project of Rawabi.

I was one of four visitors who reached Rawabi on a Tuesday in March 2018, however I was the only one arriving there independently: a group of civil engineering students from al Tireh near Ramallah, and a class of Yale undergraduates in peace and conflict resolution studies made it to 'Palestine's new town on a hill', as well as the Egyptian ambassador to the Palestinian Authorities, Issam Ashour, who was received after my mid-morning visit. Many more journalists, politicians, investors and students followed suit in the weeks before and after, touring the spectacle of everyday life that was slowly being constructed in Rawabi. Lacking a diplomatic vehicle or the comfort of group transit, I resorted to the good spirits of a Ramallawi cab driver, who knew how to take me to Birzeit, the university town a few kilometres north of Ramallah, and only approximately understood where exactly to drop me off in Rawabi, nine kilometres away from his work hub. 'I never go there', he said to me in Arabic and shrugged.

Driving up the green slopes from the epicentre of Palestinian life to the dreamed-up city, whose name literally signifies 'hills', seemed like leaving a busy family gathering through a narrow fire escape, finding oneself on a breezy rooftop, overlooking everything and seeing nothing. Leaving the crowded and often male-dominated transit hub in Ramallah never fails to make it clear that the opportunity to not zero in on something in particular, and let the gaze wander, is a considerable luxury in urban Palestine; departing from Ramallah means leaving a peculiarly saturated brand of Palestinian everyday life behind. The continuity between Ramallah and Rawabi is unmistakably given by the characteristic pastoral landscape, but much like the taxi driver suggested, and Masa made clear by omission, the transit connections between the cities are as yet feeble.

Although Ramallah has been called an incubator for a new globalised middle class urban ethos and lifestyle, it still operates within the conventional spatialities and structures of the Palestinian Territories. The real estate boom that it experienced in the 1990s was mostly designed by and catered to wealthy returnee elites, as pointed out by urban scholar Eyal Weizman, representing a twofold ideological reproduction of neoliberal modernity and traditionalist nostalgia. Moreover, being the home of the Palestinian Authorities' headquarters and many Nakba migrants, and due to its proximity to the checkpoints' spaces of contention, Ramallah counts as an 'oasis of normalcy' only if one considers the latent swarming presence of occupation to be absolutely normal. So while post-Oslo Accords Ramallah has indeed adopted a neoliberal agenda, there is not a lot of space left for the dream, or illusion, of liberation.

Rawabi, in contrast, has all the semblances of a Palestinian (optical) illusion: When I exit the taxi followed by the gaze of my bewildered cab driver, I walk past a few brand new, still empty residential buildings, behind me the untouched and occupied hills of the Oslo Accords' Area A, until I catch a glimpse of my meeting point, appearing indeed like some type of consumerist *fata morgana*: The Q Center, a squeaky clean open air mall at the heart of Rawabi. The square is flanked by fancy eateries, flagship stores of both Ferrari and Swarowski. One of the buildings in the Q Center houses the headquarters of Massar International, Bashar Masri's investment and development company, and its subsidiary Bayti Real Estate. Co-owned by Masri with Qatari investors, it has been the sole significant development force behind Rawabi. Bayti and Massar have been actively using their contacts and partners, encouraging them to open more businesses here. At this stage, a variety of more affordable clothing brands and a food court are about to be opened. At one end of the mall, between the framing buildings, the hills reappear, my view of them only obstructed by a large, fluttering Palestinian flag on a mast. I take a seat on one of the benches in the middle of the square. The morning is active, but in a quiet manner, with construction workers buzzing around and small groups of employees having meetings over lattes.

On this calm spring morning, the Q Center looks like a three-dimensional render of a swanky mall, one possibly built far away from any geopolitical conflict – the people, most of them female, moving through the square are young and dressed in expensive high street wear, they sip on iced drinks and work on their laptops, some juggling two other electronic devices at the same time. This is not the face of the Occupation one expects; not now, not the year after the fiftieth anniversary of a strenuous and vile military rule on the one million Palestinian people living in the Occupied Territories. I think of the many stories I have read about Rawabi leading up to coming here: now I know that the scripted narrative of the project results in a seemingly scripted reality. What I see here is the face and the performance of capital, success and, as some of the local women would argue, of feminist empowerment.

In the middle of the Q Center, Ruba Qadi, one of the many civil engineers working in Rawabi, stands tall facing the group of engineering students from a vocational school in al Tireh. She gesticulates in a reassuring and confident way; she smiles and nods while she takes questions from her audience. She keeps her sunglasses on, blinded by the reflection of the sun bouncing off the pale gold of limestone all around us; until now, a lot of international observers have focalised precisely on that limestone, and the controversies arising from its assemblage by Israeli contractors and workers; after all, Masri's employment of Israeli suppliers and labourers did spark several alarmed discussions in local circles. Grandinetti has termed this the weaving in of Israeli occupation in Palestinian development, 'creating an economy whose very structure is built upon a foundation of continued occupation and settler colonialism'. All the while aware of these critiques, in the moment, my focus does not shift to the brand new façades; it remains on the space and spectacle created by Ruba and her audience. I observe them from my little benched aisle in the Q Center. I can hardly hear Ruba's voice over the drills of the workers and the mellow jazz permeating the square through hi-tech speakers.

Behind her, I spot Bashar Masri, the real estate magnate behind Rawabi, sitting amid the group, listening and patiently giving answers. After having spent many years in the United States, he returned to the Palestinian Territories with returnee wealth and the fully fleshed idea of a 'new' Palestine. To his eager audience, he recounts the tale of his Rawabi, but lets Ruba take the lead of the Q&A. Even from afar, Masri is convincing with his charismatic but humble demeanors. When he leaves the group of students and disappears into the Massar office building, accompanied by Masa, the public relations manager who serves as his assistant and who I had emailed to arrange my visit, the students seem to be in awe of the man.

While Masa and Bashar hurry back into the building and to their next meeting, Ruba takes her time parting ways with the group of students. She takes pictures, exchanges contacts and engages in brief conversation. Later on, Ruba apologises for making me wait. She tells me that after the Q&A, she felt compelled to talk to some of the girls of the class. 'They need to change their attitude', Ruba says. 'I did not get one question out of them! Whereas the few boys of the class kept firing them at me. This has nothing to do with the girls' capabilities, it is just how society wants them: quiet. I did not get here by being quiet.'

Ruba graduated from Al-Najah University, the largest in Palestine, in the past year and would have left Nablus for Canada two days after graduation if it hadn't been for Rawabi, she recounts jokingly. After a number of internships as a civil engineer in large companies during her studies, she found herself demoralised. She was talked down to, not taken on sites, and led to believe that her career would not sum up to much more than a low prestige desk job. 'When I got the job here with Mr Masri I was really surprised, because people cared about what I had to say. Since I started here with my fellow female engineers, sites in Beit Jala and Hebron also see more and more women employed. We have an impact.' About 40% of the engineers here in Rawabi are women. Although both perceptions and laws regarding female representation in the workforce in Palestine are changing for the better, numbers such as the ones of Rawabi are still unusual: according to the World Bank, female participation in the formal labour system is still staggeringly low in Palestine, with around 16% and among the lowest in the Middle East. Both the detrimental military law of the Israeli occupation as well as the weak and non-unified Palestinian law make for insufficiencies in the legal enforcement of women's rights at the workplace.

Rawabi thus attracts women with a number of pathways to personal independence. Not only does the female workforce face and embrace opportunities here that would be negated to them otherwise in the actual urban development processes, the living quarters, according to Ruba, also catered to them. 'There are over 150 different apartment layouts that we offer', Ruba explains while guiding me through the already inhabited neighbourhood of Rawabi. 'But mostly we just want everyone who moves in to decide how and with whom they want to share housing.' In fact, about 10% of the over thousand apartments sold to this day, go to what Ruba calls the 'single movement': one-person households, often women, who decide to buy an apartment before marriage, defying longstanding Palestinian traditions, such as the patrilocal extended households and the heteronormative reproductive and domestic role of women. There are things here that clearly indicate that the architecture and structures of Rawabi bear some remarkably female potential, way beyond what Masri was once anecdotally quoted as saying about wanting women to jog in Rawabi, 'with or without veil'. Rawabi might very well not be just about small gestures of freedom; not only about the performance of the capitalist success narrative that precedes it, but about women tailoring a self-fashioned type of success for themselves that is not easily accessible to them in many other places in Palestine.

After a visit to the model apartment and the already built neighbourhoods, for our more extended tour of the city, we are joined by Duna Kafri, the business manager of the only school in town – a Cambridge certified K-6 school. The brief tour of the school building is given by Duna in a flawlessly recited presentation. She shows me the impeccable science labs, the spacious sports court outside, and the fingerprint check-in system the children now use with remarkable ease. Rawabi aims to attract young families with a private school of highest international education standards, adorned with all the over-the-top amenities I have come to expect at every corner in this city.

Ruba, Duna and Masa keep on telling me about Rawabi and all that its still imagined future has in store with the intensity and enthusiasm of dreams that depend on money, but that no money can buy: about an Extreme Sports Centre with a zipline crossing the hilltops, a winery that will yield the fruits for a yearly Wine Festival, the largest amphitheatre in the region with 15,000 seats, that will hopefully host acclaimed entertainment acts in no time – the superlatives sometimes blur the boundaries between what is already real and financed, and projects that are still waiting to get a green light. In fact, these women's eagerness to share these ideas takes the edge off their reality; they manage to shift and shape my attention towards their collective excitement rather than towards the hardships of a private development effort in Palestine. More so, they shift my attention towards a modernised and commodified version of Palestinian everyday life, one that they are able to malleably co-create. Ruba, Duna and Masa perform an exercise in imaginative persuasion – even if their imaginations are an echo of Bashar Masri's vision. Their ability to voice their ideas of growth, and partake in their realisation, might not seem like the peak of emancipation; but in Palestine, it is a quite significant act of subject formation.

The tour I receive guided by the eyes and minds of Rawabi's women exemplifies the complexities of what gender empowerment means and provokes in neoliberal societies. As political scientist Hanna Muehlenhoff recently argued, the terms of empowerment may have been carelessly perused by feminist scholars, much to the chagrin of political theorists: a largely positive reading of female empowerment neglects the processes through which 'gender equality becomes part of an economic calculation, which makes it a resource for more security and development'. Is Rawabi's female success story merely one that makes 'gender equality solely an instrument to achieve more security and development' along strictly neoliberal economies of the sensible, as Muehlenhoff suggests? And if so, what exactly is inherently reproachable about a feminism that navigates the mechanisms of neoliberalism to experiment with emancipatory tactics? There would be something deeply problematic about holding Ruba accountable to a different feminism than I personally want to stand for, measuring her against a different scale. So I try and question her feminism in a similar way that I would anybody else's: by being critical, and at the same time by hoping to understand her as a situated subject, taking her into account as both an ally and someone with a personal trajectory radically different to mine.

The project of Rawabi is an achievement of neoliberalism, which aims at provoking a shift in society to embrace the perks and open doors that capitalism grants its favourite children – those with the right resources. But while these critiques are in order, it is crucial to mention that Rawabi is not only the nightmare locus of Marxist academics, postcolonial scholars and who Ruba calls 'people of Palestinian heritage who sip their cappuccinos and criticise everything that contradicts what is *radical chic*'. It is also, both obliquely and concretely, a thorn in the side of those who want the Palestinian narrative to be a monolithic recitation of grief, war and struggle: for instance, the Israeli settlers of Ateret, an illegal outpost just a hill slope away, who see their race for land counteracted in a mimicking way. However, it is certainly not only Israelis who seek to portray Palestinians as people who are incapable of competent governance and development and hell-bent on violence fuelled by hatred towards Israel. As Bashar Masri declares, Rawabi is a concrete proof that 'we will live like normal people'. He and Rawabi's inhabitants see 'normalcy' as their own form of resistance – one that is supposed to reach international crowds as much as those who are daily affected by the conflict. Moreover, and this is a detail that exemplifies the multidirectional complexities of Rawabi, the urban project is a fastidious reality to many a Palestinian traditionalist and patriarch, afraid that their daughters and sons will choose a path of personal emancipation over more conventional family life.

It would be too easy to argue that those who benefit most from the 'Rawabi movement' are not those who are afflicted the most by the hardships of the perpetual Occupation, limiting an analysis of the project to an obvious critique. As Léopold Lambert, author of *Weaponised Architecture*, argues, this would lead to an "essentialisation of Palestinianness" – creating a monochrome Palestinian pawn that only wants modernisation and innovation if it directly spits in the face of Occupation. What is more, this essentialising claim also disregards the gender dynamics and its narrative, vital to a thorough understanding of Rawabi, and more generally Palestine. The media frenzy around 16-year old Ahed Tamimi, the activist female teenager who became the face of Palestinian resistance overnight in late 2017, as well as the more recent instrumentalisation of Palestinian doctor Razan al-Najjar, murdered while volunteering during protests in Gaza, show that the sensationalised tale of Palestine's women as either victims of the occupation or sensualised figures of dissent and martyrdom is as relevant as ever.

The voices of Palestinian women are often sought to investigate the silences of the history of occupation: oral histories of survivors of the Nakba, the mothers of martyred freedom fighters, young bodies exuding the allure of female resistance. The history-making agency of Palestinian women has been explored, but often limited by a heteronormative gaze and the restricting expectations shaped by the vicissitudes of the Israeli occupation. In that, not only the capitalist agency but also the epistemic role of women in Palestine has been subject to a double reduction: it is contained within hegemonic narratives by the Israeli occupier as well as by the public eye – both Palestinian and not. And perhaps, Rawabi's flirt with its own version of a neoliberal imaginary and reality disturbs the ideals of what we believe Palestine to be.

Back in the Q Center after our tour, the women and I discuss the quality of life in Rawabi. Ruba is the proud owner of a single apartment in Rawabi; Duna still resides in Ramallah and Masa lives with her family in a town nearby, but both of them don't exclude moving to this new city altogether. When I ask them what relocating here would mean for their Palestinianness, Ruba is the first to rebuff what she thought I was hinting at: 'You mean if this compromises my Palestinian identity? I come from a village older than Jericho.' Rawabi, in her words, is built to be in touch with tradition through material homages to its Palestinian land and heritage. What becomes clear, both in Bashar Masri's vision and in these women's idiosyncratic iterations, is that Rawabi is not supposed to remain an insular project. While Rawabi is made to look like Palestine, with the traditional limestone forged from the local stone quarry and the Palestinian flags crowning its hills, the larger goal would be to make Palestine look, function and work more like Rawabi. While the real estate billionaire behind Rawabi has been boasting about building more cities resembling his 'city upon a hill' in the near future, the young civil engineer Ruba motivates her wish to expand the 'Rawabi movement' in a more immediate, relatable way: 'My little sister still goes to school, and now that she has visited me in Rawabi, she wants to become an engineer, too.' She should be able to work wherever she wants, Ruba states. While I tell her that I wholeheartedly wish her the same, I remain rapt in the question: What does all of this mean for the liberation of Palestine? 'Freeing Palestine has nothing to do with throwing stones, freeing Palestine is also this', Ruba says, standing just as tall as earlier in front of the engineering students, while Masa arranges for a private driver to take me down the hills back to crowded Ramallah. Of course, Ruba's statement is saturated with unfair polarisations, excluding all the important grassroots activist work done by Palestinians, relentlessly fighting for liberation; from the non-violent struggle in the First Intifada, to more current Feminist and Queer organisations, women have played a pivotal role in Palestinian social justice. Ruba's is also a statement that oozes with utopian stubbornness, disregarding the potential negative impact an elite project such as hers might have on the surrounding area. Her boisterous statement indeed suggests that measuring the future of Palestine against the blindingly clean façades of Rawabi might still be premature. The fissures and pitfalls of a privately funded city, created out of nothing on pristine hills, have yet to be seen in Rawabi; after all, the only 4000 inhabitants do not fully account for the urban life that exists in its self-crafted narrative. As such, the establishment of a sustainable female-driven workforce and public life is also still to be assessed.

Nonetheless, the women of Rawabi already unmake and complicate what is understood as Palestinian identity and the place that women occupy traditionally within the Palestinian narrative, steering away both from Palestinian conformist ideals and the attested roles which the Occupation assigns them. Taking issue with the women of Rawabi as political subjects, if nothing else, raises the concern of non-archetypal ways to understand what it means to be female and Palestinian; or perhaps, by performing their self-styled role as Palestinian women, Ruba, Masa and Duna hold up a mirror to us, questioning what *we* want them to be.

BEING MUSLIM

Onaiza Drabu

It is said that on the Day of Judgement, the Prophet Muhammad will open the gates of heaven to his *Ummah*, the worldwide community of Muslims united in faith. However, for a religion whose followers cannot even agree on a date to celebrate Eid, universal solidarity is a tough call. In its essence, Islam is simple. The one sentence you hold dear defines your identity as a Muslim for life. You testify that there is no other God but Allah and with that utterance and belief are granted access into the *Ummah*. The universal in Islam does not run much further than this. Culture and politics, context and circumstance step in as mediums for interpreting the religion.

Some view Islam as a culture into which they were born, and others see it as a rigid set of rules, but there are so many in between. There are fanatics, liberals, secularists and even atheists who identify as Muslim, not to mention the many who do not neatly conform to any labels. We disown radical terror outfits, dismissing them as not Muslim but are they not Muslim or does their interpretation of Islam not correspond with ours? Do we have the right to question their faith when we denounce their actions? What makes a believer if not self-identification?

Over the last few years, I have been travelling around the world asking – mostly, but not exclusively, young - Muslims how they see Islam and how Muslim do they feel. Here are some of my encounters.

Kahveh and Francine

Kaveh begins most conversations with his love of the beat generation. He grew up on a steady diet of modern American poetry and literature. He brews his own alcohol, smokes a heady dose of pot and spends his weekends mixing the two when perhaps he should not be. In his mid-twenties he graduated from university in the US a few years ago and is now discovering his writing style; it's a mixture of self-loathing narrative laden with pop culture references. Characteristic of an Iran you read about in popular media, Western in consumption yet burdened with conflicting heritages of a glorious East, Kaveh lives with his parents in a smart apartment in Tehran. He went to school there and knows Islam as it was instilled in him in his early school years as part of the curriculum. Yet, none of this has been stirred in his conscious memory in years. The conversations within his social group often revolve around literature and Western popular culture. When discussions do steer towards politics, he is contemptuous of the Iranian regime. His argument is reductionist; there is denial of the religiosity of most of his country and he considers an overhaul of the theocratic government as the only solution. He is devoid of cultural or religious Islam. The only clue is his Iranian passport and his last name; a heritage not easy to shrug off in the regime he lives under. For everyone else, he is Muslim. For him that is not a tag he identifies with and one he uses solely for entertainment and now, Trump jokes.

As we overlook a lit Tehran skyline from his balcony, he tells me about the ennui that has settled around the city; he loves it and hates it too. He blames it on religion, he says and uses a common slur for religious people, synonymous with smelly feet. Majoritarian societies influence how one engages with an Islamic identity. There is a disdain stemming from religion that can only emerge under a theocracy. In Iran, where an elite, secular, sub-culture – a small percentage in a large conservative country - exists, this is strongest. Kaveh stresses that antipathy toward religion in this regime is important to be seen for what it is; rebellion against religion is rebellion against the state.

Kahveh's antithesis in many ways is a quadragenarian, blonde, British lady I meet. Francine no longer goes by her name of birth. In many months, no one has actually seen her face. Her piercing blue eyes stare out dartingly. But that is possibly all you can use to identify her with her *niqab* on. She confides that she doesn't even take her *abaya* off at night because she fears the *jinns* would see her naked. She converted to Islam a few years ago and now carries the zealous convert's burden of enforcing 'true Islam'. There has to be a circumstance that drew her to Islam but I am hesitant to ask lest I be accosted by the *jinns* that police her. She lives in Cairo studying Qur'anic Arabic at a local institute. It is a far cry from her home town of Liverpool where she lived before moving to Egypt a few months ago. She does not quite know where her new religion fits so she takes it to extremes, redefining her identity while carrying around a self-proclaimed, purified version of Islam.

How we engage with religion especially when it is not a choice or is the religion of your birth depends on what is shaping it; governments, cultures, families; even destiny and fate. Its pedagogy is as defining as the regime it is served under. Kahveh may not be Muslim by his admission but he is Muslim to an outsider. The fatalism of Islam that he criticises as weighing down the air in Iran is an essential part of him too. He is a manifestation of the culture he grew up in and can do little to escape it. Francine on the other hand, adopts all she reads minus any cultural context. In a religion where most followers do not even understand the language they utter to pray every day, religion is a ritual. How that ritual translates into an identity is defined by the politics and circumstance that surrounds it. Francine is probably an easier target for a radicalised action against the United States but it is Kahveh, whose social references are so tied to the nation, who is currently banned from entering it.

Marianne and Khadija

Marianne insists her name is spelt the French way. If you did not know her last name, her blonde mane and perfectly tanned skin would not betray her Arab ethnicity. Her outfit is on-trend and she talks animatedly about the countries she has holidayed in the past few months. I meet Marianne at a barbecue in Amman. In her early forties, she is gloriously single and smacks her lips at the mention of the Turkish men she reveals made her recent visits to Turkey particularly enjoyable. She bursts out laughing as she recalls her romantic interludes. Marianne could be a character in a TV show; her energy is palpable and the drama is alive. As she offers me a drink that I politely decline, her friends join her in declaring that they are not 'proper' Muslims; that it is okay for us to drink in their house, after all, what joy is there in life without alcohol? Religion is for others. Throughout the afternoon, I hear many such disavowals of religion. Constant assertions of how they are bad Muslims, yet never not Muslims. Marianne is brash, outspoken and incredibly fun. Her demeanour, her sassiness and her irreverence construct an image of a Muslim who sheds her religious baggage the moment she throws off her *abaya*. Marianne is animated and theatrical yet as the evening ends, I feel certain she hasn't sipped her full glass of beer at all.

A few days later, I meet Marianne's friend, Khadija, who takes me to a gathering of her *tariqa* or Sufi sect. As I tie my hair up and my scarf tight around me before stepping in, she laughingly asks: 'Who do you think we are? *Hijabis*? Loosen that up a little and slide it back. We are liberal Muslims.' She then proceeds to respectfully pray, bow, and kiss the hand of the *shakykh*. As she leaves the shrine compound, she takes off her scarf, adjusts her hair, applies another coat of lipstick and drives on. A few hours later, Khadija sits in the privacy of her room and quenches her thirst with a beer while discussing the events of the day. She says she does not like to drink before going for prayer as it would leave her unable to perform her *wuzu* or ablutions.

Often we place too much emphasis on Muslims looking the part. Marianne and Khadija are at ease with being Muslim without the *hijab* and the *abaya* and while drinking alcohol. Members of a largely secular social circle in a conservative country, they drink freely and openly but continue to practise Islam in private. Negotiating oneself in secular settings is difficult in countries where shedding religion is equated with enlightenment. Both say they are Muslims but not in a conventional way. They, says Khadija, are not the Saudis or Iranians. They classify themselves as 'born Muslim' but liberal. Bedouins, after all, hold nothing too dear.

Mustafa, Hamza and Rizwan

Mustafa is a high-ranking army officer in India. If it were not for his name, I would never have guessed he is Muslim. I am invited to his house for Eid lunch. Plates of *biryani* and customary *sewiyan* are served and devoured. The family has not fasted this month; or ever. They do not consider themselves to be particularly practicing Muslims but since no one else in their social circle are Muslim, it has become a tradition to host these obligatory Eid parties. He'd much rather do without them, frankly. Throughout most conversations, he spews disdain for Pakistan and declares how by and large, most Muslims give the rest a bad name. He quotes from the *Bhagwad Gita* often when he is invited for talks and is lauded for his secularism. I wonder if he feels he needs to be secular or celebrate Hinduism in order to find his place in Modi's India.

Mustafa supports the ruling, right wing Hindu government for its development narrative. I look up some of his public commentary after meeting him and it reeks of apologies for his identity and faith. He must not fall in line with the other Muslims, is what he certainly seems to be thinking. It is no wonder that he is the ideal Muslim poster-boy for the media and politicians; Muslim in name and Hindu in practice. Practicing has never been an option for him, to prove his patriotism he must overcompensate. He escaped the neighbourhood he grew up in; areas where people felt safe, he felt stifled. He attributes a large part of his success to his personal grit and hard work, leaving little to circumstance. One wonders if the same could have been said for him had his relationship with religion been different. No matter, with another heap of biryani on his plate, he goes on with his tirade against regressive Muslim states.

In nearby Lahore, only ten hours' drive away in distance but a vast chasm in political and religious landscape, Hamza's friends don't believe that his new avatar will last too long. Hamza turned 24 a few months ago and the realisation of all his two-dozen years has caused him to completely change his life. Attending a friend's wedding, I see him hold his *tasbih* as the music plays, reciting prayers under his breath. It has been six months since he decided to revert to an Islam even his parents thought was beyond him. They are now looking for a suitable bride. His only condition is that she should be *hijabi*. Up until six months ago, Hamza was the black sheep of his well-to-do Lahori family. They are deeply religious in a Muslim society yet like all regions of repression, Pakistan too, harbours an intense underground scene. He and his group of male friends would regularly hire escorts to party with. Drinks would flow, as would other intoxicants. The rebellion was never acknowledged by the family who felt that eventually, he would come around. And he did. Social obligations like those of a society with a strong family system are the leash of restraint on these youth. In a society that values a morality based on religiosity, he was eventually worn down. Hamza grew a beard and with that grew a distance from the many excesses of his youth.

Tangled in a tussle between Lahore and Delhi, Rizwan grew up in downtown Srinagar feeling a strange solidarity for Pakistan. He was taught to identify with it as a nation, support it over India because of their religious solidarity with this Muslim soil. Now, he uses the very same to claim an independent nation and cry for *azaadi* (freedom). Each life lost is portrayed as martyrdom or *shahadat*, in a holy war or *jihad* by the resistance. India is seen as the *kafir* (infidel) other that they must fight. Such is the rhetoric Rizwan has adopted especially after a heady consumption of separatist social media propaganda. The months he spent loitering under curfews and in protests during his impressionable teenage years, have shaped who he is today.

Lest they be homogenised into the larger India, Kashmiris feel a need to cling on to an Islamic identity. The jihadist-separatist campaign has left behind a puritanical Salafi identity, one that tries to cure Kashmir of its idolatrous, saint-worshipping Islam. Rizwan vehemently explains how visiting shrines is wrong. He is disapproving of his mother going every week. She is adamant she will not change; it is a tradition that originates from her forefathers. She, however, cannot stop Rizwan from reading what he does and going out with his friends to proclaim religion to passers-by. She fears for his life and wants him to leave Srinagar for studies in India. He is reluctant. Over the past few years, he has sported a long beard without a moustache and his trousers have steadily risen a few inches above his ankles. He often tells off girls dressed 'immodestly'. They need to know what our true culture is and support the cause, he says. We cannot get rid of *kaafir* India when our own women dress like them.

Social impact interacts with the faith you are born into. Religiosity was a coming of age ritual for Hamza, in a society like Lahore. In a secular state like India, in a multi-cultural, majority Hindu society, Mustafa recognised early that he needed to keep religious signs on low to move up in the ranks. In Kashmir, its linkages to the resistance movement have changed the social landscape of the valley. Young men like Rizwan have embraced this new firebrand Islam that seeks to purify Kashmiri Islam for a tomorrow in an independent Muslim state.

Reza, Jasim and Anum

Back in Iran, in Kashan, a smaller town, we meet Reza. He has a beaming smile with a physique right out of a wrestling match. He is introduced to us by one of his female friends, who is undertaking a research project in Iran. He talks with bashful confidence, via the help of his friend who is translating. At his home, we notice a large painting that looks holy, much like photos of Christ we see with the halo, except this man has a green turban. We think it is Ali, but we are mistaken. It is a painting of the Prophet Muhammad. In a world where Muslims protest and bombers bomb because of controversies over imagery of the Prophet, in a small town in this devoutly Muslim country, they use photos as a mark of reverence harking back to the long tradition of imagery in their culture. He looks at us, smiling pointedly and asks if we are Muslim. Giggling we reply that we are, and continuing the same wide smile tilting his head to the right, he indicates that the response is insufficient. 'Sunni or Shia', we match the high-pitched fake giggle to break the tension as we sheepishly admit that we are Sunni. Merely being Muslim wasn't sufficient, which is interesting. His demeanour changes, we aren't that foreign after all. He recognises some element of the other in us. The awkwardness is now palpable. He says something to our Farsi speaking friend, cautious lest it offend us. The tomb we pass by is Abu Lulu's the man who killed Caliph Umar. He wasn't sure if he should tell us, but he says that up until recently, effigies of Umar were burnt and the day of his assassination celebrated. Abu Lulu holds an honorific title for this act, Baba Shujauddin (defender of the religion); ironic given how he was Christian. This tale makes us acutely aware of the different versions of the religion we follow. Reza wraps up the conversation, showing off the nicer, less controversial parts of Kashan.

Reza does not identify with us. The solidarity we experienced from him dies the minute he realises that we are not Shia. Such is the case of minority faiths and sects worldwide. Stores in Pakistan refuse to sell to Ahmedis but not to Sikhs or Hindus. They are angered by a version of the same faith that goes against their own; one that tethers to the *shahada* but only loosely. Yet, isn't that the case for every identity one seeks to claim as one's own, taking offense to appropriation that defies its inherent authenticity?

On a particularly care-free day in Amman, I, being a woman, make the grave mistake of instinctively taking the front seat as my friends slip onto the back. The cab driver's chattiness reminds me of the many warnings against this seemingly innocent act. I berate myself for not remembering it but advice from my office security rang loud, 'In case of trouble, tell them you are Muslim. You'll be fine.' So, when Chatty Abu-Chatty, my Jasim, asks me where I was from, I tactfully lied, Pakistan, to hint at my faith. Then when he offered me a cigarette I pointedly exclaimed, digging into my vocabulary of all five Arabic words that I knew, *haram*! Abu-Chatty lights up momentarily, asking me if I am Muslim but soon I sense sharp judgment. He points to my forehead while driving like a daredevil and tells me I cannot be Muslim because I don't wear a headscarf. I tell him, pulling out another from my repertoire of Islamic ammunition, *tawhid* or the concept of Allah being the only God, pointing to my heart. He just laughs and kept on shaking his head saying, 'No, no. No Muslim', till he drops me off. I slam the door in his face but do not stop thinking. Clearly, the solidarity of the *ummah* did not save me from harassment but rather provoked him further. This man did not understand my Islam. To him, it was a pleasant joke. The *Ummah* may be together in *akhira*, but certainly not in this world. Judging piety and stereotyping each other is a fault we ourselves are guilty of before we point fingers at outsiders.

The first time I met an Ismaili friend's grandmother, I was surprised she responded to my *assalamualaikum* with a *ya Ali madad* (may Ali the exalted help). Where I grew up, I had heard it being used only by people lifting heavy objects, or during physical exertion. When Anum decides to take me with her to the grand old Jamatkhana in Nairobi's city centre, learning to greet with a *ya ali madad* is the first part of my training. As a non-Ismaili, I am not allowed into this prayer house but if I play and look the part, I can get away. All I have to do is remember to greet with a *ya ali madad*, and end the prayer with a *shah'jo didar* (may you be blessed with the Lord's glimpse). For the rest, I can look devout and pray with my *tasbih*.

Anum had told me much about her upbringing as a liberal Ismaili. A historically persecuted community, the Ismailis maintain a strong network and preserve their religion and practice wherever they go. It is a tight-knit community who have high expectations of each other, yet they participate wholeheartedly, lending their time, money, skills and networks to the community. She tells me how she can move to practically any country in the world and will find a fellow Ismaili to house her, feed her and introduce her to their *jamatkhana*. Many of her childhood summers in the US were spent at Ismaili summer camps that teach how to be a responsible part of this small, yet strong, global community. This was fascinating enough for me to plead until she agreed to take me along to witness their dua.

The majority of Ismailis are converts from Hinduism and mostly from the Gujarat belt of the Indian subcontinent. Many migrated to East Africa on the advice of the Aga Khan who recognised the economic benefits of setting up life in this new land. With subsequent help from the early settlers in Kenya, they established themselves as a prosperous community. Many of their traditions stem from this history of staying close together as well as influences from their past Hindu culture. Their prayers are a mix of Gujarati and Arabic, which to my ear sounded like Hindu prayer songs or *bhajans*. I was mildly surprised but very intrigued. I was told that they do not pray the *namaz or salah* and that it is reserved for special occasions like Eid but there is a service like this every day.

They began with a *kalma* that I recognised but trailed off into something I didn't. I thought I caught a reference to the Hindu Lord Ram and thoughts of *shirk* (idolatry) floated through my mind. At the end of the evening, I was about to describe my experience as very interesting but not really Muslim before I caught myself. Was I any different from my Jasim, the cab driver? Was I guilty of doing the very thing I was so critically writing about? Where is my acceptance and tolerance when I recognise something that is very distinct from my interpretation of Islam? Although if I extend this logic, would I consider the Daesh or ISIS to be Muslim just because they call themselves that despite going against the many fundamentals of Islam? Answers to such musings remain contentious.

The complete plurality of Islam is beyond my brief narrative stories: myriads of sects, numerous intersectional identities, queer Muslims, the trans community, feminists, those who are troubled by some tenets of Islam and others who seek to define their own path in or outside the religion. Who is to say who is Muslim and who is not? After all, the Qur'an declares, 'to you be your religion, and to me mine' (109: 6). As each of us bows our heads towards the *ka'aba*, some turn East and some West but we all bow in the same direction.

POSTNORMAL WORDS

C Scott Jordan

It was a swastika.

It is such a strange word. Even by English standards. Swastika. This odd combination of consonants and vowels makes for something almost as startling as the symbol itself. The symbol which lies burnt into the lawn before me on a particularly steamy summer morning. It is a peculiarly cruel form of cultural genocide to so bastardise a religious peace symbol. Peculiar still that I find this pyrotechnic graffiti in Omaha, Nebraska: a micro example of the city's famous tradition. That being, the destruction of tradition. Out with the old, in with the new. Gentrification in Omaha takes on a meaning no other city could fathom. Excise the historical and lay out a new rug to forget. No memory to romanticise, no past to draw fear from. Only the newer and the better. A noncanonical interpretation of the American Dream.

If Omaha didn't invent gentrification it has, at least, perfected the model, making it widely available and applicable. Packaged for home use, cultural genocide has been neutralised to the point of it almost being a fun family outing for the weekend. My roommate and I laugh with a nervous accent as we drive by the numerous gentrification projects at work all throughout the streets of Omaha.

This nature dates back to the first staking out of the Nebraska territory during the United States' western expansion of the nineteenth century. Nebraska comes from the native Oto tribe's word for 'flat water' referring to the Platte River which bisects the contemporary territorial borders. Omaha itself was one of the tribes that roamed the great plains. The first white people to call Nebraska home were nicknamed 'tree planters.' This unusual moniker comes from the annual tradition turned state holiday known as Arbor Day. Arbor Day traces its origin back to the sojourn of one of the original American mythological figures, Johnny Appleseed. Barefooted with a tin pot upon his head, Johnny marched across the American frontier with his bag of apple seeds in a nigh biblical fashion ridding the land of useless grassland to lay the groundwork for the industrialised, production-ready landscape that Manifest Destiny called for. Indeed, the American Spirit! The first inhabitants of contemporary America rolled with the punches. Whatever nature gave, the early tribes made it work and in such a way that did not destroy the hand that fed them. They would attempt to teach the first Europeans how to farm so that they may survive those first treacherous winters. Leave it to the Western tradition to take a model and find a way to exploit it and bleed it for all it has to offer. The gift of the first thanksgiving would, unbeknownst to the givers of the first American tribes, be the instrument for their undoing. Military campaign, mass over-farming and slaughter of the Buffalo would provide the first wave of genocide and gentrification against the native peoples. The second wave would not only strike against the way of life for Native Americans but be a slap in the face of mother nature. A mass terraforming event that would set the ball rolling on the demonic mind of early developers of the largest Midwestern cities.

Year after year, more and more trees turned the endless sea of prairie grass into odd forest as the nineteenth century waxed and waned. The tradition of gentrification would not stop there. The twentieth century brought cars and industry, turning Omaha from a pit stop on the Oregon Trail, to a metropolis, a true American city. The fathers of contemporary Omaha had the Pacific Ocean in their sights but found that fortune and glory would be found easier in the journey than the destination. They settled in Omaha to finance those set on California gold and most importantly in transporting it back east. Bankers and businessmen sought to make Omaha the ultimate capital of a pan continental empire of business, managing trainlines, telegram (and eventually telephone) lines, and safe transport of mail and money to and fro. To the northern part of the town, the first kings and queens of Omaha (to this day they actually hold a ball every year where the city elites elect a King and Queen of Aksarben, which is Nebraska spelled backwards). A new way of life had taken root in the loose soil of the former plains. Symbols of the old Native American way were transformed and "made better" with the heavy use of Art Deco.

The mass immigration from Europe at the turn of the century created a refugee crisis for the Eastern coast of the United States. Just as the founders of the East fled the persecution of the Old World, the new immigrants moved west to flee the new persecutors. Tribes of Bohemians, Italians, and Slovaks built ghettos within the modern-day city limits of Omaha. Like any true American city ought to, the city developed along a classic grid system. North to south. East to west. Block by Block. The streets became as good walls as modes of transport, making sure every different group stayed in their own place. Eventually the rich elites of the North set their eyes for the West to recreate a Stepfordian paradise in the yet untouched land Johnny Appleseed left them. The South, the landing point for newcomers (due to the railroad's placement) became the labour capital and home to the working minorities. First Europeans, more recently the Latin Americans. The abandoned castles of the North would become a good a place as any for the recently freed slaves to settle upon the conclusion of the American Civil War. Malcolm X was born in the leftovers of Omaha's most royal families. The construction of major interstates would help solidify the artificial borders of segregation that keep all the different citizens of Omaha away from each other.

Omaha today is a microbrewery for racial and class tensions. Numerous structures in society seek to maintain the physical borders that the architects of Omaha put up to frame Omaha from the Missouri River westwards. Fairy tales told to scare children are reinforced by the five o'clock news. The South is for the lazy foreigners and is ruled by gangs imported from Latin America. The North is the capital of crime and hate, also noted as the most likely place in all of the United States for a Black Male to be murdered. Downtown (the East) is just where you go to work, but try to avoid the homeless and their plight. Even the mighty police force has trouble properly herding them away from the general public. They inspire an instant of empathy, but in truth the average American hopes they would carry on with decreasing the surplus population. West Omaha is safe. That is where home is, reeking of cleanliness and success. The American Dream imagined. No crime happens here (except of course for the crime which happens within the family unit, or within the closed boardroom, or any of that sexual misconduct occurring in front of the blind eyes of university campus leaders or church officials).

Omaha is America. That wonderful melting pot of culture, where only the filmy crud rises to the top and temperatures and tensions remain constantly high. Come visit our world-famous Henry Doorly Zoo. It houses a wide variety of species from all around the world! Like this world-famous zoo, Omaha itself is always tearing down old buildings to build new and better yet keeping little bits of romanticised memories in the façade. Shuffling new groups of immigrants around being careful not to let them mix too much. The immigrants of Yugoslavia and Africa from the nineties and the noughties are just beginning to carve their little bits of the city out, just in time as the latest influx of global refugees is beginning to develop bringing in new groups from the Middle East. Everyday more and more projects gentrify the old and decrepit. Upon the ashes of the old, Omaha builds up and outward, prices soar, and the class gap is kept well fed. Yet each group is kept sectioned off from each other, each in their own cage. A proud zoo of humanity. Something truly postnormal comes in Omaha's pride over its heritage, steeped in multiculturalism, yet emphasised in segregation and division.

What keeps it all together. The lie upon which the plot of the American narrative is carefully constructed. The lie is that America defeated racism, or at least that we have managed racism so effectively that to even count it as still existing is statistically superfluous. The Civil War, the Civil Rights Movement, Black History Month, the multitude of pan cultural holidays and school lesson plans. They all succeeded. Congratulations America, we did it. Blacks and Whites, Asians, Mexicans, Middle Easterners, even the Russians. We can all live in tolerant harmony. Even religious, gender, and sexual identity come together to sing Kumbaya or enjoy a cup of Joe, consuming and gentrifying *ad infinitum*. Score one for humanity!

This was the education I was served growing up an American millennial. It was the 1990s and we were at peacetime, things, by American standards, were quite weird. We were told to look around, there was no forced segregation, and to look at all the minorities that we share this wonderful country with. Measures had even been taken to pay for the sins of the father such as Affirmative Action and issued public apologies. It was the highest crime for our generation to make fun of anyone for being different, to refer to disliked things as being "gay" was outlawed, and a sort of

Ludovico sickness would develop in our stomach just for thinking of certain racial slurs. Change had finally come.

And then there was 9/11. No, that must have been a fluke. Americans are past hate. We love our differences. That which makes us unique. We stand together in our differences as one nation. We would rally behind the stars and stripes. The struggle occurred, and we progressed to the mountaintop. But had we? Why did the older generations use certain words or avoid certain places or banish certain types of music and film? Was this story more complicated? Did we miss a part? What if we had been lied to? It is a hard and nauseating thought, to realise that you might have been indoctrinated.

And then there was the election of 2008. Barack Obama. And just like that, the hate returned. Racism resurfaced, alive and flourishing. Those differences shifted into focus. To be American meant something different overnight. While we didn't fully understand it, it was something that none of us really liked. And then there was the election of Donald Trump. The seemingly impossible, now a reality.

And then I found myself in Omaha's Memorial Park on a phenomenally humid day. Sweat dripping and my morning jog reduced to a dumbfounded loiter with an exhaustion-induced *contrapposto* stance. My lungs rapidly disrupting the air pressure around me. The salinity of my sweat burning my eyes. And a swastika lay burnt into the hallowed ground of Omaha's highest war memorial. Aside from housing the granddaddy of all high hills for snow day sledding, Memorial Park is the sight of memorials honouring those who died from Douglas County in America's various foreign conflicts. World War I, World War II, Korea, Vietnam, all meshed together. Memorial Park is a collage of patriotism, organic as with the tallying of each new death toll for each new American military operation, one could bet that another statue or plaque will be added to the grounds. Among the names of the fallen Nebraskans is an exorbitant number of American flags and the fast and loose use of classic patriot phrases. Each one more mind numbing than the last, derived from sound bites delivered to force homogeneity amongst a people ready to tear each other apart in accordance with Hobbes' nightmare.

Give me liberty or give me death. United we stand, divided we fall. Live free or die. You're either with us or you're against us. Forgive but never forget. Freedom is not free. All of them dated. All of them ridiculous. Pathetic attempts to unite a people simply to be against the other. Simple platitudes and threatening contradictory mind traps. If Freedom is not free, then perhaps what it is that we are talking about is anything but. We utter these words without thought or reflection just as we recite the anthems and light the fireworks and gather around the heart-warming glow of patriotic nationalism.

And then, as I wipe the sweat from my forehead, I realise I have discovered what it is that Omaha is missing in all its infinite diversity. Nazis.

Just as it takes the latest fashion trends time to travel from the coasts to Middle America, perhaps postnormal times has also lagged in reaching the Heartland. But it is unmistakably here. This swastika was no random event. This is not something that can be passed off as a childish prank or the ravings of an isolated lunatic. A ripple of thunder is rocketing across America as Nazis are returning, if it is the case that they actually went away. Even in Omaha, reports spoke of Nazi propaganda leaflets appearing in various neighbourhood Little Free Library boxes. While defamation of property is a bold statement, do we know what is actually being talked about?

Language is a strange thing and postnormal times has made it even stranger. What I propose here is not some duel of wits and semantics. Instead I wish to point out the fragility of the very semantics by which we structure our logic and the fundamental fallibility of our wits. The damage already done leaves us with words, starved of definition, which we take for granted. Wilfully sipping this nectar of ignorance, we pass through time and space with reckless regard speaking to such phenomenon as unpatriotic nationalism, contingent independence, and subjugating freedom. A blissful ignorance side kicked to an unrelenting uncertainty self-perpetuates the postnormal state. Those in the know, or, perhaps at best, aware of their own unknowing, are perplexed to a crippling degree. The problem is an issue of not having the correct tools. The physicist finds their theories reaching beyond their experimental range. Thus, their practice is more philosophy than fact challenging science. The postmodernist attempts to eradicate grand narratives, creating a grand narrative against grand narratives. The posthumanist dives head first into the robot revolution untroubled by the multiverse of potential ironic consequences that can and are resulting in such neglectful investigation. Each master tries to capture the future in their own image and direct it towards their own utopic ideal.

At this point we are faced with two problems. First the future is not singular, it is a plurality of futures. Second the future cannot be controlled, managed, or placed upon a shelf. The complexity and contradictions, uncertainty and chaos of our times, coupled with breathless accelerating change, does not allow for the old-fashioned luxuries of control, efficiency and management. The present is not just weird; it is constantly getting weirder. Our systems and routines are becoming obsolete. The jogging paths we've come to know by muscle memory are not taking us to the destinations we desire. So, is this where the road ends?

Where to go next. This is an interesting dilemma. The approach favoured by the most academically minded is to grapple this problem, wrestle the angel, dissect and experiment, and look for the definite solution. But the beasts of uncertainty and ignorance cannot be defeated. We need to learn to navigate our way from postnormal times. Beyond this point, we require tremendous creativity, distillation of foundational value, acceptance of rapid change, living with uncertainty, awareness of our ignorance, and thinking the unthought. Even mastery of those tools does not guarantee smooth seas for navigation. There is no assurance of safety, sanity, or indeed survival in postnormal times.

Postnormal times does not come without signs. Indeed, those of us wrestling with postnormal times are constantly refining and building up our awareness of these signs. The menagerie of postnormal times serves our purpose best here. Black elephants are the first member of the menagerie. Black elephants are those events which are otherwise easily identifiable possibilities that had been ruled out due to confirmation bias or simple ignorance. The second member of the menagerie are black swans. Black swans are the inconceivable, at least within given worldviews and systems, the seemingly impossible. These game changers alter our imagination's ability to perceive what is possible, trigger a flurry of positive and negative potentialities. The third member of the menagerie are black jellyfish. These creatures are the true bulls in the china shop of postnormal times. Rapidly becoming the symbol of these climatically challenging times, black jellyfishes are those events that, though often starting as small, 'normal' occurrences, are driven, through positive feedback, to grow in geometric proportions challenging the structural integrity of global systems. They are 'high impact' and have a great potential to make things postnormal – rapidly.

It is important to note here that the menagerie is largely dependent on perspective. One individual's black swan could easily be a black elephant to an individual halfway around the world in a different socio-political context. But the purpose of the menagerie is to highlight uncertainties, our ignorance, and the limitations of our own worldview and situation. It is a much better way of navigating futures beyond the end of the road.

Jogging on the road, the body is in a super-heightened state. Smells, signs, sounds, feelings are all on their highest alert as the body struggles to maintain homeostatic control of itself. During a proper run, things out of place can startle, sending the body into a state of shock. On the numerous jogs I have taken in my life I have been startled by the happening upon of roadkill, animal scat, and even unnoticed fellow joggers. This was the first time I had been startled by the discovery of a symbol. I snap out of it, moving away from the swastika, reigniting my run for home, still a few miles down the road. My mind is racked by various words. Words we over use and others we don't use enough. And then there are the words we use and don't actually know the definition of what we are talking about.

Freedom. It is a most curious contradiction. Worse yet, it is a seductive contradiction. Like capital, it is never just satisfied with a unit or two of itself, it must always be more. Insatiable, freedom fights for itself even at the consumption of the freedom of others. Just as Adam Smith convinced the Western world that acting in one's self interest magically worked in the interest of the common, my freedom is your freedom and we must be willing to die for it at any given moment!

This could not be illustrated more perfectly than through the Constitution of the United States of America. While I could write volumes on the contradictions this particular document eludes to, I will try to remain focused on this one. Naturally, the first two amendments are the only ones the common American will remember by heart without having to consult Google. While the second amendment gets more airtime on the news (for the unfamiliar, that's the gun one) the first amendment is the one which tends to be invoked on a more regular basis. Within that one run-on sentence lies over two hundred years of legal philosophy, fundamental building blocks responsible for American angst and arrogance, and a dangerous contradiction. It speaks to freedom of expression, speech, and assembly. It promises that if this great experiment fails, we have the right to tear it all down and build something better in its place. It allows one the freedom to be. But, it also allows one the freedom to take others freedom. Common sense and jurisprudence have done a little good in history. For instance, it is illegal to yell "Fire!" in a crowded theatre, as this would invoke mass hysteria. Though it gives both the oppressed and the oppressors the right to march in the streets with police protection. This freedom gives you the freedom to bind your fellow human in bigotry, racism, and xenophobia, of course with the adage that you ought to be able to consume what you dish out. The first amendment of the U.S. Constitution gives one the right to hate. It also turns freedom into a commodity, our commodity and one which can be stripped from the other if they don't play by our rules. A day doesn't go by in the United States without us proclaiming the sacred word freedom, with each use, we further bastardise its meaning deepening the contradiction. This black elephant is ripening towards postnormal fruition and soon those cries for freedom will find themselves being answered by something very different.

As the Americans have overused the word freedom into its own undoing, both Europe and the United States have underused another word allowing for a faded memory to return proudly and display its ugly face unabashedly. Fascism. Even to see the word written, carries with it an entire context. Yet, today we are told not to use this word. Not for fear of offending others or because it has become outdated. We have become so afraid of Fascism's return to global dominance, that we shun the slightest use of it beyond historical context. In fact, a black swan is identifiable in the concept of fascism ever rising to power again in Europe, or anywhere in the world for that matter. Those of us who find some or all of our life having been uploaded to the internet may be familiar with Godwin's Law. This is the law which states that eventually all online arguments devolve into comparing one's competitor to Hitler or the Nazis. The use of this comparison had become a cop out for finding the most insulting thing to say to one's opponent. Understandably, for the preservation of professionalism and dignity, many have refrained from making such comparisons entirely. But what of the events in the contemporary era that actually are fascist and look a lot like or even one-up the deeds of the Nazis?

Former US Secretary of State, Madeleine Albright throws the word at us in giant red letters on a black background in her latest book. In *Fascism: A Warning*, Albright seeks to re-inoculate public discourse with the word. She rightly points out that fascism has often been chalked up to meaning 'What Hitler or Mussolini did'. Distilling it from historical conceptions, Albright defines fascism as the belief in one opinion standing for the whole of a nation or state and the defence of that opinion being the justification of violence. She lays out a historical primer in fascism's approach to the twentieth and twenty-first centuries and highlights the creep of fascism back into global politics. Most importantly she pushes for further study of the phenomenon so that it can be curbed and prevented from being the decay of contemporary political order.

Freedom and fascism have taken an interesting path into contemporary political rhetoric. Trump, Brexit, Fake News, Social Media, Big Data. Little of it has retained any intellectual value. As in Albright's work, there has been a small revival in reflecting on fascism and freedom. Thinkers like Timothy Snyder are not afraid of pointing towards a soft hijacking of contemporary democratic processes by tyrants and fascists. Like a good Aristotelian should, in his latest book, *The Road to Unfreedom,* he pits extreme political views of the now against each other so as to find a mean, the principle itself. Ultimately, this exercise proves futile in postnormal times. The extremes of the now are contradictions that fracture our opinions. There is a value to Snyder's discussion though. The struggle between extremes is important for beginning to comprehend the contemporary world. He also points out important historical trends we must remain cognisant of. He asks the reader to take control of the past so as to build a more preferred future. In terms of postnormal times, the past he speaks of is more properly stated as the Extended Present. This is the future before us if the status quo is maintained. Trends continue uninterrupted and all is business as usual. As things become more and more postnormal, the probability of this future coming to be is less likely. Understanding this limitation is key to fulfilling the request to the reader that Snyder states. Power is never given. No one is just offered the keys to history.

Postnormal times is not a spectator's game. It requires participation. This conversation must be kept alive. Reflection and constant correction control is needed to refine the language we use. Fear, irrational assumption, and hate have been allowed to control discourse at an unprecedented rate. Words need to be constantly on trial. What do we mean when we cry freedom? What are we doing when we mindlessly spout off patriotic diatribes and nationalist oaths and songs? What is truly being risked when we turn freedom, in its myriad of forms, into a motivation for action? Fascism is scary. But will we ignore it as it quietly grows in the dark? The confounding nature of the potential danger laced within language can quickly be manipulated into convincing people of their own opinions. This is populism at is most malicious. The calls for a return to the 'good ole days' or to make (insert your nationality/state identity here) great again are the smooth romanticising of the familiar and ultimately destructive.

Language has a unique power. It can time travel. At this particular point in time, we humans cannot. Because of this fact, we must rely on memory. Language travels through time and space, often unscathed by the journey. Memory is constantly recast and edited before the might of perspective, cleaver story telling (often by the winner of a particular historical moment) and the ever-flexible impact of emotion. The more eloquent of society can attempt to use words as they please and, if they sing a pretty enough song, can weave lie and fractured reality into language. We can be convinced to disregard history and let the sins of the father be just that. But remember, history matters. Futures matter and are always there before us. We can allow our words to be misused and morphed. Slowly they become the black elephants and swans that haunt our reality and historical trajectory. Heaven forbid they become the black jellyfish that can disrupt all, positive and negative, for better and for worse. Yet, words are words. Just as we can lose our own identity in the wake of populism, it can be recovered. Definitions must be held accountable. This is the first step towards owning the future, that together can begin the construction of a trajectory towards our preferred futures.

I am not sure if a dictionary can be made in postnormal times. Perhaps the philosopher in me needs that stability, and perhaps that stability may come in a form of unthought to our present selves. What is important is a self-awareness check on the language we use and the complexity, contradictions and chaos that takes it to radically new trajectories. The confinement brought on by structures in language and society can equally be an opportunity and impediment. If a dictionary is to be attempted, it mustn't be a dead, hardened set-in-stone law text; it has to remain flexible and a living dictionary subject to change and to changing times.

I adore running in the rain. There is a comfort in the hazard. The combination of a thinned-out atmosphere and a slight temperature drop makes for an all too familiar world being made a new. You notice things you have once taken for granted. Postnormal times is like running in the rain, but that only means our bodies must be all the more alert for the dangers that accompany roads and rain. Be aware that the path you once knew so well might take you to an entirely different destination. We are blinded by the rain drops of our own uncertainties and ignorance, but we can take comfort in identifying the elements of the menagerie, judging the awareness of our limited perspective and begin to take the first steps that become the full-on sprint. We stand to be startled out of our run by things far stranger and more fear-invoking than swastikas burnt into a public green space.

ARTS AND LETTERS

ANTIGONE AND SHAMSI *by Boyd Tonkin*
SHORT STORY: THREE BLIND MICE *by Tam Hussein*
KEMBON AND CALLIGRAPHY *by Norhayati Kaprawi*
FIVE POEMS *by Mozibur Rahman Ullah*

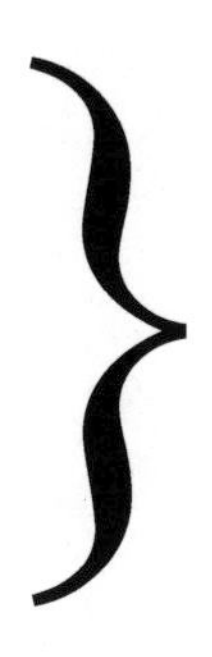

ANTIGONE AND SHAMSIE

Boyd Tonkin

In March 2017, students of Edwardes College in Peshawar won admiring reviews for their production of *Antigone* by Sophocles. The young actors enrolled at this late-Victorian foundation – now affiliated to the University of Peshawar – live in a province of Pakistan where the tragedy's backdrop of fratricidal strife, family division and murderous combat between clashing sources of authority could hardly feel more urgent. As I write, the recently-concluded election campaign in Pakistan has witnessed a suicide attack on a party rally in Peshawar that killed 21. In December 2014, a co-ordinated assault on the city's Army Public School by six fighters affiliated to the Pakistan Taliban left 156 dead.

Peshawar, and the Khyber Pakhtunkhwa province as a whole, remains a place where centralised power struggles to enforce its legitimacy. Rebels and rivals, without and within, seek to challenge the state. The forces of order, embodied by the Pakistani army, prove at gunpoint that they heartily endorse the demand of Sophocles' embattled ruler Creon: 'that man the city places in authority, his orders must be obeyed, large and small, right and wrong. Anarchy – show me a greater crime in all the earth!' Meanwhile, Sophocles' defiant heroine still casts her far-reaching spell. For Professor Nasir Iqbal, director of the Edwardes College production of *Antigone*, her resistance to sacrilegious despotism should give to young women 'the lesson to stand against all odds and face every condition courageously'.

Like so much of what counts as 'Western' culture, Greek tragedy has long found a welcoming home in the Indian sub-continent. Writers, directors and actors absorb, adapt and repurpose the few surviving texts from the heyday of European classical antiquity with never-failing ingenuity. In early 2018, for instance, *Antigone* returned to the stage in Delhi, at the Theatre Olympics festival, in a production by the Mandala

Theatre of Nepal. Performed in Nepali, in a translation by Som Nath Khanal and Bikram Pariyar, this latest incarnation arose from director Rajan Khatiwada's search for a way to respond in drama to 'political dishonesty and corruption'. For Khatiwada, 'Though written in an ancient timeframe, the play *Antigone* depicts the contemporary issues of Nepal.'

That ancient timeframe dates to around 442BC, when Sophocles wrote *Antigone* for the drama competition that marked the annual Festival of Dionysus in Athens. Its composition preceded *Oepidus the King* and *Oedipus at Colonus* – the two other works conventionally grouped in Sophocles' 'Theban trilogy' – by around a decade, although the action of *Antigone* follows that of the other plays. Antigone, daughter of the incestuous liaison of Oedipus and Jocasta, defies the edict of her uncle Creon, ruler of Thebes. She gives formal burial rites to the dishonoured corpse of her brother, Polynices. He has revolted against the state and died fighting against their brother Eteocles, who stayed loyal to Thebes. Creon condemns her to living burial in an underground cell despite the protests of Haemon, his son and Antigone's betrothed. Shocked by the prophecies of doom uttered by the seer Tiresias, Creon repents and tries to save her. Antigone has already hanged herself, while both Haemon and Creon's wife Eurydice take their own lives.

Whenever and wherever Greek drama has found audiences or readers, *Antigone* has been hailed as a summit of the form. Writing two centuries ago, the philosopher GWF Hegel – whose long, deep engagement with the play shaped countless later interpretations – called it "the pre-eminent, the most satisfying work of art". *Antigone* has travelled the world, and still does. Whether one believes in the "universality" of classical Western art, or detects in that familiar claim another mask for Eurocentric hubris, successive waves of contact, conquest and commerce have certainly ensured that it has the capacity to put down new roots in many soils. Look, for instance, at a 2011 volume of essays devoted to global productions of *Antigone*. *Antigone* on the Contemporary World Stage rounds up accounts of translations and adaptations in Argentina, Ireland, Manipur (north-eastern India), Haiti, Poland, Egypt, Lebanon, Japan, Georgia and Finland – not counting more predictable venues, such as Scotland, Italy, the US and Greece itself.

However, the staging of *Antigone* in northern India and present-day Pakistan complicates the routine narrative in which the production of a hallowed foreign text confirms its relevance to some far-flung region thousands of miles from Athens. In one light, we even can view a performance of Sophocles on the north-west frontier not as a transplantation but a homecoming. In the 1900s, the archaeologist Sir John Marshall excavated and described a fragment of a locally-made pot near Peshawar. It dated from the period and culture of the Indo-Greek kingdom in Gandhara after 200BC: one of the legacy states that flourished in northern India and Afghanistan in the wake of Alexander the Great's expedition in the 320s BC.

Marshall was in no doubt that the painted fragment depicted the scene from *Antigone* in which Haemon pleads for the life of his betrothed with the king. Archaeological or written traces of drama in Indo-Greek society are scanty. But since their sophisticated cities, such as Taxila, boasted all the amenities and practices of mainstream Greek culture, it seems highly unlikely that theatre did not flourish in them too. Some historians claim to find a reciprocal relationship between Greek plays and Sanskrit drama of the time. The Sanskrit term for 'curtain', yavanika, may mean 'Greek thing'. WW Tarn, historian of Indo-Greek civilisation, argues that since the Peshawar vase 'was of local manufacture it proves at least that somebody in Gandhara was interested in Sophocles'. So the distinct possibility exists that *Antigone* reached the stage, or was at least read, in the northern sub-continent around 1800 years before publication of the first English-language version of the tragedy: Thomas May's *Antigone, The Theban Princess* in 1631.

Two millennia later, in an elite institution such as Edwardes, *Antigone* survives of course via the medium of the English language. The play still moves in the distant slipstream of a colonial government whose senior officials often merged their own ideals and methods with those of ancient Greece. Famously, the philosopher John Stuart Mill claimed in 1846 that 'The battle of Marathon, even as an event in English history, is more important than battle of Hastings.' If the Athenians and their allies has not resisted the 'oriental' Persian empire early in the fifth century BC, then the spiritual heirs of Greece in Victorian Britain could never have ruled the waves – and the Raj. As Greece and Rome invigorated the British mind, so – fortified by the art and learning of the ancients – British culture would revitalise India. In his epoch-making 1835 *Minute on Education* (which advocates the creation of 'a class of persons, Indian in blood and colour, but English in taste, in opinions, in morals, and in intellect'), Thomas Babington Macaulay makes this chain of command explicit. 'Nobody, I suppose,' he writes, 'will contend that English is so difficult to a Hindoo as Greek to an Englishman. Less than half the time which enables an English youth to read Herodotus and Sophocles ought to enable a Hindoo to read Hume and Milton.' Not to mention Herodotus and Sophocles in English translation.

In the (almost) two centuries since Macaulay wrote, subcontinental writers, teachers and intellectuals have registered the imperial impulse behind his words but sought to reap the benefits of the educational system he helped impose. Although imported as a conqueror's cargo, its Greekness (and its antiquity) overlaid by the language and conventions of the Raj, Athenian tragedy could still speak across the borders of time and culture. A play such as *Antigone* might, in this perspective, resonate anywhere, and everywhere. It still can. In 2008, to take a noteworthy recent case of re-engineered Sophocles, the Bangladeshi film-maker Tanvir Mokammel set his version of *Antigone*, Rabeya (The Sister), amid the slaughter and displacement of the 1971 independence war.

If *Antigone* and other classical masterpieces can withstand the loss of the political superstructure that first lodged them in Asia, then what accounts for their endurance? Theories about the portability, and versatility, of the ancient Greek myths that fed the tragedies spread almost widely as the plays themselves. For Karl Marx, in a notoriously reductive formulation, these stories belonged to 'the childhood of mankind'. More sophisticated, and influential, Sigmund Freud found in them narrative templates for the drives that determine the psychic, sexual and social lives of every human subject. Antigone herself, after all, is the daughter of the unwitting incestuous union of Oedipus and his mother Jocasta. The play's directors (and audiences) have often registered an erotic charge in her ardent attachment to her disgraced brother Polynices. Other analysts cast the net even wider. In his comprehensive study of the play's cultural afterlife, *Antigones*, George Steiner argues that 'It has... been given to only one literary text to express all the principal constants of conflict in the condition of man.' That work is *Antigone*. For Steiner, these 'fivefold' constants are 'the confrontations of men and of women; of age and of youth; of society and of the individual; of the living and the dead; of men and of god(s)'. *Antigone* delivers the full house, or royal (and divine) flush.

Above all, critics and philosophers since the time of Hegel have framed the story as the archetypal tragic conflict not between right and wrong, but right and right. The play sets Creon's commitment to public law, and the security of the state, against Antigone's devotion to the ancient family pieties mandated by the gods, by kinship and by love. Hegel views the tragedy as 'a collision between the two highest moral powers'. Creon's 'right of the state' wrestles Antigone's 'law of the nether gods' into a catastrophic impasse that must end in mutual destruction. This irresolvable dialectic of human and divine justice also becomes a signal instance of female revolt against patriarchal order. It mounts, in Steiner's words, "a final, supreme clash between the worlds of man and of woman".

II

The British-Pakistani author Kamila Shamsie published her seventh novel, *Home Fire*, in 2017. It confidently, and creatively, joins and enriches this long history of re-interpreted *Antigones*. Set chiefly in north London today, with a prelude in Massachusetts and a finale in Karachi, *Home Fire* maps Sophocles' treatment of the myth onto a story of jihadi violence, state repression and torn loyalties.

Sophocles' Antigone becomes Aneeka Pasha of Wembley: daughter of a Londoner of Pakistani origin who has abandoned his family to fight in Bosnia, Chechnya and Afghanistan, then mysteriously died after torture at Bagram while en route as a captive to Guantánamo Bay. In the novel, jihadi combat – an accursed inheritance passed down from father to son – becomes the principal taboo that afflicts the Pasha family. It replaces the incest that dooms the dynasty of Oedipus. After a process of 'radicalisation', Adil Pasha's embittered son Parvaiz – Shamsie's equivalent of the rebel Polynices – joins the media unit of Isis in Raqaa. As a soundtrack specialist, he helps edit videos of tortures and executions. Soon, he feels utter revulsion at the task and thinks better of his impetuous flight to 'this joyless, heartless, unforgiving hellhole'. Via Aneeka, the chastened Parvaiz seeks to return to Britain. In Istanbul, awaiting repatriation after escape from Raqaa, his former Isis comrades execute him.

While a postgraduate student in the US, their sister Isma (Sophocles' Ismene) accidentally meets Eamonn Lone, the Haemon figure. He is the son of a British Muslim politician and his Irish-American wife. In Shamsie's hands, Creon turns into Karamat Lone: an aggressively patriotic champion of assimilation and 'British values', foe to traditionalists and fundamentalists, and scourge of 'outdated codes of behaviour' among Muslim families. He becomes a hardline Home Secretary just as Aneeka befriends, and begins an affair with, Eamonn – first as a strategic ruse, with a view to persuading Eamonn's father to allow Parvaiz to return, although a genuine bond between the pair then forms. After Parvaiz's death, the elder Lone stonily resists his own family's entreaties to mercy. He forbids the repatriation of the 'traitor's' remains: 'I don't have a son and I don't have wife. I have a Great Office of State.'

As a political stunt, Pakistani politicians allow Aneeka to fly to Karachi instead, along with her brother's coffin. In the city's relentless heat, as in Sophocles's play, the final showdown between family and state, conscience and law, unfolds via real-time online video amid what Shamsie calls 'rot-drenched horror', and Steiner the 'primal dread of decomposition'. Aneeka's obduracy makes her reviled by portions of the UK press. But her devotion prompts the aghast Eamonn to defy his father and post a video which asks (in a scene that echoes the illustration on that Peshawar pot): 'Is Britain really a nation that turns people into figures of hate because they love unconditionally?' All the while, the fearful, conservative chorus of citizens in Sophocles's play mutate into the alarmist or agitated voices of the British media – either hysterical and inflammatory, in red-top style, or else hand-wringing and high-minded.

Modern terrorism, however defined, has lent an edge and bite to many other *Antigone* revivals since the mid-twentieth century. As the French Resistance took up arms against the German occupiers, the dramatist Jean Anouilh wrote his re-interpretation of the tragedy in early 1944. At that moment, the refusal of the German authorities to hand back to their families the corpses of murdered Gestapo prisoners gave a special frisson to the theme. Yet Anouilh's notably (to some critics, deplorably) even-handed negotiation between the claims of state and family ensured that the

Occupation censors in Paris permitted the original production. Other Antigones set in occupied Europe followed the Nazi defeat in 1945, almost all tilting the scales decisively towards the heroic sister's side. For example, Bertolt Brecht's version, in 1948, shows Polynices as a deserter from the forces of a Nazi-style dictatorship.

In the 1970s, when outbreaks of political violence returned to western Europe during a crisis of authority in many states, Antigone staged another of her periodic comebacks. In Ireland, especially, the Troubles in the north seeded translations and productions in abundance. The poet Tom Paulin recast the language of Sophocles in the flinty Ulster idiom of *The Riot Act*. Seamus Heaney only published his translation of the play, *The Burial at Thebes*, in 2004 – along with the poet and classicist Anne Carson's version, it is one of the re-tellings that Shamsie has acknowledged as a guide and inspiration for *Home Fire*. However, Heaney roots his transposition of the tragedy in a bitter and brutal phase of conflict between UK state forces and paramilitaries in the Northern Ireland of the 1970s and 1980s. In a lecture, he recalls the army disruption of a Catholic funeral and the sense among mourners 'that something inviolate had been assailed by the state'. At this time, he writes, Antigone had begun in Ireland to feel like 'our own special allegory'. For all its Irish overtones, the poetic mood of *The Burial of Thebes* also draws on the more recent outrages of Bagram and Guantánamo Bay, during the post-9/11 coalition wars in Afghanistan and Iraq.

In West Germany, as terror attacks by the Baader-Meinhof group and Red Army Faction shook the post-war Western and democratic order, Sophocles also found a new voice. The portmanteau film *Germany in Autumn*, made in 1978, splices episodes from different directors into a collective portrait of an uneasy nation still haunted by phantoms from its past. In the segment directed by Volker Schlöndorff, and scripted by the novelist Heinrich Böll, a television channel considers if it can allow the screening of a production of *Antigone* just after the jail suicides of Andreas Baader and Ulrike Meinhof. Their isolation cells become the equivalent of Antigone's burial chamber, where Creon vows to wall her up alive in a rocky vault. In death, as in life, Antigone disturbs the peace and subverts the state's exclusive claims of right. Censorship will re-bury her moral challenge to despotic power.

Shamsie's novel often shares the means and the mood of these European terrorist *Antigones*. However, the specifically Islamist forms of armed conflict against the West and its allies add a fresh dimension to the cycle of reinterpretation. *Home Fire,* arguably, maintains a finer Hegelian balance between its twin poles than those post-war versions that simply depict a freedom-fighting Antigone as the virtuous antagonist of a tyrannical state. Yes, we see how and why Parvaiz cherishes the memory of his militant father, succumbs to jihadi grooming by the sinister, charismatic Farooq, and comes to agree with the radicals' case for the necessity of violence. From Isma's sarcastic, nit-picking interrogation by immigration officials at Heathrow to Karamat's distorting diatribes against conservative family life, scenes of casual or official anti-Muslim and anti-migrant prejudice strengthen Aneeka's hand. And we share the 'vein-flooding pleasure' of revenge as, before his departure for Raqaa, Parvaiz reflects that at last he knows 'how it felt to have a nation that wielded a sword on your behalf'.

Yet Shamsie never forgets that Isis is not the French Resistance, nor even the armed wing of Irish Republicanism. Home Fire no more sanitises their barbarism than it denies the liberal attractions of Wembley, of Amherst, of the West in general. The novel begins not with Aneeka but Isma – the sensible, moderate sister, who in Shamsie, as in Sophocles, represents the virtues of compromise and accommodation. Although an opportunist and, at times, a rabble-rouser, Karamat Lone thinks of himself as a lifelong anti-racist, cherishes a vision of Parliament as 'the engine of radical change', and privately whispers the traditional prayers that his secular, public self treats with utter indifference. (Remarkably, Sajid Javid – a secular Conservative politician from a Muslim family background – became the actual UK Home Secretary a few months after the appearance of *Home Fire.*) Karamat errs, and falls, not because he wishes to defend representative democracy against jihadi violence but thanks to his wilful, cruel and – in every sense – blasphemous refusal of the decent rites of burial to a fellow-citizen.

III

So this Wembley Antigone stays far nearer the 'perfect equilibrium' that Hegel celebrated in the play than many recent adaptations, with their saintly Antigones and fascistic Creons. It hugs Sophocles close, too, in the ambiguity of the heroine's faith. The Theban princess defies Creon's order in the name of the gods and their laws, 'the great, unwritten, unshakeable traditions' that honour the dead and consign them to the care of their family – above all, to their womenfolk. Yet she applies her own gloss, her own spin, to the demands of tradition and kinship. In a famous, and still disputed, passage, Antigone asserts that she would not have stood up so adamantly for a child or a spouse ('a husband dead, there might have been another'). To her, only love for an irreplaceable brother, this brother, could justify the rebellion. This is not just conservative piety; and no more does Creon's punitive and malicious animus against Antigone embody reverence for the laws. Both figures have customised their own, self-justifying faith. Likewise, almost every major figure in Home Fire – Aneeka, Isma, Parvaiz, Karamat – reengineers the idea of Islam to suit their individual aims.

In this way Shamsie stays true both to Sophocles, and to the way that people in many cultures today inherit, and transform, the precepts of traditional belief. In a key remark, Aunty Naseem, who has raised the orphaned Pasha siblings in Wembley, says that 'In my days either you were the kind of girl who covered her head or you were the kind who wore make-up. Now everyone is everything at the same time.' After they start their affair, as her disingenuous seduction deepens into real affection, Aneeka continues to baffle Eamonn Lone: on the one hand, the turban, the prayers, the zeal; on the other, the frank and open sexuality, the wilful autonomy. 'Everything at the same time': just as with his father Karamat, that imam-bashing connoisseur of fine wine who has never quite cut loose from his God-fearing Bradford migrant home. 'Reverence toward the gods', enjoined by the Chorus as the tragedy concludes, now means very different things to different folks.

In the jihadi headquarters of Raqaa, we see the 'Islam' concocted there in blood and fear as a hi-tech fabrication. It rests on state-of-the-art media equipment and super-modern online propaganda – religion as an empty pretext for atrocity in 'a place of crucifixions, beheadings, floggings, heads on spikes, child soldiers, slavery and rape'. Yet it seems that self-evident or uncontested piety had also vanished from the theatre of Athens by the time that Sophocles wrote. The blind soothsayer Tiresias, who denounces the crimes of Creon and foresees the ruin of his clan, berates the king for the 'violence/ You have forced upon the heavens'. But he says almost nothing to confirm Antigone's faith in her own righteousness.

In Thebes, the gods punish manifest injustice but otherwise remain unknowable. In Wembley, the creeds upheld by the characters in Shamsie's novel remain subjective, idiosyncratic. They may result in good or evil, justice or oppression. But no clinching verdict will ever descend from the heavens. By the time she travels with her brother's ice-shrouded corpse to Pakistan, the frantic focus of a global media gale, Aneeka has drifted far from any traditional model of faith and law. She dwells now in a self-created, solitary place where private love and loyalty hold sway. Her desperation recalls the words of Antigone when, condemned by Creon, she asks: 'Why look to the heavens any more, tormented as I am?' By speaking out against state law as a woman and a relative – Creon is her uncle – Antigone herself has already crossed the threshold into civil disobedience. In extremity, she seems to doubt the wisdom of the gods as well.

The religious or post-religious idioms of *Home Fire* echo the arguments of Creon and Antigone herself – two stubborn innovators who believe they are just adhering to time-honoured laws. For the feminist theorist Judith Butler, the revolt of Antigone herself 'is the occasion for a new field of the human, achieved through political catachresis' – creative re-interpretation – 'the one that happens when the less than human speaks of the human, when gender is displaced, and kinship founders on its own founding laws'. The deeds of both niece and uncle will bring the city down. His son dead, his clan and kingdom wrecked, Creon himself appears in the end not as a stern upholder of civic right but a hysterical, grieving bungler, who curses his own 'mad fanatic heart' and writhes in despair at 'the heartbreaking agony of our lives'.

Even in Sophocles, then, truly solid ground lies beneath nobody's feet. For her part, Shamsie refuses to frame her updated myth as a stereotypical contest between the Western secular state and Muslim kinship networks. Karamat Lone's own immigrant origins and culturally mingled family, as much as Anneka's pick-and-mix interpretation of religion, mark this story as one that pits several competing sorts of modernity against one another. None can exclusively claim the absolute precedence of custom and tradition. The great parliamentarian, Karamat has broken with the past he reveres. He tweaks the law to strip British citizenship from jihadi volunteers. Orphaned, adrift, outcast, Aneeka must in every way compose herself. Parvaiz falls, fatally, into the gap between warring identities and affinities. Thus, kinship in Wembley proves as problematic as it does in Sophocles's Thebes, where the incestuous destiny of Oedipus has knocked all authority out of its true course.

Both tales, in Wembley and Thebes, also dramatise the terrifying – and irrevocable – loss of the idea of home. In a celebrated passage, Antigone laments that 'I have no home on earth and none below, / not with the living, not with the breathless dead'. She speaks of herself as a resident alien, *metoikos*. That word-choice pushes the political meaning of the term into a realm of metaphysical alienation. Creon punishes her with confinement in the death-chamber, a limbo stranded between the domains of the living and the dead. 'Dead or alive,' he proclaims, 'she will be stripped of her rights, / her stranger's rights, here in the world above.'

'Stranger's rights' had a particular sense in ancient Greece: the protections, short of full citizenship, extended to the long-term guest; the resident alien. But Antigone, of course, is no more a non-citizen than Creon himself. In a parallel manner, Karamat Lone seeks to delegitimise Parvaiz and his family; to suspend or annul their British citizenship. Here Shamsie adds an additional layer of meaning to the story, one seldom highlighted before in modern Antigones. The peril of not belonging in a civic or legal sense – that perennial burden of migrants and their descendants in the West – spreads outwards from Parvaiz's crime, or error, or madness, to touch his whole family. What was given may be taken away: in life, or in death. This sense of soul-devouring insecurity threads through Home Fire. It runs from the crass questions about TV shows and the monarchy flung at Isma at Heathrow ('Do you consider yourself British?') to Karamat's posthumous curse on the remains of Parvaiz as he decrees that 'we will not let those who turn against the soil of Britain in their lifetime sully that very soil in death'.

As Steiner's history shows, the story of Antigone has changed its shape and altered its focus according to the fault-lines and raw wounds of every society in which it has found an audience. 'New Antigones are being imagined, thought, lived now; and will be tomorrow.' In Shamsie's case, contested citizenship – what it means to belong to a community; which powers do or should have the right to grant or rescind that belonging –

adds an especially topical twist to the confrontation between individual and society that Steiner numbers among the 'fivefold constants' of the drama. By early 2018, it was reported that around 200 dual nationals who fought for Isis had been stripped of their British citizenship. At the same time, many British Caribbean elders from the Windrush Generation were finding that the Home Office refused their claims to UK citizens' rights and, in some cases, demanded their deportation. It was this scandal that forced the resignation of the previous Home Secretary, Amber Rudd, and led to the elevation of Sajid Javid. As Home Fire gained readers and awards (it won the Women's Prize for Fiction in June 2018), Britons of immigrant origin far beyond the close kin of jihadi volunteers had reason to echo Antigone's cry: "I have no home on earth and none below."

This contemporary focus on Antigone and her siblings as *metoikoi* – in-betweeners, border-crossers, wanderers in perpetual transit between values and worlds – also brings to the fore a quality always inherent in the myth, and the play. No narrative has ever proved more mobile, more adaptable, than Antigone. And, if we credit the evidence from the pot in Peshawar, it began its journeys to the east many centuries before much of the West had ever heard this tale.

In an interview, Shamsie herself noted the depth and range of Greek-Asian dialogue: 'I actually think it is quite amusing that Ancient Greece is considered the cornerstone of Western civilisation. To me those divisions simply aren't true. You had an Indo-Greek kingdom and some of the greatest art that comes out of the subcontinent is infused with Greek artistry and mythology and the gods. But it's also infused with a very local, native influence. There's that marriage of the two.' When her Antigone-Aneeka howls over the decaying body of a beloved brother in a Karachi park, 'in the singed grass, beneath the banyan tree, rose petals desiccated around her', a core myth of the West has not ventured into some exotic land. Rather, a vast, slow wheel of historical debate and exchange has turned through another circle. For Shamsie, work on the novel cemented her belief that 'the Greeks are part of everything really. Certainly they're a part of life in Pakistan.'

SHORT STORY

THREE BLIND MICE

Tam Hussein

Driving to my mother's house, my nine-year-old boy was indignant. He sat at the front with his knees up, listening attentively to Radio 4. Being the son of a news man, he was already developing that habit of listening to 'The World at One'. The international community, namely America, Britain and France, had launched air strikes overnight hitting three Syrian targets. It was done to signal their disapproval of the use of chemical weapons in Douma, Syria.

'Dad,' he said with the frankness that came from not grasping diplomacy yet, 'if Assad is bad, don't we need to stop him? This is why I would never want to be president.'

I was pleased at his aspirations. He was already considering the presidency of another country, and more importantly, the implications of wielding power. I agreed with him, how could the world sit and watch as children my daughter's age were frothing at the mouth and screaming. I glanced in the mirror and she was writhing, pretending to be in immense pain due to her tummy ache. How could Ghouta and Douma have turned into such scenes of insanity? Ghouta used to be the place where one sat under shady trees barbecuing meat next to the Barada river during hot spring days. Those were idyllic times. Sure, I wanted to stop the chemical attack, who wouldn't want to stop the perpetrators?

I relished those sorts of questions from him because it allowed us to to explore the consequences of one's actions. What was the right thing to do when such an event had occurred? How does one separate a devotion to Humanity from its causes? As I got older, I didn't know who to be wary of;

that activist who was a slave to his own activism, who shot the archduke Ferdinand in Sarajevo thinking that it would solve all of the world's problems, or those mad suits in London who squabbled over maps, drew lines in the sand and sabre rattled in the Bullingdon Club. Little gods in their own little way. There were of course other questions I wrestled with. Sometimes what was legal was not the same as good, and perhaps being good was sometimes the choice between two bad decisions.

'Well, son', I said, 'what do you think could happen if we stumbled into a war that we cannot control?' I explained that Syria had powerful backers whose interests, if encroached, might lead to an all-out world war at worst, 'we also don't want people thinking that we can just interfere in the business of other countries.' I parroted the line about creating a rules-based order in the world, etc.

'What about the children?' he asked me as if he represented all of the children of the world. I glanced in the mirror and my girl was still holding her tummy making those same faces I had seen on the TV screens. He was right. What does one say to that? He kept on searching my face for answers as we neared my mother's house. Somehow, I managed to turn our attention to whether the tactics employed by the International Community were correct. The outcome was a sham, since the three countries informed the Russians of the locations they were going to strike. But then again should one let a brutal regime act with such impunity and get away with it? And so whilst my little girl moaned and intermittently demanded that I apply Vicks Vaporub – the solution to all her ailments – we discussed the various issues to do with war. I concluded, I admit with a quiet satisfaction, that my son understood; one does not enter into war lightly. I also felt he grasped that power was not something one should ever wish for. Power is very much like the Seven Rings in Tolkien's the *Lord of the Rings* saga; they consume you and turn you into the Lord of Darkness if you aren't too careful.

I parked my car in the garage; my boy scrambled off to his grandmother and my girl's stomach ache vanished miraculously at the sound of her. Father taught son. Father kissed daughter on tummy. The sun was shining. Douma and that dusty terrified girl being carried by a frantic ambulance driver himself covered in rubble and blood became distant once again.

I found my mother preparing lunch, rice, beef stew and chicken curry. For the children she made a beloved childhood dish which my kids loved too: rice, milk and crushed bananas with a dash of salt and sugar. Watching her do what she did to my kids reminded me of what she had done for me. She had made me into a man all by her lonesome. Of the three of us, I was most like her and perhaps like her, also the most rebellious. I always felt guilty for all the worry and grief I had given her in my teenage years. I pray to God she forgives me for the heartache I caused her. She had cleaned hospital toilets, worked ungodly hours, turned down offers of marriage from good men devoting all of her being to us. It was she who made us pick up the rubbish off the pavement, hold doors for old ladies, watch our tongues, watch our manners and remember our duties to God. She even forgave the man who killed her mother when she came face to face with him in an East London wedding when he had become a decrepit old man. Seeing her thus, with strands of white in her hair, her body no longer listening to her indefatigable determination as the arthritis slowly seeped into her, made me happy and sad – the job was done.

Whilst the kids went off to play I decided to wash the car. As I opened the garage shutter again I noticed little black pellets on the floor. The place was a mess. My mother tended to hoard things because of the acute shortages she had experienced in her life. She tended to do it with certain goods. She bought rice, bleach, tinned goods and forgot where she had put them. Then you had a pound shop inside the garage. Other members of the family stored old suitcases and furniture there, too. It was difficult to navigate through this accumulation of goods and memories. I noticed my mother unwilling to enter the garage. This wasn't like her at all. I detected her hesitation as she watched me clean the car. I soon realised we had a mouse infestation in the garage. After all, the place was nice and warm and close to rail tracks; the perfect habitat for those critters.

This mess needed to be sorted out. So once I finished washing the car I started to clear out the garage and removing the flotsam and jetsam of life. I blocked the holes, set traps and cleaned up the mouse shit. I had a clear strategy: I was going to throw out things she didn't need, hoovering as I went along, inventory the boxes, emptying them and putting them in see-through plastic boxes so my mother could walk in and see what she had on the shelves. Initially, things went well. The old VCR, Sony tape deck, several laptops, endless amounts of rope, folders, incomplete homework files from year seven, toys, all were going out whilst my boy threw the frisbee and my girl ran around outside. As I cleared the mess I could hear the mice moving around increasingly perturbed by my presence.

And then disaster struck. I found a shopping trolley. Mother had deliberately left it untouched for a long time. With its mock tartan pattern, the trolley had an exceptional amount of shit pellets on its top cover. She definitely didn't take that to North End market. I began to hoover the poo pellets up in no time. Then I opened up the trolley and found that it contained shredded newspapers. Here was one devoted mother mouse who had shredded them with her teeth to create warmth for her babies. I carefully put my hand in to see what else was in the trolley, half expecting to be bitten by a large black death carrying rat, but instead there emerged from the shredded paper three blind mice. They were cold, tired, shivering and only a few days old. I picked them up in my palms. They were immensely cute.

In theory all I had to do was close my fist and crush them there and then or put them in a plastic bag and suffocate them. Then perhaps put them on display in the garage to send the right signal to its inhabitants and the problem would be solved in no time. But as I contemplated signing their eviction notice through their murder, I felt like those powerful rulers of ancient times who sought to set an example to its unruly citizenry. Was this how Pontius Pilate felt as he crucified a rebellious citizen and treated him like a common thief in order to make an example of him? Whilst the heart no doubt inclined towards that unruly Nazarene citizen, the mechanics of power were different. What was Pilate meant to do? He was answerable to Rome after all. How was he to explain away the disorder in the temple? He was being lobbied by notables daily and here was this man causing problems amongst the usurers and such like who kept the country prosperous. Trade and taxes is a language all rulers understood. What was he to do? This one citizen, even if he was good, was trouble. What could he do but take him out? It was for the greater good.

At that crucial moment as I held them in my palms, my little darling entered the garage. She saw what I was holding and asked me to show her. I was reluctant at first, but she insisted, so I gave in. She gushed, 'Oh, how cute!' She ran to call her brother.

My son came in and looked at the babies in wonder, 'they are tiny babies, Dad!'

'Sylvanian families!' said my girl giggling, 'they are like the Sylvanian families!' The grey babies reminded her of the toys she had at home. She played with them for hours dressing them up playing mummy and daddy.

Had they been adult mice I don't think I would have had any compunction in killing them. But for some reason I couldn't. Something within me started to whisper: what if He holds me to account? I looked at my baby girl. Would I want someone to crush her to set an example to others? There was of course another voice which said quite rationally that it was perfectly fine. That my argument was a fallacy, my analogy was incorrect. And in any case, God would understand. So I fudged it, I tried to absolve myself of responsibility. It was legal, I said, but my heart asked, was it morally good? Did I have the right?

I took the blind mice to a small patch of green where my car was parked, put them under some soil for warmth, 'since they are yours' I told God, 'you look after them.'

At that very moment I left the mice, my mother came to survey my handiwork. She saw the extent of the mess that the vermin had caused and started to curse them like she had done to me when I was getting into trouble. The same voice, the same tone. I told her to calm down as I continued to clean up the mess in the garage. But then her attention was drawn to my children who were huddling over the little patch of green where I had left the mice. 'What are they doing?' she asked.

'Oh, nothing' I replied.

She went over and saw my girl bending over adoringly over the little babies in the soil. My mother took the children away, then came to me and said 'what do you think you are doing?'

'What? I'm hoovering.'

'You have to kill them,' she said. I was surprised. A woman who had given birth to three children asking me to kill the children of another mother-albeit a mouse. How did it work? They only look after their own? Was that the reason the Begums of the palace didn't bat an eyelid as a half-brother was killed off with a silk cord? Were they so selfish that all that mattered was that their son was crowned Sultan? Was that the reason they could purchase makeup that kept them beautiful irrespective of the hundreds of white mice that were martyred for the sake of their eyelashes? Causes, as James Baldwin put it, were notoriously blood thirsty.

'Be a man' she said urging me to kill the babies.

'Be a man?' I asserted, I am a man. 'I'm not going to be held accountable by God for that.'

'You can do it' she said, 'it is allowed, you can't have mercy over these vermin. They have terrorised me for far too long! Too long! Go to the back garden and take a look.'

I don't know what she was talking about, so I went to the back of the house and found the bloody rascals, those same ones whose shit I was having to touch, smell and have fall on my head as I moved the boxes had slunk through the holes under the floor boards and arrived at the back garden. They were frolicking in the garden whilst I was trying to set my house in order! I grabbed a broom and was about to enter the garden ready to massacre every single one of them when my girl came in to the kitchen. She saw them and whooped with joy raising her hand to her chest and looked at the brown little creatures in wonder. She had discovered a new world where no darkness lived. She saw my hands firmly clasped to the broom and surmised my intent. 'Daddy' she said, giving me the same stern look my wife gave me at home when I did something wrong, 'what have you done?'

'Nothing' I said trying to hide my intentions, 'nothing.'

'Daddy. Daddy, they haven't done us any harm.'

'What do you mean?' I said dropping my broom. How did my wife infuse herself in her? How did she manage to get a five-year-old to lecture me? This must be the End of Days. 'What do you mean?' I said defending myself, 'those animals are tearing the garage apart, eating our food!' What was more, my skin was crawling with the phantom sensation of the tiny vermin all over me.

'We have lots of food daddy, what's wrong with sharing? Why can't we just share? If we did that we wouldn't have this mess.'

'But they cause a mess! You don't understand? They carry disease!'

'Daddy' she said, 'do you really want to kill the mummy of the Sylvanian babies in the garden? What will God say to you then?'

I put down my broom wavering and went back to my work and she followed me to ensure that I didn't lunge after the bastards. I worked morosely turning to see my girl by the green patch looking at the babies, talking to them, she was even trying to feed them McVities biscuits! She never did that to me. Why is she doing that to them? I wanted to stop her but something within asked whether I should really prevent her from doing that? And all the while I imagined those mice in the garage laughing away, shitting their black and white pellets. Plop, plop, plip just shitting away everywhere. I could see their faces scrunched up, whiskers like Don Juan dropping a few just to spite me in the place I had just cleaned. I moved one bag and one of these terrorists emerged. It paused for a moment, looking me up and down insolently and then ran off to the back.

'Bastard!' I said shaking my fist at it. For the first time I understood Mr McGregor in *Peter Rabbit*, and I swore I would show Peter no sympathy whenever my girl wanted me to read his story.

My son, perhaps sensing my frayed temper, brought me a cup of coffee and a transistor radio. I turned on Radio 4 and we listened as the leader of the opposition asked the prime minister whether taking unilateral action without Parliament's consent was a sign of her poodlehood to US foreign policy. After the prime minister's reply, my son asked me what unilateral action meant. I explained somewhat frazzled, that it was to act alone without consulting others.

'Like you do?'

'I don't' I said, 'I don't.'

An irate Syrian government official came on next. He berated the presenter for understanding things completely wrong. 'It's the terrorists!' he said, I could see him waving that fist and thumping it on the desk, 'they did this, the president doesn't use chemical weapons. You should be fighting the terrorists! Not us.'

The presenter in that classic Radio 4 tone asked again, 'so you are saying that the Syrian rebels in order to fool the world, in order to beat Assad used chemical weapons on their own children?'

'Yes! It's all fake news!'

My son picked up on the word fake news, it was something he had heard often in the car, 'Dad,' he said.

'Yes.'

'Who is worse Trump or Assad?'

'Assad.'

'Are you a Trump supporter?'

'No. Son, no, no I'm not,' I stated indignant whilst spotting one of them critters skulking in the shadows, 'son, let's talk about it later.'

'But he dropped a massive bomb in Afghanistan, remember?'

'Okay. Later. Out!'

I removed the fryer that my mother used to fry potato chips in when we lived in a bedsit hotel many years ago in Earl's Court. All these years she had kept it. I found one of my brother's books which accused me by its very title: *If not now, when?*. I turned to the blurb and the late Primo Levy stared out at me in that haunting manner of his. I felt almost guilty to throw him in the recycling bag.

I opened up several boxes, there were canned beans from yesteryear perfectly edible. Mum had squirrelled it away and forgotten about it. I opened another box and found two mummified mice completely dry in gentle repose, having no doubt died of gluttony.

As evening came, I told my children to go in. My girl was in tears, 'They are going to be cold, can't we give them some blankets?'

'No' I said. 'Bad daddy' she said crying.

Before I went in, I walked over taking one last look at the three blind mice. They were still there, still breathing, writhing, sleeping, their little tummies shivering. They must have been hungry. Their mother hadn't fed them. She was probably scared off by the strange smell of human on their bodies. Perhaps they missed their mother too, perhaps that is what some of the peeping noises were all about; cries of pain and separation from the source. Maybe a cat would find them. I wished my wife was here. She knew what to do and what to say to the kids. I went in, my mother had turned the boiler on for me, so I could scrub myself clean.

'Have you killed them?' she asked. I didn't say anything. 'What are you? A man or a mouse?' She laughed at her own witticism.

Her words stung me. Why couldn't I just go out there and step on them? I am allowed to do it, all religious codes except perhaps the Dharmic religions allowed for it. Why couldn't I just do it? Am I not a man? Wouldn't these creatures turn out to be like their parents and terrorise my mother who raised me alone? And in any case, weren't they suffering now from hunger and cold? Wasn't it better and more merciful if I just finished them off there and then? My mother gave me another look of contempt.

But I couldn't utter a word of reproach to her, that was a sin. I still gave my boy a clip round the ears if he gave me or his mother lip, so of course I had to suck it in. I went upstairs and showered, scrubbing myself fervently imagining that I was covered in mice shit.

After my shower I went to the kitchen and mum had returned to being the saint. She had prepared rice with runner beans and prawns. It tasted lovely. I watched her lovingly read my children their bed time stories. Whilst they closed their eyes she worshipped and recited Qur'an too. Tomorrow, I said to myself, tomorrow I would put an end to the mice. I told myself that I was over-thinking the issue. I just had to be a man. I had seen this in my line of work. I had covered plenty of stories like this: Ghouta, Douma, Houla, Aleppo and more: none differed from the other. As the Arabic proverb goes: 'there are many ways to die but death is one and the same.'

Next day, my mother was up at the crack of dawn. She let me sleep in. As I came downstairs my coffee and toast was already on the table and my kids were just finishing breakfast. After breakfast, I went to the green patch praying to God that they were dead. But they were still alive, moving and breathing. How? There were ants crawling over the tiny creatures. I was just going to step on them when my girl came out of the front door skipping towards me. So I stilled my foot.

'How are they Daddy?' It was clear she had now adopted them, they had become her children.

'Fine,' I said feeling again like a murderer, I walked away leaving it to God's plan. She stayed there talking to them and explaining that I just didn't understand the world. That everything would be alright. Then she went inside again.

My aunty came into the garage inspecting my handiwork. My mother had probably called her. She was a tough hard woman having been through the same struggles that my mother had encountered. After saying hello she went straight to the green patch and stepped on them. She checked that all of them were dead, and then another stamp just to make sure. I was upset with her for doing it. I even reproached her, but I wasn't sure as to why. Perhaps it was due to the brazen way she had done it. A murder done so shamelessly in the sun, in front of everyone and she felt no two ways about it. When she saw my look of reproach, she laughed at me, as if she implied

I had to grow a pair. 'They are only mice,' she said, 'a fart in the wind, you are turning proper Islington. Next minute you know you'll even question circumcision. Come on. You were starving them.'

She was a no-nonsense woman, in her world view only white people from Islington had the time and the leisure to be concerned with veganism, organic food, GM free; the stuff that non-whites, that is poor folk, had little time to consider, let alone afford. To her, veganism and people worrying about the cruelty of halal food was one and the same thing, knives had been used to kill animals from time immemorial. 'Why' she would say, 'was a bolt to the brain less painful or cruel?' This was just about Islington imposing itself everywhere and anywhere in the world.

But to me at least, they weren't just three blind mice that had been crushed. Perhaps I should have done something instead of doing nothing. 'Give me any adult mice and I will slaughter them!' I said waving my fist at her as she went in to see my mother. She said she would make me a nice cup of coffee and added that I had completely lost perspective. I turned on the radio and I heard an Arab commentator likening the impact of the three countries, America, Britain and France bombing the Syrian regime to an Arab proverb: 'the mountains went into labour and gave birth to a mouse.'

KEMBAN AND CALLIGRAPHY

Norhayati Kaprawi

Norhayati Kaprawi, or Yati, as she is affectionately known, is a Muslim woman artist-activist from Malaysia. Trained as a civil engineer in Wales in the 1980s, she transitioned into full-time activism in the early 2000s. Her work involves engaging with grassroots women's communities so that they are aware of the full range of their rights within Islam, many of which have been systematically withheld by Malaysia's Islamic bureaucracy because of its patriarchal, restrictive interpretation of the religion. But her activism is far from dreary – her sense of humour and lightness of touch always bubble up. In order to gain the trust of one village community, for example, she spent hours with the menfolk, stirring communal *dodol*, a traditional toffee made from the aromatic durian fruit, until everyone was charmed by her wit and passion.

Through her activism, she caught the filmmaking bug, and has now made numerous documentaries on topics such as the *tudung* (headscarf), Muslim women *ulama* (scholars), and religious conversion and child custody, all fraught issues under Malaysia's Syariah legal system. She takes it upon herself to screen her films at university campuses and independent festivals around Malaysia – often to packed halls.

Her first love, however, is painting, as she explains to *Critical Muslim* Deputy Editor, Shanon Shah. They have been friends since the early 2000s, when both were actively involved Sisters in Islam, the Muslim feminist non-governmental organisation. In Yati's words:

My paintings have primarily explored two themes – *batik jawi* (or the Arabic-influenced batik of the Malay Archipelago) and *kemban* (the traditional Malay women's torso wrap). But I don't feel that I have to be bound by any particular style of genre. I love Jawi (the Arabic alphabet for writing the Malay language) because I am from Johor, the southernmost state in Peninsula Malaysia, and we were all taught to write in Jawi from young. I went on to take a short course on *khat* (Islamic calligraphy) at the Islamic Arts Museum in Kuala Lumpur. But I don't produce 'proper' *khat* – I use it as a concept to create more abstract works. And I absolutely love batik because my first venture into visual arts was making batik prints on silk. When I got busier, I started painting on canvas, but using the batik-making style and approach, without the use of wax. I integrate Jawi and batik because I want to convey that religion and culture are often intertwined and inseparable. Sometimes I add the element of human relationships, in whatever form, because they are part of the signs of nature that the Qur'an encourages us to appreciate and reflect upon.

Motivasi (Motivation)

This is for lazybones like me. It's inspired by a friend of mine whose mother saw her sprawling on the sofa while watching a Jane Fonda exercise video. The mother said, deadpan, 'Right, at this rate, you'll be losing weight in no time.'

Picnic
This is how my family used to do picnics – go to the park, eat, and lay down the rest of the afternoon. We wouldn't take walks – we'd watch other people take walks.

Oops
When I was a child, my siblings and I used to bathe in the pond near my uncle's house in our village. My sister's sarong would balloon upwards every time she jumped in.

Love
I don't feel like I have to be bound by any particular style or genre.

Abdul Aziz
This is a painting requested by my sister in memory of her late husband, my brother-in-law.

Bersiar dengan Miaw (Gallivanting with the cat)
I sold this at a charity event organised by a trans woman activist, Nisha Ayub.

Panas sungguh (It's too hot)
This was sold at another charity event, organised by the Women's Aid Organisation.

FIVE POEMS

Mozibur Rahman Ullah

The Poet and the Pir

The Poet, living in his moment
Does not survey the whole field until his last
And then, looking back
Sees the whole staring back with a deaths head

The Pir, surveying the whole field
Acts not, retreats into the green forest light
There he kindles his fire
Casting light
And makes his meditations
And makes his prayers

Here, the whole paranoma
Here, all the masks

And the Poet says to the Pir
Whither goest thou sunk in forest gloom?

And the Pir says to the Poet
Thy ecstasies will not last!

The Poet blind to reality
Drunk on the moon
Sings on
Like the nightingale in a clay cage
His heart red with his own admiration

The Pir seeing the real
Beyond Maya
Beyond the masks and the mirrors
Writes his writing on the wall

Here, he says, when you have reached your last
And literate at last
You will find what it is you had yearned to know
Before you drown'd in human voices
Before you slumber'd in a woman's bed

Now, awake at last
You see the field in all it's bloody garb
And the moon turned black

Speaking of love, you spoke of self-love
Sinking all in the self

Now seek ye the greater love
That shines through the dark night
And chain thy light to the greater light

And the Poet says to the Sage
I have felt all, and written all
Had I not written, the people will not have read
I am the mouth through which
Allah Almighty spoke
I have fountained blood
But I have also fountained joy
Now, my body is as a burnt offering to the gods
I am the sacrificial lamb

The people look here
Celebrate what is to come, what will not last
And enter the field with capacious hearts

Thy heart is as steel and as cold
And thy path a straight one

My heart is as warm as a new born doe
And as dewy
And my path a rocky one

Yet we are here, now
At the edge of the world
Raising our voices in harmony
To the tumultuous crowds below
They will not hear, nor will they see
A few always listen, and a few will always see
But no man can be king in the kingdom of the blind
He will cast his lot with the crowd
He will bear his wounds
Becoming as witnesses and shahids

It is good that Allah is compassionate
For man is a weak vessel
He chose weakness when he chose
  Freedom to act
  And knowledge of Good and Evil

The Mountains refused it
But man, foolish man, did not
Taking on his shoulders the weight of the world
And it is hard
And hardens his soul
Until it breaks
And his soul caged, cries out

Is thy soul a philosopher?
  Said the winged wind.
Where is thy heart?
  Mourned the circling dove.

And the people listening,
Mostly smile and laugh
And a few struck by deep yearning
Look away weeping

Their hearts as wet as the billowing clouds
In the newly budding spring fields

Arjunas War

Arjuna, lift up your blow

Your brothers have commanded war

And if you do not shoot, you will die

If you do not command the field,
They shall, and you will rue the day

You wife will be taken captive
And your sons and daughters will be slaves

And your seed will become as dust
Blown in wind, hither and thither
Never finding rest

Take heart, and hearten yourself
Thy arm is as strong as ever
And thy eye as keen

Now is the time for action
That poets will memorialise forever

Doubt

Doubt can be no foundation
It undermines itself
And then the mind
And then the man.

Doubting doubt - can you doubt?
I sat on doubt and wondered how and why.

I want a cloud to hang my doubt upon
Like a chain around my heart to uplift my heart

To cast my doubt upon a cloud
And let the cloud carry the burden I cannot bear

Doubt floods the rivers and the lakes
It has monsooned doubt
And cleared the air
And runs into the sea of doubt

Nobody wonders why,
now.
We are all used to it.
Living with it.
Pickled in it.

Doubt hammered my mind.
When I should have been walking
or talking or doing.

Instead, the mind spins on its spindle
Going where the West Wind blows
Or the East

Instead of finding its true direction

And setting its course

Here, there are no signs to guide me by
The sky is dark and stars have blanked out

And the world words has turned dark
Like a dull and dark insidious mist
Obscuring the earth, the sun, the stars

O Griefs! O Sorrows!
O Hatreds! O Hate!
O Rage! O Anger!
O Love! O Lost!
And the tears of children.

Where are you going,
                    Little one?
                      Little lost one?
Do you know,
  And your mother who watches over you?
  Does she know?

In my mothers home,
                      My home
She had woven a picture of flowers in a garden
In bright reds, greens and blues
And lettered underneath
God is Good

Now and then – it guides me still

The Sorrows of Old Hindenburg

Tonight, new sorrows coffin my brain
In a hearse through the streets of old Berlin

I should have shot the man

But I gave him the emblems of power

He has taken our country into his hands
And crushed it

And though I had seen the shadows in his smile
I doubted my own eyes

And though I had seen the shadows in his eyes
I doubted my own mind

Everything I have known has come now to no good

Dark eagles fly overheard

Cities burn

O My Madonna, cradle thy son in thy arms

Azaan

If I am a hole in the air,
 O Allah, then fill me up
If the ground is stony and dry
 O Allah, then stir the sap up

Thy falcon has flown the wide and wild
 Tides of the sky, O Allah

And now he seeks thy hand
  To alight there, to perch there

The hills and mountains in the clouds
  He has seen
And the crevasses and abysses underneath
  He has seen

He had hidden himself in the wind

Thy light, O Allah, thy light
Is thy truth

  And is everywhere

Seeding the world

Seeding the voids

There is none to compare

REVIEWS

REWORKING IBN KHALDUN *by Shanon Shah*
SHELLEY'S SHADOW *by Hassam Mahamdallie*
NOT AFGHANISTAN *by Sabil Warsi*
BEING BRITISH *by Misha Monaghan*

REWORKING IBN KHALDUN

Shanon Shah

It's best to start with an excerpt from a classic text:

> One of the greatest injustices and one contributing most to the destruction of civilisation is the unjustified imposition of tasks and the use of the subjects for forced labour. This is so because labour belongs to the things that constitute capital. Gain and sustenance represent the value realised from labour among civilised people. By their efforts and all their labours they (acquire) capital and (make a) profit. They have no other way to make a profit except (through labour). Subjects employed in cultural enterprises gain their livelihoods and profit from such activities. Now, if they are obliged to work outside their own field and are used for forced labour unrelated to their (ordinary ways of) making a living, they no longer have any profit and are thus deprived of the price of their labour, which is their capital (asset). They suffer, and a good deal of their livelihood is gone, or even all of it.

If you think this is something out of *Das Kapital* by Karl Marx, try going back about five hundred years to North Africa. It is taken from the magisterial *Muqaddimah* (*Prolegomena*) by Ibn Khaldun, the renowned fourteenth century Arab scholar (d. 1406). The *Muqaddimah* covers much more than economics – it is no less than the author's self-proclaimed 'introduction to history'. Impressively, it contains insights that appear ahead of its time, including passages, such as the one quoted above, that seem to pre-figure Marx's theory of wage-labour and capital.

Robert Irwin, *Ibn Khaldun: An Intellectual Biography*, Princeton University Press, Princeton, 2018

The *Muqaddimah* dazzled me, a sociologist of religion and an ethnographer, when I first read it not too long ago. My post-graduate training involved, firstly, becoming familiar with the birth of the social sciences as modern, post-Enlightenment disciplines that attempted to make sense of social change. Modern sociology's formal origins in Europe meant that the works and thinkers I initially came across were invariably white, male, and Western. The textbook illustrations of their insights were overwhelmingly Eurocentric – whether these were about the explanations for social cohesion by Emile Durkheim; the analysis of multi-layered relationships between religious belief and social action by Max Weber; or the attention to class, injustice and social conflict by Marx. Coming to the *Muqaddimah* a bit later as a Muslim social scientist was, in many ways, a revelation. For example, it was, and still is, tempting to regard Ibn Khaldun's concept of *asabiyyah* (often translated as 'group feeling') as foreshadowing and complementing Durkheim's ideas about social solidarity. This and other gems in the *Muqaddimah* are almost advertisements for the study of history to not only understand the present, but to anticipate the future.

I am hardly unique in my reaction to the *Muqaddimah*. As Robert Irwin points out in his intellectual biography of Ibn Khaldun, from the nineteenth century onwards, there has been a 'conscious or unconscious drive' to present Ibn Khaldun as a man before his time – a 'modern', 'rational', and even 'Western' intellectual. In addition to Marx, Weber and Durkheim, Ibn Khaldun has been claimed as a precursor of other totemic Western figures such as Machiavelli, Hobbes, Montesquieu and Vico.

According to Irwin, the *Muqaddimah*, with its long and sprawling passages, contains an ambiguity that lends itself to divergent readings. Yes, it has several moments of clarity and insight for the modern reader, but these are interspersed with numerous cryptic extracts about more esoteric stuff. Irwin argues that the 'modernised' and 'rationalised' readings of Ibn Khaldun have often been selective, glossing over these murky sections, and they have served different political and scholarly agendas.

There was, for starters, the belief among French colonialists that a thorough understanding of Ibn Khaldun's opus would assist their control and subjugation of North Africa. As part of this project, the architects of French colonialism elevated Ibn Khaldun as a 'genius' who was utterly 'unique'. Unlike the vast Arab and Berber mob that they had to rule over,

Ibn Khaldun was a 'gentleman historian' who had a 'perfume of the Renaissance' about him.

This co-option of Ibn Khaldun as an imperial Frenchman-in-essence was soon contested by anti-colonial French intellectuals. In the 1950s and 1960s, as France was battling to retain its control over Algeria, significant numbers of French academics campaigned for Algerian independence, including Louis Massignon, Yves Lacoste, Maxime Rodinson, and Vincent Monteil, whose translation of the *Muqaddimah* was published in 1967-68. Yet this anti-colonial trajectory did not displace the Eurocentric ennoblement of Ibn Khaldun – Monteil presented him as a forerunner of not only Machiavelli, but also of French Enlightenment thinking and of Darwin, and credited him with inventing sociology.

Insights such as these make Irwin's narration of what he calls 'the strange afterlife' of the *Muqaddimah* one of his book's several strengths. Irwin meticulously elaborates how Ibn Khaldun's legacy became transported and transposed differently in different contexts. For German intellectuals, for example, Ibn Khaldun's grand narrative of civilisational growth and decline recalled the thinking of their very own idealist philosopher Georg Wilhelm Friedrich Hegel. In the English-speaking world, the historian Arnold Toynbee identified Ibn Khaldun as one of his intellectual ancestors and described the *Muqaddimah* as 'undoubtedly the greatest work of its kind that has ever been created by any mind in any time or place'. Meanwhile, for the British-Czech philosopher and social anthropologist Ernest Gellner, Ibn Khaldun was 'a superb inductive sociologist'. Ironically, their works and numerous other European publications were to catalyse the rediscovery of Ibn Khaldun amongst modern Arab intellectuals in the nineteenth and twentieth centuries.

Yet the main point in Irwin's book is that these selective readings of Ibn Khaldun do not reflect how conventional he was as a man of his time. 'When I read the *Muqaddimah*,' Irwin writes, 'I have the sense that I am encountering a visitor from another planet…' Irwin stresses, however, that this is what makes the work so exciting. In his own words: 'It is precisely Ibn Khaldun's irrelevance to the modern world that makes him so interesting and important.' Thus, according to Irwin, while reading Ibn Khaldun might not illuminate anything about our world of globalisation, digitisation, and nation-states, it can illuminate just how radically different his universe was from ours. The realm that inspired Ibn Khaldun's thinking, for one thing, was one where human beings were joined by angels and demons in determining the outcome of battles and foretelling the future. This is hardly the stuff of 'modern', 'rational', post-Enlightenment thinking.

Before expanding on this aspect of Ibn Khaldun's thought, it is perhaps worthwhile to provide a summary of his life and his work. Wali al-Din Abu Zayd 'Abd ar-Rahman Ibn Muhammad Ibn Khaldun al-Tunisi al-Hadrami was born in Tunis, North Africa, in 1332. A son and grandson of scholars, and a great-grandson and great-great-grandson of court diplomats in the powerful Hafsid dynasty, he was primed for a career amongst the political and scholarly elite. He studied politics, literature, Qur'anic exegesis and jurisprudence from some of the best teachers of his day. Some of these included refugees from Moorish Spain or were the descendants of such refugees, who were driven out by the centuries-long Christian Reconquista of the Iberian Peninsula. Ibn Khaldun's own family were from Andalusia but claimed their origins in the Hadramawt in Yemen. According to Irwin, this Hadrami lineage could have been fabricated, albeit unknowingly – the *un* ending was usually added to the names of Christian converts to Islam in Moorish Spain.

Disaster then struck in Ibn Khaldun's late teens. First, the Merinid army from Fez conquered Tunis and sent the Hafsids into exile, introducing a period of chaos and instability. Then the Black Death swept through North Africa via Egypt, killing more than half of the population. Ibn Khaldun lost his parents as well as several of his teachers and friends to the plague. It is against this backdrop that Ibn Khaldun began working as a politician and court advisor in his youth, followed by a career as a jurist (*faqih*) and then chief judge (*qadi*) of the Maliki school of jurisprudence in his middle and old age. He was on the move throughout his life, spending time in Fez in Morocco, Granada in Spain, and Alexandria in Egypt, eventually settling in Cairo until his death. It was when he arrived in Cairo that he sent for his wife and children in Tunis, but they drowned at sea. Towards the final years of his life, he visited Damascus to seek a meeting with Timur, the ruthless yet erudite Muslim conqueror and leader of the Chagatai Turks whose troops had laid siege to Syria.

Ibn Khaldun began composing the *Muqaddimah* in 1375, while taking refuge at Qal'at Banu Salama, a remote castle in what is now western Algeria. The manuscript took two years to write, and it was finally published in 1378, with Ibn Khaldun dedicating it to the Hafsid ruler Abu al-'Abbas. The combination of political chaos, the lingering aftermath of the Black Death, and Ibn Khaldun's own aristocratic background were all influential in shaping his approach to history. It has even been suggested that the *Muqaddimah* was Ibn Khaldun's way of making sense of his own failed political career.

In a nutshell, the *Muqaddimah* lays out a set of principles for Ibn Khaldun's new – for its time – approach to history. Instead of simply recording events that floated on the surface of history, Ibn Khaldun sought to uncover history's inner meaning. For him, the historian ought to provide 'a subtle explanation of the causes and origins of existing things, and deep knowledge of the how and why of events'. To do this, he built the work around three core ideas – the first distinguished between nomadic and sedentary peoples, focusing on the different requirements of their lives; the second explored the importance of *asabiyyah* (group feeling) for a group's ability to organise itself and stay united; the third argued for the role of Islam in augmenting or transforming *asabiyyah*.

This analytical concern with the 'causes' of history and social change is what made Ibn Khaldun so appealing to the founders of post-Enlightenment European social science. Yet, for Irwin, Ibn Khaldun has become over-modernised and over-rationalised. In fact, much of his writing was concerned with subjects that 'modern', 'rationalist' thinkers would consider bonkers. For instance, unlike Durkheim, Marx and Weber, Ibn Khaldun inhabited a spirit-haunted world in which plants, stones, and planets had 'talismanic' powers. This is why, according to Irwin, Ibn Khaldun 'was obsessed with the occult'.

Ibn Khaldun characterised occult practices – sorcery, alchemy and astrology – as being, like philosophy, part of the *'ulum al-awa'il* (sciences of the ancients). All had the power to do much damage to religion, but sorcery (*sihr*) was particularly heinous and deserved the death penalty. According to the *Muqaddimah*, there were three ways in which sorcerers might achieve their objectives – through the exercise of their own will; by drawing on the magical properties inherent in the celestial spheres or contained in letters and numbers; or by acting on the imaginations of their audience. Sorcery was a form of idolatry because it entailed the veneration of spheres, stars, or *jinn* (invisible, capricious beings made of smokeless fire mentioned in the Qur'an).

This attitude towards the occult was actually quite conventional for its time – and, it must be added, amongst many contemporary Muslims – since it conforms to the Qur'anic worldview. Even so, Ibn Khaldun's condemnation of the occult contained a proto-sociological layer that was quite unique. According to him, the study and practice of the occult arts were particularly dangerous not simply because they went against religious teachings, but because they were damaging to social stability.

In this sense, contemporary readers still have an entry point to grasp Ibn Khaldun's stance on sorcery. This overall rationale can be extrapolated onto his attitude towards other practices that might perplex us now, including letter magic, treasure hunting, numerology and geomancy. Yet even then, some things remain a bit too baffling, especially Ibn Khaldun's fascination with a device called the *za'iraja*. He came to know of this instrument – 'half divination machine, half parlour game', as Irwin describes it – in 1370, during his stay in Biskra, Algeria. The *za'iraja* consisted of a circular diagram containing complex concentric circles, connected by 'chords', with everything set within a rectangle divided into numerous segments. It operated as an oracle of sorts, with the questioner preparing with a *dhikr* (devotional chanting) and then presenting the question in written form, breaking it down into its 'component letters'. A series of complex operations with these letters in connection with a verse written on the *za'iraja*, ascribed to the diviner Malik ibn Wuhayb, would eventually produce an answer.

When Ibn Khaldun used the device, he asked who had invented it – the response was that it was the Qur'anic sage, Idris (or Enoch in the Old Testament). Remarkably, Ibn Khaldun did not think that sorcery was involved in the operation of the *za'iraja*, nor did he believe that there was any sleight of hand employed by its operators. He maintained, however, that it would be wrong to use the *za'iraja* to foretell the future, suggesting that perhaps he did think there was an element of the occult about it after all.

It is this caveat about the power to foretell the future that underpins Ibn Khaldun's obsession with the occult, and his caution about it. Ibn Khaldun did not discount that the future was knowable but this ability rightfully belonged only to the prophets, who were guided by God. This is why Ibn Khaldun also took great pains to distinguish between prophets and those who practised divination, which is an entirely conventional and commonplace Muslim approach.

These examples certainly demonstrate, as Irwin argues, that Ibn Khaldun was a product of his time and place, and that he is not the exceptional harbinger of post-Enlightenment rationalism that he is made out to be. But neither were many medieval thinkers in Christian Europe who were purported to have been ahead of their time. For example, the thirteenth century English philosopher Roger Bacon, acknowledged as one of the first European advocates of the scientific method, was also fascinated by magic. Many of the purported founders of the European Enlightenment also straddled convictions in the scientific and the supernatural. Isaac Newton, the forerunner of the Enlightenment who theorised the Law of Gravitation, was preoccupied with the occult. Charles Darwin's relationship with religion fluctuated throughout his life – he never considered himself an atheist and *On the Origin of Species* was written at a time when he believed in a creator God. But perhaps it is Auguste Comte, the founder of modern sociology, who takes the kooky cake by trying to turn sociology into a religion. This was far from ironic – Comte's religion included a liturgy, hymns and sacraments in which the worship of God was substituted by a worship of Humanity. This is why Comte's introduction as the founder of sociology in many introductory undergraduate courses is often followed by a 'moving-swiftly-on' segue to more 'respectable' figures like Marx, Durkheim and Weber.

Therefore, while I appreciate the case for contextualising Ibn Khaldun's work and life more robustly, I do not fully agree that he or his work are irrelevant to the modern world. This is not the same as claiming that he was the first economist, or sociologist, or anthropologist. How could he have been, when these disciplines are all post-Enlightenment inventions? Yet his insights on social organisation remain interesting and significant. Again, this is not to claim that they are without flaws – but then so are many of the theories posited by the modern European founders of the social sciences. This is, after all, how scientific theories are built – they need to be tested against available evidence, according to which they may be accepted, refined or rejected. And while we must surely discard some of Ibn Khaldun's more outlandish or empirically unsupportable claims, we can also acknowledge the enduring usefulness of some of his ideas. For example, the sociologist of religion James V Spickard suggests that, as a concept, *asabiyyah* remains a corrective to several strands within modern social scientific thinking that compartmentalise ethnicity and religion as separate analytical constructs. Rather, '*asabiyyah*' enables us to recognise the fluidity and porousness of group feelings that are based on a mix of tribal affiliation, ethnicity and religion. This is but one amongst many noteworthy aspects of Ibn Khaldun's thought that justify the celebration of his legacy.

Irwin confesses that he was hesitant to add yet another title to the numerous books already published on Ibn Khaldun. This reticence is understandable but unnecessary – this intellectual biography is a fascinating, critical introduction that should enthuse many newcomers to Ibn Khaldun as well as experts. It gives much-needed context to Ibn Khaldun's narrative of history and the future, as well as to the many modern narratives that have emerged *about* Ibn Khaldun and his worldview.

To me, this juxtaposition of viewpoints also raises a crucial question about the nature of Islamic jurisprudence. Because isn't it fascinating that so many modern, Western thinkers – especially social scientists – would be enamoured by a book described by its author, an Islamic jurist, as an analysis of 'history'? Growing up, my *ustazes* and *ustazahs* (male and female religious instructors) would repeatedly drum into us that Islamic law was divinely ordained, unchanging, and infallible. It was only later that I learnt to distinguish between *fiqh* (jurisprudence) as the well-meaning but fallible human endeavour to interpret and apply shari'a as Divine guidance. And *fiqh* was historically suppler and more flexible than what was presented to Muslims like me, simply because it evolved in response to its immediate social circumstances.

The social circumstances surrounding Ibn Khaldun – the aftermath of the plague, intra-Muslim warfare, inter-dynastic competition, the growing Reconquista, and his own personal tragedies – were nothing less than chaotic and uncertain. In his attempt to understand and explain what was going on, he could only but resort to the intellectual tools that were available to him as a jurist, including Qur'anic exegesis and an analysis of *isnad* (chains of transmission of particular historical reports). The exceptional turmoil surrounding him, however, seems to have catalysed his creative application of these traditional resources, combined with original insights based on his own direct observations. This is probably why, in some parts, the *Muqaddimah* appears so conventional for its time and yet, in others, it is as though *fiqh* has been distilled into something new and exciting – something that many now recognise as inchoate social scientific theorising.

If so, the story of Ibn Khaldun and his work is also a story of the creative and analytical potential of Islamic jurisprudence. Notwithstanding *jinns*, letter magic, and the *za'iraja*.

SHELLEY'S SHADOW

Hassan Mahamdallie

In Ahmed Saadawi's award-winning novel *Frankenstein in Baghdad*, Hadi the rag-and-bone man picks through the debris and carnage after the daily explosions and suicide attacks terrorising his city. It is 2005 and Hadi and his fellow Iraqi citizens are living an increasingly calamitous existence under the US-military invasion and occupation that has unleashed chaos and murderous sectarian hate. Thousands of people, including civilians, are dying at the hands of US forces, sectarian militia or proliferating criminal gangs, or being blown apart by bombs, with Baghdad bearing the brunt of the violence.

Hadi, a Baghdadi version of the 1970s British TV comedy creation Albert Steptoe, complete with horse-drawn cart, unkempt appearance and ongoing hygiene problem, has never been the same since his younger partner Nahem (and the firm's nag) had been blown to pieces by a car bomb. 'It had been hard to separate Nahem's flesh from that of the horse'. Now, Hadi trawls bombsites, selecting remanants of victims he finds to put into his canvas sack and take back to his half-collapsed ruin of a house, situated in the poor Al-Bataween district of the city. In his scrapyard shed he sews together a whole body, made up of the different bits and pieces he has found. The discovery of a blown-off nose completes the project. He tells his cronies with whom he hangs out with at a local coffee-shop that his idea is to hand over his creation to the authorities 'because it was a complete corpse that had been left in the streets like rubbish', that deserved a proper burial.

However, before Hadi could carry out his plan, a suicide bomber driving a stolen rubbish truck detonates his load, and amongst his victims is a young man whose body is completely blown to bits, down to a pair of smouldering boots. There is nothing left of him for his wife and family to put into a coffin and bury. His soul is left stranded without a body to go back into. Alarmed that it will be stuck forever in this limbo, the soul of the young man searches Baghdad for a corpse to inhabit so that he can be properly laid to rest. Hovering over Al-Bataween he spots Hadi's creation – a body without a soul – and descending, sinks into it. The post-modern Promethean monster thus animated comes back into being; resurrected to go forth and seek out (at least initially) all those responsible for the deaths of the victims from whom he is composed and deliver them the ultimate retribution. The monster becomes popularly known as the *Chismah*, or Whatsitsname, and as the city's military and police authorities gradually become aware of its diabolical existence, the hunter becomes the hunted.

Saadawi's novel was first published in 2013, on the 200th anniversary of the publication of Mary Shelley's gothic original. However, Saadawi is not principally concerned with producing a modern remake of a classic, or even to give a familiar story a modern twist. He assumes only that the reader knows the basic Shelley narrative, either through the text or through the countless film versions we are familiar with, and then riffs off it to tell the story he wants to pass on – the apocalypse visited upon the city of his birth, and the enduring suffering of the ordinary people he sees around him, living and dying amongst the ruins.

Ahmed Saadawi, *Frankenstein in Baghdad*, translated from the Arabic by Jonathan Wright, Oneworld, Oxford, 2018 (Originally published in Arabic in 2013).

Saadawi has a natural empathy with the city's working class and transient inhabitants. He was born into a proletarian family in Sadr City, uncharitably described by Rajiv Chandrasekaran in his account of post-invasion Bagdad *Imperial Life In The Emerald City* as 'a squalid warren of 2.5 million Shiites' wedged into 'the slum's labyrinthine alleys', mired in their own filth. The events in Saadawi's *Frankenstein* are centred on the Al-Bataween district, that sits hard by the eastern bank of the Tigris river, across from the city centre and a few kilometres away from Sadr City. Al-Bataween was once a prosperous and well-regarded area originally developed by Baghdad's Iraqi Jewish population, known for the distinctive Art-Deco houses favoured by its residents. Its Jewish inhabitants have long since left or been driven out, it remains only the site for the city's Jewish cemetery and lone synagogue. Al-Bataween also became home for the city's Christian, including

Orthodox Armenian, population, before a long slide into urban decay through the latter half of the twentieth century. During Iraqi's 1970s and 80s economic boom it drew a mainly African migrant worker population housed in residencies converted into cheap boarding houses and hotels. It became regarded as a poor multi-ethnic ghetto, its elegant past now a distant memory. In Saadawi's novel Al-Bataween is kept alive by a disparate band of inhabitants, thrown together by history or circumstance, who struggle through good means or foul to cling onto what remains of the place they all call home. We can imagine that at the time the story is set our characters are sustained somewhat by the hope that the bad days will at some point come to an end, and even that the good times will return. However, we know that in reality Baghdad and the rest of the country is perched on the edge of a sectarian precipice and will shortly freefall into an intensification of cruelty, murder, mayhem and despair.

Saadawi was one of the few Baghdadi writers and members of the literary and intellectual class who stayed behind in Baghdad after the US-led invasion in 2003 and witnessed its aftermath. Although he is the author of three novels – *The Beautiful Country* (2004), *Indeed He Dreams or Plays or Dies* (2008), *Frankenstein in Baghdad* (2013) and a volume of poetry *Anniversary of Bad Songs* (2000) - his stock-in-trade is journalism and documentary film-making. It is the journalistic attention to economy of language as well as an ear calibrated to the voices of those overlooked or rarely listened to, that marks out Saadawi's approach to novelistic form and content.

The author was in London in May 2018, promoting the English translation of *Frankenstein in Baghdad* on the eve of the International Man Booker prize award, for which his novel was shortlisted. At a London book-reading, accompanied by his fine translator Jonathan Wright, Saadawi explained the incident that gave rise to the original impulse for his story.

One time while he was reporting from a Baghdad hospital in the wake of a bombing, Saadawi came across a man crying in the autopsy room. 'When I asked him why he was crying, he said his brother had been killed by a bomb, but that his body could not be found. A hospital attendant had told the man "I have a part of your brother – his foot". When the man asked the attendant "Can I have that part of my brother' the attendant had replied "Shall I gather other parts together to go with your brother's foot and put a full body together?" This is why the man was crying'.

For Saadawi it is not so much a narrative about a monster, but an attempt to encompass the monstrous things that humans are capable of inflicting upon each other. As Saadawi says, 'the problem here is that I cannot escape "Iraq". I mean, this is the place I know, and it is the one place that primarily matters to me more than any other. I want to create a vision that is honestly constructed about what is going on. I believe that many of us in Iraq – artists, intellectuals, and average people – are still unable to comprehend the dramatic and monstrous events that took place since April 2003, and until this day'.

The style of writing Saadawi employs in *Frankenstein* has the feel of reportage about it. He argues that his technique sits within the Arab oral folk storytelling tradition: 'I treat classical historical writings in Arabic as narrative texts. Although they claim to address real events, they are full of miraculous events and mythical and metaphysical stories'. Saadawi also knowingly plays with literary post-modern devices – as we read the novel we are always aware that Saadawi the author is pulling its narrative strings on our behalf, playing with us and the characters. He inserts a version of himself into the story in the guise of the libidinous young and ambitious journalist Mahmoud al-Sawadi, eager to impress his cynical editor, Ali Baher al-Saidi. The young man with the surname closely resembling that of our author, has managed to get an exclusive interview with Whatsitsname, recorded by its creator/father, Hadi, on the reporter's Dictaphone. He writes the story up and hands it over to his boss.

Mahmoud gave Saidi an article headlined 'Urban Legends from the Streets of Iraq'. Saidi liked it immediately. When Mahmoud did the layout for the magazine, he illustrated the article with a large photo of Robert De Niro from the film of Mary Shelley's *Frankenstein*. Mahmoud wasn't happy when he got a copy of the issue, especially when he saw that his headline had been changed.

'Frankenstein in Baghdad,' Saidi shouted, a big smile on his face.

The clipped sentences and spare descriptive passages Saadawi employ carry the responsibility of honestly describing the terrible cyclical nightmare that Iraq has yet to shake itself from., Fantastical and the real have merged. And fiction appears more succinct than fact.

It is as if we are reading the testimony of a survivor, attempting to carefully recall what happened, and using 'matter-of-fact' language as a way of tamping down and avoid triggering the deep emotions and trauma the event has lodged in their psyche. Take this example of an early passage in the novel describing the aftermath of the latest car bomb: 'Trails of black smoke continued to rise from the cars, and flames licked small burning objects scattered on the pavement. The police came quickly and set up a cordon. Injured people were groaning, and bodies were lying in heaps on the asphalt, covered in blood and singed black by the heat'.

This distancing, or *Verfremdungseffekt* in Brechtian terminology, also takes us out from the individual sense memory towards a more collective overview. After all, as Saadawi told his London audience, 'history is not concerned with our personal feelings'. He sees the role of the countless venal self-serving figures that have paraded across Iraqi's political stage since 2003 as shameless manipulators of the raw emotions of those they seek to influence and direct. Saadawi has, at least for now, abandoned his early belief that post-Saddam 'there would be freedom, that change was still possible. I believed as an intellectual and a writer and journalist I could contribute to this task of making us great again'. However, he went on to say, 'it isn't the role of literature to cast a positive light on things – to satisfy society's view of itself. All societies see themselves as great civilisations. But I think it is the job of literature to lay bare the truth. Beautiful things are rare and far between'.

Beautiful things are few and far between. Reading Saadawi's work and listening to him talk, his despair at the seeming inability of any force to break the cycle of murder and revenge that is inexorably grinding his country and its people into the dust comes to the fore. The *Chismah* embarks on a series of nocturnal murders that it regards as a simple matter of natural justice: 'The prayers of the victims and their families came together for once…the innards of the darkness moved and gave birth to me. I am the answer to their call for an and to injustice and for revenge on the guilty'. It complains that some, particularly those in authority, have misrepresented its acts: 'they have turned me into a criminal and a monster, and in this way they equated me with those I seek to exact revenge on. This is a grave injustice'.

However, after an initial bout of bloodletting, the *Chismah* finds itself suffering from mission creep. It is alarmed to discover that bits of the reconstructed body are starting to rot and fall off. One night he finds his eyesight going cloudy as his right eye disintegrates. 'I pulled at it gently, and it moved with my hand. Then the whole thing came out, like a dark lump, and I tossed it aside'. Thinking that it will literally fall apart before it's work is done, the *Chismah* is compelled to kill random people in order to keep going. The *Chismah* reconciles itself to this new development by arguing that the end justifies the means – his innocent victims become 'a sacrificial lamb that the Lord has placed in my path'. Thus, the canker of revenge begins to eat away at its host. We are horrified by this macabre turn of events. But who would not acknowledge that justice always contains a greater or lesser element of retribution and vengeance? Saadawi touches on our complicity in the use of violence as a legitimate method of bringing about societal and political order. As Saadawi has commented elsewhere: 'There are many messages [in the novel]. One of them is that with this war and violence, no one is innocent'. This is what finally halts the murderous progress of the *Chismah*: '"There are no innocents who are completely innocent or criminals who are completely criminal". This sentence drilled its way into his head like a bullet out of the blue...This was the realisation that would undermine his mission – because every criminal he had killed was also a victim'.

Saadawi also examines the way in which religious justifications smooth the path towards immoral acts committed on a grand scale. He talks about how the early days of strife in Iraq produced a series of men, each one claiming to be the *Mahdi* who successfully attracted numbers of fanatical followers before being killed by rivals or sinking back into obscurity. In the novel the *Chismah* is surprised to finds itself the focus of religious fervour: 'I was amazed how many young gunmen bowed down to me in the street. All of them believed I was the face of God on Earth'. Saadawi turns this phenomenon into a dark comedy but the serious point is still made.

Although Saadawi avoids any relationship between his novel and the 1813 original, I do think there are tentative parallels to be drawn between the two authors and their particular historical circumstances. In both cases there is a rejection of previous grand narratives and ideologies that promise to deliver heaven on earth, but seem only to succeed in dragging us all that little bit closer towards hell. In Saadawi's case there is the monolithic falsehood of Baathist socialist national unity, torn down by the Americans, only to be replaced by another lie embodied in fragmented religious, ethnic and sectarian identities stoked by mirror-image competing demagogues. As Saadawi told his London audience: 'The figure of the *Chismah* is full of symbols. For example, the primordial Iraqi citizen is a body made up of the different sects and ethnic groups of Iraq. This appears in the novel in the form of satire. Behind it is the idea that since the foundation of the nation state to the fall of Saddam that we have forged all Iraqi identities into one Iraqi identity. This has proved to have failed as an idea, and an ideology. The other face of the *Chismah* is that in times of crisis, especially in the Middle East, the idea of a religious saviour emerges'.

In Mary Shelley's case there was a growing disenchantment with European Romanticism as a radical political expression of Enlightenment ideals. Her husband Percy Bysshe Shelley on the other hand was steadfast in his belief in the French Revolution. He refused to be infected by 'the gloom' that pervaded his fellow Radicals, many of whom had become disillusioned in the revolutionary project. In the forward he wrote for the third edition of *Frankenstein*, Shelley held up his wife's fictional creation as 'a tremendous creature' who had been driven to monstrous acts by its mistreatment.

However, Shelley's later interpretation appears at odds with his wife's original intentions. As she was writing *Frankenstein*, Mary Shelley was starting to challenge the certainties of the Radicalism espoused by her husband and her parents Mary Wollstonecraft and William Godwin. She seems to have come to the belief that the promise of the French Revolution and what she saw as its violent excesses had cleared the path for reaction, embodied in the expansionist dictatorship pursued by Napoleon Bonaparte she had witnessed first-hand during a trip across Europe. *Frankenstein* was, and remains, as a nightmare of Romantic idealism, the dark side of utopias that propelled the imagination of Romantic myth-makers.

Thus, when Ahmed Saadawi told his London audience of his conviction that the most important thing about literature was 'to give victory to man[kind], not ideologies' he was perhaps drawing himself closer to the creator of the original Whatitsname that he has so stylishly resurrected in present-day Baghdad.

NOT AFGHANISTAN

Sahil Warsi

We arrived late for Friday prayers from a meeting in the city centre. Carried on a warm May breeze, the sermon droned over the little loudspeakers of the dome-less, minaret-less mosque to an audience of motorcycles, chained handcarts, and an avalanche of footwear. The audience inside was mixed: middle-class men in crisp *perahan-tumbans* (tunics and trousers) sat with their sons alongside street vendors and young men in distressed jeans and logoed t-shirts.

The imam began the second part of the sermon as we entered, describing how Muslims of yore gave all they had, including their lives, to safeguard their community and faith. It was our duty, he explained, to protect the nation, our families, and our belief! I deliberately continued ignoring my colleague's nervous glances. 'And we need to begin with our mosques!' the imam suddenly exclaimed, launching into a list of outstanding repairs and the mosque's construction needs. A cart-puller stood up, interrupting the imam. 'With your permission Mullah Saheb,' he began in Pashto-accented Dari, 'we've no food for our children, the cost of living increases daily, where will this money come from?' Amidst a cacophony of encouraging cries, bids to shut up and sit down, and *astaghfirallahs* (heaven forbids), the cart-puller stubbornly continued, emphatically suggesting that the government, the police, and religious officials bleed everyday people dry; that perhaps early Muslims did not face similar problems of inflation and lack of social support.

The sermon and prayers came to a quick end. The cart-puller's frustrations seemed forgotten as people streamed out to begin their weekend. Heading back to the office, my colleague apologised repeatedly for the scene on my first Friday in the city. His contrition rang with embarrassment; he had, after all, invited me to this mosque to 'see the real Kabul', and whatever happened reflected indirectly on him. 'These *karachiwan* (cart-pullers) have no manners,' he sneered, betraying an anti-

Pashtun bias I had yet to catch, 'they come from the village with no idea of how to talk to people. But these mullahs are no better. They just chase after money, even when they say the right things.' Every Friday after that, despite my suggestions, if we prayed together it was always at a larger mosque where a banal, government-approved sermon was delivered to a mostly bored, socially-mobile audience itching to finish the obligatory prayer.

This incident occurred in 2009, toward the end of the reported period of information collection for *Taliban Narratives*. Yes, Kabul is among a handful of international, cosmopolitan urban centres in Afghanistan, but rural Afghanistan is no isolated time-capsule as the book might lead one to believe, especially not Kandahar, where much of the data collection took place. Like anywhere else, people in Afghanistan are complicated. As with people's reaction to the imam's sermon, individuals in Afghanistan receive and consider religious and political discourses packaged in cultural vernaculars in multiple ways. Their reactions reflect varying personal mores and interconnected social divisions including socio-economic status, ethnic identity, political affiliation, or religious belief. This understanding and nuance is markedly absent in *Taliban Narratives*.

Thomas Johnson, *Taliban Narratives: The Use and Power of Stories in the Afghanistan Conflict*, London, Hurst, 2018

The thesis of the book is, in part, indisputable: before invading and during seventeen years of presence in the country, US military forces have not effectively communicated a consistent or relevant narrative around their presence in the country. The book's contention, however, that US military failure to attain territorial hegemony and garner popular support stems from a 'Western' inability to replicate Taliban use of traditional and religious narratives in propaganda, ignores the political and historical realities of Afghanistan and US involvement in the region. This assertion also supports, perhaps inadvertently, a misguided Huntingtonian narrative of 'cosmic struggle' (a term attributed to Taliban views in the book) between an alleged 'West' and Muslim polities.

Overall, *Taliban Narratives* leaves room for improvement in form and content. The introduction presents a theoretical framework for considering narrative and audiences in the context of Information Operations (IO) and Psychological Operations (PSYOPS). The subsequent two chapters suggest Taliban and other Afghan insurgents' narratives and stories be understood in terms of religious, cultural, and political messaging aimed at audiences across Afghanistan (supporters, neutral, and opposers), neighbouring countries (Pakistan and the Gulf), and the international community (the US and its allies). Chapters four and six respectively list descriptions of print media and electronic media outlets (somehow including graffiti) employed by the Taliban and other insurgent groups, with an interluding fifth chapter on Taliban night letters (*shabnamaha*). The seventh and longest chapter of the book provides numerous examples of Taliban poetry and *taranas*, followed by an eighth chapter reviewing the 2009 and 2010 Taliban codes of conduct. Focus is shifted momentarily in the ninth chapter to the Hezb-e Islami Gulbuddin to describe its history and use of media, though the group does not feature again in the book. The penultimate chapter examines examples of US military propaganda materials to demonstrate how neither culturally appropriate messages nor media were used, and the book concludes with a chapter reiterating observations from across the book on simple, consistent, and culturally framed Taliban messaging works, and 'Western' ignorance or inability to engage in these narratives that consequently led to military failure.

The ten chapters hang together loosely and lack internal organisation, making for a disjointed read. Rather than being led through a series of systematic arguments, readers are presented with documentary artefacts and repetitive commentary that is rarely thematically organised and often communicated through bulleted lists or series of statements resting on the authority of the authors. The constant repetition of similar observations renders the writing tedious and unengaging, but also only tells readers what material presented might mean to Afghans, rather than showing how or why this is the case.

Terminological confusion also spans the book, diminishing clarity of its message. 'Afghan', 'Pashtun', and even 'Afghani' (the name of Afghanistan's currency) are employed interchangeably, without an explanation of the plasticity or history of the terms or any delineation of how or why they are being used. The text similarly uses 'the West', which is never really defined, to stand for US forces, US allies, the NATO-led International Security Assistance Force (ISAF), and even the Government of Afghanistan by extension. The Taliban, also treated as a unified category despite being an umbrella of multiple and competing groups, are interchangeably described as Deobandi or Salafi: two distinct and non-commensurate ideological schools. This last confusion connects to a broader generalisation across the book regarding Muslim belief and practice and misunderstanding of religious positions held by different Muslim groups. Ultimately, while a statement or two are made to the effect that not all Afghans or Muslims are the same, the writing and analysis demonstrate little appreciation of this fact.

Inconsistent assertions further weaken the book's overall argument. Where most chapters suggest the Taliban enjoy popular support because of their ability to employ culturally appropriate narratives, chapter seven avers the Taliban's focus on military objectives prevent them from capturing the 'true will of the people', weakening their appeal and tactical position. This argument is never returned to nor reconciled elsewhere. Relatedly, where chapter five begins by asserting that the tactic of clandestinely distributing unsigned 'night letters are part of the Afghan tradition and one can assume that people are more receptive to them than to any other/new means of communication that would be foreign to their culture,' it ends with a caveat on the impossibility of determining the extent to which night letters resonate with people and effect support for the Taliban. These are just a few examples. Such contradictory statements are not necessarily wrong or unrepresentative of the situation in Afghanistan, but insisting on a simplistic rubric to present them makes the book's argument less compelling.

While it is clear some research was conducted in Afghanistan, little detail is provided on what this entailed. In some cases, broad statements about society in Afghanistan are attributed to authors' conversations with 'many Afghans' or 'many Kandaharis'. No indication is given as to who was consulted, in what context, or how representative their views might be. Again, such telling of what people in Afghanistan believe without showing why or how this is the case makes the argument less convincing.

The methodological opaqueness in *Taliban Narratives* is most notable in its translations. Original texts of poems and songs, comprising the bulk of the book, appear sporadically without rationale as to why or when they are provided. In most cases, following a literal translation, readers are furnished with what is suggested to be an 'Afghan-centric' translation of what people would understand, which is chased with a summary explication by the authors. The 'Afghan-centric' translations and explications tend to employ tropes of 'cosmic struggle' between Islam and the West, with references to 'infidels', 'apostates', etc., that are not present in original poems. In one striking example, the title '*Arman Khudaya'* is translated using a nonsensical English-Arabic mix of 'Wish Allah', rather than the actual translation of 'My wish, O God', and even though the Arabic word 'Allah' is not in the original title.

A stylistic decision has clearly been made in the 'translations' to present a perceived Muslim extremist aesthetic that does not resemble the language of the poems. Whatever the motive, presenting these interpretations as translations hides the licence taken in their construction and misrepresents the multifaceted nature of the poems. It also betrays an unfamiliarity with literary devices of metaphor, imagery, or tropes in the Indo-Persian poetic tradition: a fact all the more shocking given the central thesis of the book on the necessity to grasp such discursive elements.

Consequently, the book's translations of poems are flat and denuded of the variegated meanings and emotions, and explications often inappropriately rely on interpretation grounded in a Western European canon. The poem titled *Every Night Somebody Hits My Door with Stones* is one example. The literal translation hints at delicate imagery of the original, tying events from the life of the Prophet into that of the poet. Following traditional form, the final couplet reveals the message of the poem as a response to the Danish cartoons. Nowhere is there an assertion of an 'infidel West' that is 'seeking to destroy the best things of Islam from art, to knowledge, to religion', which the explication suggests is 'the language of the jihadist'. The poem is about the sadness of the poet who loves the Prophet, and the senseless futility of such aggressions. The symbolism of throwing stones at the mountain, alluding to Mount Hira where the Prophet received guidance, is completely lost, with the translation suggesting it is the 'mountain of Islam'. That the poem might resonate differently with individuals differently oriented toward the Taliban or 'the West' is not considered.

Despite linguistic failings, claims made in *Taliban Narratives* also rely on weak sources and selective research. It is disappointing to see many serious assertions on Afghan religious, cultural, or political attitudes attributed to online articles in sources like *The Daily Mail, The Independent*, or *The Observer*, or even more critical sources like *The Washington Post*, *The Guardian*, or *Huffington Post*. While op-eds and news articles can be credible sources of information, it is surprising they are favoured at the expense of extensive professional research on society and politics in Afghanistan.

As an anthropologist, I was encouraged to see references to ethnographic work on the country. The book, however, dismayingly focuses uniquely on research from the 1950s-80s, even if published later in the 1990s. Much of this research was conducted from outside Afghanistan due to political unrest, and is concerned with explaining the fractured politics of the 1980s. Following anthropological interests of the time, it concentrates on tribal and ethnic identity, pitting tribes against the state and sometimes introducing Islamic religious networks as a kind of third estate. David Edwards' *Heroes of the Age* is cited as representing the 'spirit' of research underpinning the book, which explains a great deal. Edward analyses three oral and written texts moralising past events in Afghanistan to suggest a 'moral incoherence' in Afghan society. This incoherence, he suggests, derives from competing moral frameworks of honour, Islam, and state rule. While stating he does not wish to suggest Afghans are slaves to tradition, Edwards' work only cements such pathologisation by excluding real voices of how people ethically navigate and manage the different frameworks. *Taliban Narratives* similarly ignores real people's attitudes or reactions, and assumes an approach suggesting a homogenous 'Afghan psyche' or 'mind', centrality of *Pashtunwali* (described as the 'unwritten rules' driving social organisation in Afghanistan), and universality of social-political imperatives of Muslim faith and practice.

The book's ignorance of contemporary ethnographic research on Afghanistan is striking given its reliance on current security studies research, especially that published by the lead author. Over the last decade, anthropological research in Afghanistan has unpacked static ideas of tribal organisation, *Pashtunwali*, etc. that the book bases its argument on. This research recognises the different frameworks identified in *Taliban Narratives*, while also providing insight into machinations at individual, group, and state levels that produce multiple competing and changing realities within Afghanistan. While expensive paywalls often place academic research beyond reach, rigorous research on Afghanistan is also available online through organisations like the *Afghan Analysts Network* or Afghanistan's premier research institution: the Afghanistan Research and Evaluation Unit (AREU).

In 2012, AREU published a report on drivers of anti-government mobilisation in Afghanistan during the last thirty years. Like *Taliban Narratives*, this research explores the current insurgency. It contrastingly highlights how changing social, economic, and political contexts have interacted with efforts of foreign forces and anti-state agents such as the Taliban to inform the situation today. The contradictory evidence and claims of *Taliban Narratives* are thus not necessarily incoherent or wrong. What is misguided, however, is the book's insistence on erasing these contradictions through forcing a simplistic framework. Doing so is both unfaithful to reality and politically dangerous.

A central argument of the book is that 'the West', and by extension the government of Afghanistan, have not used media, especially electronic media, as effectively as the Taliban to garner support and spread their messages. Yet, one need only look at the numerous official and unofficial Twitter handles, Facebook pages, and Instagram accounts and the outpouring of support and 'sharing' they receive to see how this media is also used effectively by forces of 'the West' to counter Taliban propaganda and further their agenda. Programming I worked on for the US Agency for International Development mirrored projects by the UK, Germany and others to employ Afghan popular and traditional music, poetry, and art to create social change and encourage political cohesion. From an armed forces perspective, General Petraeus even ordered the learning of Dari and Pashto by recruits in Afghanistan, even if this might have been too little too late.

The fact is, somebody who is influenced to vote by watching a mobile-phone version of Farhad Darya (an Afghan pop icon) singing a Pashto song on social cohesion and political participation, might also be legitimately enraged by US forces' indiscriminate killing of civilians two villages over; they might be influenced by numerous other considerations in developing a stance vis-à-vis the government, occupying forces, or insurgents. Framing of conflict in Afghanistan as merely a clash between a united

'West' and a monolithic Taliban representing Islam or *Pashtunwali*, precludes an appreciation of the very complexity required to address the situation at hand. It requires the book to conduct an amnesic sleight of hand ignoring 'the West's' role in nurturing the Taliban, the byzantine arms networks connecting both the Taliban and 'the West', and myriad other factors undermining any facile dualistic understanding of conflict.

While I can support the aim of the book to the extent it encourages appreciation of language and culture in Afghanistan by US forces and sheds light on a tactical mistake that could have been avoided, I would not recommend it as a piece of popular writing or rigorous research on Afghan society. The assertion that US military failure lies in a 'Western' inability to use religious discourse in mobilisation is untrue. Religious language has been used to legitimate state violence both inside and outside the US and the separation of church and state continues to be a contentious issue in the US today.

I'm reminded of an incident when a friend invited me to the US embassy pool for a rare afternoon off. A brawny soldier from Hawaii with 'كافر' (*kafir*) tattooed on his bicep struck up a conversation with me after one too many drinks. He was bemused to find out I worked with religious officials on civic participation, and that I was a Muslim. Becoming increasingly agitated, and after using several expletives to describe Afghans and Muslims, he suggested 'people like me' were undermining his work. His friends pulled him away just as he began explaining that people in Afghanistan could not be saved except through renouncing 'Allah' and accepting the true God. Such outbursts by soldiers were not rare. One would, however, likely not take this soldier's statements along with the pledge of allegiance, the motto on US currency, and teleological assertions of 'values' and 'truths' espoused by US leaders grounded in religious imagery of America's founding documents to suggest an unequivocal Christian design undergirding US political involvement in Afghanistan. Yet this is effectively the operation performed by *Taliban Narratives* on religious and cultural vernacular in language used by the Taliban.

In forcing a simplistic and dualistic lens on conflict in Afghanistan, *Taliban Narratives* ultimately perpetuates myths around Afghanistan and Muslims that underpin the quagmire the US finds itself in today, in Afghanistan and elsewhere. Suggestions in the foreword and preface that the book's lessons would serve well in other Muslim contexts dangerously encourages further US military intervention in the world, which I could not support as a US tax-payer or as a conscientious human being. Perhaps *Taliban Narratives* is seeking to emulate what it sees as the Taliban's forte of simple and consistent messaging. Perhaps this would work to attract some audiences. Such messaging will not, however, help in understanding and addressing the conflict in Afghanistan.

BEING BRITISH

Misha Monaghan

Identity is important. It helps you find your clan, it engenders a sense of belonging, and it can – and should – have many dimensions. But in Britain, it seems, only certain identities are thought to belong. That's because Britain is a nation in denial. It is a nation in which the default narrative is set to 'white'. Until recently I had struggled to find appropriate vocabulary to articulate why there is so much wrong with the notion of alleged 'colour blindness' in Britain. Afua Hirsh's *Brit(ish)* helped me to express to others why a nation such as Britain – which colonised half the world and then proceeded to colonise its own education system so no one could learn the true extent of the horror it inflicted – cannot be 'post-racial' until it addresses its inherent and deep rooted history of oppression against people who do not conform to that narrative.

I was never more acutely aware of my lack of belonging than when I was asked the dreaded question: 'so where are you reeeeeeally from?'. This is a probe that is all too familiar to people of colour in Britain. For many years I was in denial, I thought I was being asked this question because of my hybrid Glaswegian and Surrey accent but any time I answered with 'oh a small town outside Glasgow called Paisley', I would immediately be asked the inevitable follow up: 'oh yes but *originally*?' The 'originally' always sounded like it was italicised. What was really being asked of me was how I had brown skin and how far back in my family history you would have to go before finding the culprit who I inherited my melanin from – the original interloper. Being Scottish and Pakistani/Indian most definitely made me feel like an outcast in Surrey and London where I spent the majority of my formative years. Struggles with belonging and identity are inherent to the process of becoming an adult. They are unavoidable, but as a non-white British person you have a variety of other adversities to incorporate into your adolescence. I never saw reflections of myself in the books I read or the television programmes and films I watched. I did not have silky straight hair or a slender frame like Rachel Green. Self-love was a hippy concept and conformity was *à la mode* so I never felt as if I had found my place. I thought I could find a home in the vast Pakistani and Indian communities of Britain and they in turn thought I was too white – I could not possibly understand their experiences as people who were less racially ambiguous than I. Of course they were right, I have the privilege of being of lighter skin, I am able-bodied and I slot neatly into hetero-normative societal structures. Nonetheless, this was a crushing blow to me; my mother had gone to great pains to make sure I had grown up fluent in Urdu and with the ability to make exceptionally round *rotis*, it seemed it was all for nothing. I lived in a limbo, a strange purgatory in which I would facetiously be called a mongrel.

Afua Hirsch, *Brit(ish): On Race, Identity and Belonging*, Jonathan Cape, London, 2018

I did not know any other people who had a similar narrative to me, one where there was a constant battle to belong because the two sides of your gene pool were fighting a silent war. Shamefully, I never explored it in great depth. Instead I accepted it as my lot to never really be understood. Hirsch expresses such a wide array of what I have internalised throughout my life and I will be eternally grateful to her for writing a book that I found myself aggressively nodding to as she details her perpetual struggle for belonging and acceptance. Admittedly, her experience varies from mine in the heritage that she has but I found in her words a companion to my life-long fight.

Originally, I had approached Hirsch's book as a study into an aspect of British history that I was completely unfamiliar with. I must admit that I also enjoy reading books on the tube in London that I think may cause some people to give me the 'side eye', books that I think are highly likely to cause an English Defence League (EDL) member distress. When I started reading the giant hardback version of *Brit(ish)* on the tube, I felt rather giddy at the prospect of enraging people with my 'woke' material. There were several moments while reading the book that I thought 'say it louder for the racists in the back'. Hirsch does not centre her own experiences but instead employs her narrative of growing up in Britain as the daughter of a Jewish man and Ghanaian woman as the foundation of an in-depth analysis into Britain's history with identity. Her work focuses specifically on the black experience. She covers Britain's long and multifaceted history with black people, the sexualisation of black bodies and the intersection between race and class. She also takes into consideration what she calls the 'New Black', namely immigrants in a post-Brexit era.

As I turned over page after page, utterly engrossed, I learned more and more about the horrors inflicted on black people by the British throughout history. Every single chapter leaves you reeling, aghast and (if you are anything like me) in floods of tears. At no point, however, did I read the information in Hirsch's book and think 'I cannot believe that happened' because I most certainly can. I believe that Mozart stole music from a black composer named Chevalier de Saint-Georges and I can believe every horrific detail of the discrimination faced by Venus and Serena Williams. These are some of the least painful stories to read and Hirsch's meticulous research and engaging prose bring every harrowing detail to life. People of colour in Britain have been conditioned to expect racism even if at times we do not realise it is racism. I became aware of this early in my life interacting with many of my Scottish relatives who – despite having known and loved my Pakistani immigrant mother for the better part of their lives – exhibit some extremely problematic behaviour with the excuse of generational ignorance. Even without the familial connection to racism I have, I grew up with the same understanding that I believe most people of colour have in Britain: white is normal, non-white is not.

Brit(ish) is a searing indictment of how substandard my formal education was. I studied history up until the age of 16 in British state and private schools. We covered Henry VIII so many times that I genuinely believe somewhere locked away in my psyche may be a detailed log of his bowel movements; but not once did I learn about the atrocities that funded the Industrial Revolution. Nor was I ever taught about Britain's relationship with slavery before it so gallantly abolished it. I was not educated about the barbarity of Admiral Horatio Nelson, Sir Winston Churchill or Cecil Rhodes. As a nation there is no escaping what has been done; Britain raped and pillaged lands but has never properly addressed its own history. Indeed, England has invaded all but 22 nations in the world. There have been black people in Britain since at least the era of Queen Elizabeth I but the history we were all taught was through the white lens, even when we talked about India.

This is the resounding message in Hirsch's book: if we want to understand why people from ethnic minorities in Britain are two to four times more likely to be stopped and searched by the police, why Islamophobia is at an all-time high and why at the end of 2017 the highest rates of unemployment rates in Britain – between 23-25% – were found amongst people of colour then we cannot ignore our own history. There is a national pandemic of people arguing that we should not look to the past but instead work to improve the present. However, when the present is as bleak as the one we are looking at now it is important to comprehend how we got here. There is also a prevailing belief that anyone who is not white and does not speak with the correct accent should feel grateful that they are being tolerated in this great and illustrious nation. I could fill this entire piece with titles from newspapers such as the *Daily Mail* detailing how British people of colour such as Nadiya Hussain (of Bake Off fame), Stormzy, Akala and many more should be kissing the feet of the immigration officers for the platform they have been given. I think a better question to ask would be how remorseful and grateful are the people calling for this gratitude, for the infrastructure and wealth that was gained by Britain off the backs of slaves and colonised subjects.

Afua Hirsch is an incredibly accomplished woman. She is a barrister and journalist and, as author of *Brit(ish)*, a *Sunday Times* Best Seller. It was the intersection of these aspects of her identity that raised concerns when I was speaking to someone recently about her work. Hirsch is an elite-educated, light-skinned black woman. She has been part of the system that she speaks of as having oppressed people of colour in Britain who have not enjoyed the same opportunities as her. She is an acceptable face for the debate on race. Taking all of this into consideration is important. It helps to contextualise how foundational and internalised racism is in Britain but it is also essential to note that Hirsch is acutely aware of her own privilege. She specifically explains that her life 'is not a story of the kind of prejudice that a young black person growing up in an aggressively policed, publicly neglected, negatively stereotyped and materially deprived inner-city council estate experiences on a daily basis', and that despite the fact that she has significantly more advantages than the people she is writing about she still experienced a ferocious amount of racism in her life. This itself demonstrates how severe the problem is.

I grew up with stories of my mother's hair being pulled in the street by an old white woman as punishment for speaking in Urdu to her cousin, my grandmother being thrown off a bus because she smelled like curry and my own encounter with a man aggressively shouting 'get out my country Paki' in my face in Southall, London of all places! *Brit(ish)* is essential reading for everyone. We must understand the crimes of our collective past, we must appreciate the diversity of our history, and we must decolonise our minds. Hirsch's work is not the first and will not be the last book of its kind, but it is a crucial chapter in the ongoing story of understanding the distorted lens through which we understand our brutish history.

ET CETERA

LAST WORD ON FAMILY NARRATIVES *by Samia Rahman*
THE LIST *Shazia Mirza's Comedians*
CITATIONS
CONTRIBUTORS

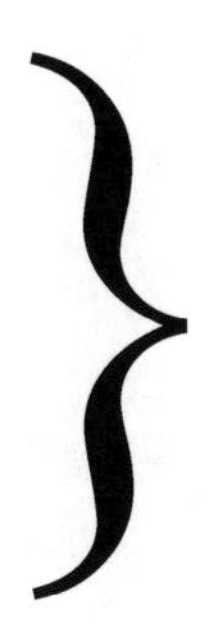

LAST WORD

ON FAMILY NARRATIVES

Samia Rahman

When you tell the story you were never told, the happy ending may not be forthcoming. But what if there is no right or wrong way to narrate the story of our lives. Do our histories make us, or were we always the architects of the futures we have come to realise? The paths we take, perhaps at random, sometimes pre-determined, supposedly by choice or more likely out of duress, occupy the greatly anticipated blank space of our forefathers' aspirations. Many of us have ancestors who endured untold hardship to secure the futures of generations to come. Who are we? More to the point, who am I? A culmination of cherished memories and a curated lineage or a blank vessel surging with misfiring neurons, synapses and vacuoles?

My own parents made great sacrifices in the hope of guaranteeing a better life for their children. Wrenched from all that was familiar to navigate a hostile environment, they strived to fit in to the postcolonial framework of everyone's expectations. Born into a tradition where family was everything, the personal thread of their existence only made sense when it formed part of the intricate cobweb of family narrative. Just as a spider spins an elaborate web of intersections and peril, family stories are mired in a nexus of compelling secrets withstanding distance or translocation.

During visits to Karachi I would listen in wonder, straining to make out the hushed conversations of relatives as they discussed the fate of some unfortunate branch of the family or pored over a past incident mythologised in folklore. I would re-tell these stories to my school friends in the UK, fascinated by a world so far removed from their own. My most prized tale was the one that still sends shivers down my spine. It was 1955 and my mum, just three years old, travelled with her family and many other relatives from Karachi, where they had settled after Partition, to a big family wedding in their home city of Allahabad, in India. On the train journey back to Pakistan, amidst the mayhem and chaos of exuberant children, piles of luggage and tightly-packed carriages, it became clear that my mum had gone missing. My relatives searched the train, she had to be somewhere on it. The tension and fear they must have felt resonates through me all these decades later. My grandmother's terror and desperation felt palpable. Child abduction was common and almost always had a horrific end. Eventually my great-uncle spotted a man who was attempting to conceal something beneath his *dhoti*. He roared at him to reveal what was hidden. Other relatives came running. It was at that moment that my mother's cries were heard and she was recovered.

Stories such as these and from even longer ago would be passed along family members, through generations, embellished and redacted at whim; mis-remembered and even sometimes entirely fabricated, yet resolutely part of the fabric of our extended family narrative. The reason? Because these are our stories and the medium through which we reinforce our sense of self. Identity becomes wrapped up in the highlights and lowlights of those we refer to as 'our blood'. We swell with pride or quiver with shame or distress as if revisiting memories involving those we knew intimately. Stories would be formulated to fortify each member's role in the jigsaw puzzle of a family dynasty. This was the wayward great-great-grandfather who frittered away the family's bountiful wealth. We would be living a life of untold opulence and not this impoverished existence if he hadn't been so foolish. And here is the story about the distant relative from one hundred years ago who eloped with her unsuitable lover and sent the line of descent along an entirely unexpected course. The story of my mum's brief abduction formed part of the narrative of her lauded beauty that morphed into a statement of fact even among people who had never actually set eyes on her. That girl's porcelain skin, huge almond eyes and pursed lips meant that she was a jewel to guard and protect even at the tender age of three years old. That my dad had won this coveted woman, that she was my mother, gifting me half my genes and with her blood coursing through mine, made me feel like the daughter of a princess; and inevitably warped my ideals of what it meant to be beautiful.

My childhood was filled with enchanting tales of family drama of yesteryear. Of intrigue and plotting and betrayal and heartache. My parents' generation, newly arrived in the UK, could re-invent themselves and recast the stories of their heritage at will. Some did. Some didn't. This was before globalisation or social media or the Internet and if you were far from home you could claim to be whoever or whatever you wanted, no one would know any different. When meeting someone of South Asian extraction for the first time they would almost if not immediately ask where they were from and what sort of family they belonged to. Your reply defines you. It would determine who they would socialise with and who would support you in your work and studies and who would want to marry into your family. I remember watching the mesmeric Indian film, *Mughal-e-Azam* with my family and coming away with the misapprehension that Anarkali, the courtesan with whom the future Emperor Jahangir fell in love, was a distant relative. How I mourned her brutal demise, even though historians remain divided on the veracity of her existence never mind her political murder.

Family friends would proudly proclaim that they were descendants of the Prophet Muhammad and it was with immense superficial reverence that this fact would be received. I would hear my parents reply that their ancestors were the Mughals, hence my baseless confidence that *Mughal e Azam* was a family home video, and that our lineage was Persian. Even now if anyone ever enquires I casually let it be known that I have Iranian blood, and allow this unfounded fact to explain away my curly hair. Stories from the Mughal Empire felt embedded in the narrative of my own trajectory as if the victories and tragedies of this mighty clan were my own. My ancestors, I was told, were respected members of the Mughal Court who fought in Agra and Delhi against the invading British colonisers and lost their wealth and influence upon the formation of the British Raj in the nineteenth century. Those that survived retreated to Allahabad and became landowners and families of renown. My fury at their subjugation remains undimmed. I would face off racism in the smug belief that my pedigree was infinitely superior to the uncivilised masses who sought to make me feel unwelcome. Family history becomes synonymous with self-respect and dignity when your world seems an alien place.

Do the stories of our ancestry illuminate our present? How many times do we hear people commenting on how a child is just like his grandparent or some other relative. We hear of a fascinating quirk of character in a predecessor and it seems as if we could be gazing into a mirror. Our family stories give us agency, belonging, they make us feel part of something bigger than ourselves, affording us our place in history. The narrative of who we are assures us that we matter in the world, that our impact goes beyond our solitary being. This would explain why the hugely popular BBC television series *Who Do You Think You Are?* has captured the nation's imagination since it first aired in 2004. Viewers continue to be gripped by shocking, scandalous and heartbreaking revelations unearthed by celebrities as they trace their family tree as far back as possible. The surprises are astounding, adding weight to the notion that our past looms large in our present. With great astonishment *Harry Potter* author JK Rowling learned she was not the first single mother in her family. It transpired she descends from a long line of single mothers, as far back as her great-great-grandmother. Is this sheer coincidence or an example of genealogical destiny. None of us are islands of isolation, but to what extent are we shaped by the reality of those from whom we have been formed? Not all of the skeletons that are uncovered are welcome. Television presenter Emma Willis was less than thrilled to discover that her great-great-great-great-great grandfather was convicted of torture and murder in Ireland and television chef Ainsley Harriot was devastated to find out that his great-great-great-grandmother had been sold into slavery in Barbados at the age of two years old. What's more, his great-great grandfather James Gordon Harriott turned out to be a descendant of white slave owners. The connection that may resonate with a relative, however far in the distant past they lived, was movingly illustrated by former BBC Newsnight presenter Jeremy Paxman's emotional response to hearing of his great-great grandmother's unjust consignment to grinding poverty. When her husband died she was unable to access his pension and resorted to poor relief in the slums of Glasgow to support her nine children. However, after an anonymous letter was sent to parish authorities alleging that one of her children was illegitimate, this financial support was withdrawn, leaving her destitute. Known for being a brusque and acerbic interviewer, Paxman was uncharacteristically tearful, remarking: 'You shouldn't go into this family history business. It's just upsetting.'

Family histories are a tumult of emotional drama that invite themselves into our private lives and render us enthralled and appalled in equal measure. This is why generational family sagas are loved by so many. Whether a period drama such as *Downton Abbey* or the dark brooding of *The Godfather*, family narratives become those stories we appropriate as our own. My mum was one of many viewers riveted by *Who Do You Think You Are?* because she could passionately imagine the treasure chest of revelations that lay buried deep within the recesses of our family narrative. For years she had been musing that she would research our family tree but it was the 2018 episode featuring Shirley Ballas, a judge on the television series *Strictly Come Dancing*, that truly captured her imagination and motivated her to entertain the idea seriously. Upon confirming a family rumour that her paternal grandfather was of mixed race, Ballas went on to trace her four times great grandmother, Caroline Otto, discovering she had been forcibly brought to South Africa as a child slave after being taken from her place of birth, Madagascar. A further twist to the tale was that Caroline was Muslim, and remained so, despite her children being brought up Christian. Ballas was inspired to draw resonance from the tragic experience of her relative and contextualise the strong women that dominate her family narrative. She explains in a tabloid interview: 'I must have got a gene from those women of a survival instinct cos being a child on a housing estate with a single family. My own mother is strong and I think that my own mother got that will from her ancestry and I've also got it from my mother's side and my father's side. And I'll never forget this journey.'

This journey to locate the stories we want to hear about our families has become one that is no longer confined to celebrities. Prompted by the dramatic account of Ballas' bloodline, my mum seriously resolved to find out more about our much talked of Mughal roots. A quick Google search brought up a dizzying array of websites and tools that promised to aid her search. It was at this point that her enthusiasm faltered but her inconsistent persistence is not typical of the average genealogy explorer. A close friend and her parents decided to actually commit to finding out 'who they really were'. It all began when planning a week-long holiday to Rhodes. My friend's grandfather had been a general in the Indian army during the

Second World War and had spent a period of his posting in Cyprus. Known within the family as 'The General', he had kept a detailed diary recording his adventures in this far flung part of Europe that was completely different to his native Bhopal. He wrote about the minutiae of life, the stunning sites he visited, and the warm and hospitable local people he met and befriended. The diary was a vivid insight into his thoughts and responses to the events and interactions that characterised his everyday existence. Life in Rhodes must have been unprecedented and unimaginable to a young man leaving India for the very first time, and he immersed himself in the experience with positivity and wonderment. When his granddaughter, born and brought up in the UK, took a holiday in Rhodes she brought his diary with her and decided to retrace his steps. The experience proved profoundly moving – walking down the same streets that her grandfather had walked along yet in such different times and under completely different circumstances, was humbling and powerful. Rhodes was now used to visitors from different parts of the world but during the Second World War his presence would not have gone unnoticed. Did he encounter prejudice or unkind treatment? As my friend viewed the island through his eyes via the words he articulated on the pages of his diary, she couldn't help but wonder how their two excursions, bound by blood yet divided by decades, could possibly compare.

Spurred on by this connection with the past and its vision in the present, she encouraged her parents to join her in taking a genealogy test, curious to see what it might unearth. After sending off a saliva sample for the extraction of DNA to their chosen heritage-hunting website, they eagerly awaited the results. What came back was a remarkably accurate ethnicity estimate, confirming what they already suspected, overwhelmingly South Asian with an intriguing 7% East Asian, an unexpected 2% Polynesian, and possibly anomalous 1% Native American. As it happened their closest matches turned out to be each other, bar one or two based in India.

What about those who find that their heritage test results throw their lives into disarray rather than confirm what they had always believed about their lineage? The advertising campaigns of companies offering DNA home-testing kits regularly show smiling mixed-race individuals who are delighted with their 'citizen-of-the-world' results. Yet this burgeoning industry, which is expected to be worth £7.7billion by 2022, comprises databases that are skewed towards different parts of the world. Despite genetic variation most prevalent in Africa, the lack of continent breakdown can prove bewildering and frustrating for those who wish to know more than that their ethnicity has been plucked from a huge swathe of the continent. Country breakdown should not be impossible but is rarely offered. In an article in the *Guardian* Georgina Lawton writes about the cynical way in which the man-made construct of ethnicity is being exploited by US and European companies in their pursuit of profit. 'For people of African descent', she writes, 'whose individual and collective histories are blurred by the legacies of colonialism, slavery and rape, what they know about their identities is particularly important.' Of one woman who her entire life had believed that she had Indian as well as Caribbean ancestry, only for the test to find no trace of Indian ancestry, Lawton explains, she 'felt that one of the narratives woven through her family had been broken'.

Aside from the alarming security and privacy issues that come with private companies holding very sensitive data, the potential for ethnicity to be used to determine race with the sliders of discrimination thrown into the mix do not bear thinking about. We may all be searching for the story of what makes us who we are but the cold hard scientific truth is that there is only so much DNA passed through generations, and once we have gone back ten generations there is no longer a genetic link.

This is surely a good reason to celebrate the mythology of family stories. The more we pursue the concept of truth in the story of our lives, the more we elude the way in which heritage and personal histories may enrich our present. Just as science cannot explain the bewildering intricacies of family ties, we must be allowed to mis-remember, to elaborate upon, and to discard our family narrative(s) in all its/their unreal reality.

SHAZIA MIRZA'S COMEDIANS

Do you remember when we did the things we were supposed to do? The things that brought us all respect, status, money and a good quality husband or wife? The things that on the outside made everyone else happy but never us? The things that bought us a five bedroomed semi-detached with concrete driveway, a top of the class Mercedes and twelve other houses that we rented out with no mortgage. We really were, as my dad would say, 'Top of the Pops'.

But then a few of us decided to throw a shovel into this bullshit. The twaddle and balderdash that enhanced everyone else's ego but did nothing for ourselves. We didn't want to be Doctors, dentists, lawyers, pharmacists, and engineers. You know those Asians who proudly stand in the middle of a party with death behind their eyes and regurgitate the tedious insipid line, 'I'm a Doctor you know', as though they were some kind of pussy magnet and that alone would make me want to jump into bed with them. Little do they know that it takes more than a ninety-six-hour shift and an MBBS to get me jumping.

Some of us had the ground-breaking, life sabotaging, marriage terminating idea of becoming stand-up comedians. I started doing comedy at a time when there were no other Asian female comedians, and no Muslim female comedians in this country (UK). I was the first, and I had to take some serious flack for it. The white males running the comedy industry, the critics, reviewers, 'experts', club bookers, promoters, TV and radio producers didn't see me as a comedian, they saw me as a professional full-time twenty-four-hour Muslim. They wanted me to go on stage and talk about terrorism, bombs, burkhas, bullets, arranged marriages, forced marriages, no marriages, women's oppression, hairy men, hairy women, Islamophobia, Muslims, Mexicans, lesbians whilst at the same time explaining 9/11, and 'Who was Osama Bin Laden?' Did I know him? Where was I when 7/7 happened? What do I think of Boko Haram? Do I know any girls that went missing? What do I think of Tony Blair taking us to war with Iraq? Would you die for your religion? And 'If you blow yourself up, will you get 72 Virgins,' a German journalist once asked me.

I wanted to talk about my friend Julie, and how I lost my knickers whilst going through security at JFK. But they weren't interested. They want you to talk about what they want you to talk about. As a Muslim person, in their eyes it's your job to represent all other Muslims and people that look like you, think like you, and come from your part of the world. They may want me to represent my lot, but it's never 'my lot' that want me to represent. While my lot just want me to shut up and get married.

We are forced to explain the actions and debauchery of terrorists and dictators, who are primarily identified as Muslim but never invited to publicly rejoice in the triumphs of people who achieve great things and who are then not identified as Muslim – Mo Farah, Marat Safin, Zinedine Zidane, Mohamed Salah.

If you stray away from your job description and talk about white people things like sex, travel and traffic, then you are a 'Waste of a good Muslim'. If you talk about being Muslim then, 'That's all you ever talk about'. Once again it is a way of white power controlling a minority. They want you but only on their terms.

When I read the reviews of white comedians, the words creative, inventive, imaginative, artfully conceived, highfalutin, brilliant career often crop up. When I read the reviews of Muslim comedians the words hack, obvious, lazy, race, religion, predictable often spring up. They see us talking about our skin colour or background as cheating, having a head start, not being creative. Richard Pryor, Chris Rock, Eddie Murphy they told that story, does it really need to be reiterated again and again?

When a new Muslim comic comes along he/she is compared to the last one, and the one before that. We are measured by the standard of other Muslims not by the standard set as normal including all kinds of comedians. Many times I have been lumped in with reviews and articles with Omid Djalili and Shappi Khorsandi – they are not even Muslim. Once a reviewer came to my show thinking I was Omid Djalili.

There are constant lists in the mainstream media '100 best comedians', '50 funniest women', '30 best comedians working in the world today'. Nobody that looks like me is ever on those lists. Nobody on those lists reflects my life experience. The people on those lists reflect the lives of the people writing them. The people they admire and wish to be.

Most of the white men writing these lists have probably never known a Muslim man or more likely a Muslim woman in their life. They don't know, or understand our experience so how can they relate to it and find it funny?

As a result of this clash of understanding, I have often received reviews, which are racism disguised as criticism, bullying, subconscious discrimination, taunting and harsh judgements on my religion and way of life. I have learnt that in order to progress you have to 'whiten up', make your comedy accessible to the white audience. That way you are inclusive of a large majority and once they accept you, everything will be ok. You'll get awards, be on TV, and be acknowledged and validated or you can talk about all things Muslim, serve your purpose, stay in your lane, and don't you dare try to move out of it. Either way you lose. The only way to win is to be the individual you. Comedy is about truth and we can only speak our truth. As the Prophet said, when asked that he joked: 'I only tell the truth'.

So, to tell you the truth, I don't want to write about the top ten Muslim comedians in the world. I refuse to compile a list of who I think is good. It is divisive, exclusive, conflicting and alienating. I know how I feel when I read lists that I am not on. I know how it feels to be excluded from lists that I feel I should have been on, I know how it feels to be considered not worthy enough because my worldview is not as celebrated. I don't want to do that to my brothers and sisters at a time in our history when we are being persecuted on a daily basis in our personal and worldly lives. We are mocked by politicians for the way we dress, far right Muslim hating leaders are labelled 'heroes' for opposing what we believe, we are being banned from entering into countries because of our religion, and our Prophet is being denounced as a predator in the name of freedom of speech.

What I want is to applaud and celebrate all working comedians who come from a Muslim background. I refuse to call them 'Muslim comedians' because they are not that. They are individuals who have many facets to their lives and personalities and Islam is just one part of that.

So all rise. Dave Chappell, Negin Farad, Hasan Minhaj, Aziz Ansari, Dean Obeidallah, Imran Yusuf, Guz Khan, Omar Hamdi, Tez Ilyas, Shazia Mirza, Nabil AbdulRashid, Prince Abdi, MoAmer, Preacher Moss, Aamer Rahman, Naz, Abdullah Afzal, Nazeem Hussain, Omar Regan, Aatif Nawaz, Aman Ali, Azhar Usman, Humza Arshad, Ali official, Rahim Pardesi, Max Amini, Adil Ray, Umar Rana, Maysoon Zayid, Fawzia Mirza, Nisti Sterk, Zinat Perzadeh, Laila Sari, Nasim Pedrad, Soimah Pancawati, Mona Shaikh, Bilal Zaffer, Jeff Mirza, Riaad Moosa, Aman Ali, and Prince Abdi.

There are probably many others that I don't know about in the many different countries around the world. I am so sorry if I have missed your name off the list.

May they all prosper and not pander to the wants and needs of a narrative dictated to us by those in power with an agenda. May it be our narrative that is true to us and represents us as we are. And may we stand at parties and gatherings and be proud to say we are comedians, may people be impressed with us as they are with doctors, engineers and lawyers, may men and women want to marry us, feed us, love us, and keep us.

In the future, we will become the new Jews of comedy. They were once a persecuted minority who had to change their names to disguise themselves against further abuse. They were taunted, mistreated, alienated, mocked. But they used their situation to retaliate with humour. There came a thing called, 'Jewish humour'; it made the world laugh. Joan Rivers, Mel Brookes, Groucho Marx, Jerry Lewis, Lenny Bruce, Jack Benny, Gilda Radna, Larry David, Gene Wilder, Billy Crystal, Bette Midler. Albert Brookes, Mort Sahl, Peter Sellers, Andy Kaufman. That will be us very soon. *Inshallah.*

CITATIONS

Introduction: Stories We Are Heirs To by Merryl Wyn Davies

The definition of culture is from the opening lines of E B Taylor's *Primitive Cultures* (volume one, John Murray, London, 1871). Margaret Hodgen quote is from *Early Anthropology in Sixteenth and Seventeenth Centuries* (University of Pennsylvania Press, 1964). Other works mentioned: Mary Midgley, *Evolution as Religion* (Routledge, London, 2002, second edition); Thomas Kuhn, *The Structure of Scientific Revolutions* (University of Chicago Press, 1962); and George Orwell, *Nineteen Eighty Four* (Penguin Modern Classics, 2004; original 1949).

Simple Stories, Complex Facts by Jeremy Henzell-Thomas

Works cited in the article: Ameer Ali, 'Islamophobia to Westophobia: The Long Road to Radical Islamism', *Journal of Asian Security and International Affairs*, 3,1 (2016), 1-19; Sindre Bangstad, 'Researching Islamophobia', *Critical Muslim* 15, *Educational Reform* (Hurst, 2015), 99-110; Warren Berger, 'Want to be a better critical thinker? Here's how to spot false narratives and 'weaponised lies'', *Quartz*, 22/2/2017 at https://qz.com/915723/want-to-be-a-better-critical-thinker-heres-how-to-spot-false-narratives-and-weaponized-lies/; Ian Buruma, 'Across continents: autocrats take control'. *The Observer*, 18/12/16; Norman Cigar, 'The Role of Serbian Orientalists in Justification of Genocide Against Muslims of the Balkans', *Islamic Quarterly: Review of Islamic Culture*, Vol. XXXVIII, No. 3, 1994; Hamid Dabashi, 'Edward Said's Orientalism: Forty years later', *Aljazeera*, 3 May, 2018, at https://www.aljazeera.com/indepth/opinion/edward-orientalism-forty-years-180503071416782.html; Alex Evans, *The Myth Gap: What Happens When Evidence and Arguments aren't Enough* (Transworld, London, 2007); Abdullah Faliq, Editorial, *Arches Quarterly*,

4:7 (Winter 2010), 7; Niall Ferguson, *Civilisation: The West and the Rest* (Penguin Press, 2011); 'Why the West is now in decline', *Daily Telegraph*, 6/3/11; Costas Gabrielatos, 'Discourse Analysis and Media Attitudes: The Representation of Islam in the British Press', Keynote lecture, Symposium on Muslims in the UK and Europe, Centre of Islamic Studies, University of Cambridge, 16-18 May, 2014; Jean Gebser, *The Ever-Present Origin,* authorised translation by Noel Barstad with Algis Mickunas (University of Ohio Press, Athens, 1985); Jack Goody, *The Theft of History* (Cambridge University Press, 2006) and *Renaissances: The One or the Many?* (Cambridge University Press, 2010); Nick Gvosdev, 'Is There an International Community?' *Ethics and International Affairs (EIA),* 23/12/2015; Fred Halliday, 'The Clash of Civilisations?: Sense and Nonsense' in *Islam and Global Dialogue: Religious Pluralism and the Pursuit of Peace,* ed. Roger Boase (Ashgate, Aldershot, 2005), 129; Victor Davis Hanson, *Why The West Has Won: Carnage and Culture from Salamis to Vietnam* (Faber and Faber, London, 2001); Gregg Henriques, 'A Passionate Call for a Commitment to the Truth', *Psychology Today,* 9/3/2018, at https://www.psychologytoday.com/blog/theory-knowledge/201803/passionate-call-commitment-the-truth; Jeremy Henzell-Thomas, *Learning from Informative Text: The Interaction Between Top-Down and Bottom-Up Processes*. Ph.D. thesis, University of Lancaster, 1986; 'The Power of Education', *Critical Muslim* 14, *Power* (April-June 2015), 78-79; John Hobson, *The Eastern Origins of Western Civilisation* (Cambridge University Press, 2004), and *The Eurocentric Conception of World Politics: Western International Theory 1760-2010* (Cambridge University Press, 2012); Samuel P. Huntington, 'The Clash of Civilisations?', *Foreign Affairs* 72: 3 (1993), 22-49, and *The Clash of Civilisations and the Remaking of World Order* (Simon and Schuster, New York, 1996); Amir Hussain, 'Muslims, Pluralism, and Interfaith Dialogue,' in *Progressive Muslims: On Justice, Gender, and Pluralism*, ed. Omid Safi (Oneworld Publications, 2003), 25; Martin Jacques, 'What the hell is the international community?', *The Guardian* 24/8/06; Daniel Kahneman, *Thinking, Fast and Slow* (Penguin Books, London, 2012); Nassim Nicholas Taleb, *The Black Swan: The Impact of the Highly Improbable* (Random House, New York, 2007); Tim Lewis, Interview with Arundhati Roy, *The Guardian*, 17/6/2018; Daniel J. Levitin, Weaponised Lies: How to Think Critically in the Post-Truth Era (Dutton, New York, 2017); Jonathan Lyons, *The*

House of Wisdom: How the Arabs Transformed Western Civilisation (Bloomsbury, 2009); María Rosa Menocal, *The Ornament of the World: how Muslims, Jews, and Christians created a culture of tolerance in medieval Spain* (Little, Brown, Boston, 2002); Pankaj Mishra: 'The Western model is broken', *The Guardian,* 14/10/14; 'After the Paris Attacks: It's Time for a New Enlightenment', *The Guardian*, 20/1/15; Darío Fernández-Morera: 'The Myth of the Andalusian Paradise', *The Intercollegiate Review*, Fall 2006, 23–31; James Winston Morris, *The Reflective Heart: Discovering Spiritual Intelligence in Ibn 'Arabi's Meccan Illuminations* (Fons Vitae. Louisville, 2005), 81; David Nirenberg, *Communities of Violence: Persecution of Minorities in the Middle Ages* (Princeton University Press, 1996), 9; Robert Parry, 'The Power of False Narratives', 18/4/2013 at https://consortiumnews.com/2013/04/18/the-power-of-false-narratives/; Edward Pearce, 'The west and the rest', *The Guardian*, 27/8/08; Fred Pearce, 'Down with data! Sagas are more likely to save Earth', *New Scientist*, 11/1/2017, at https://www.newscientist.com/article/mg23331080-500-down-with-data-sagas-are-more-likely-to-save-earth/; Ransom Riggs, 'The Sherlock Holmes Handbook: Opium Dens and Narcotics in the Victorian Era', 26/10/09, at http://mentalfloss.com/article/23097/sherlock-holmes-handbook-opium-dens-and-narcotics-victorian-era; Barry Rubin: 'Western Civilisation is not Really a Civilisation': 'Westophobia' in Arab Culture', 20/11/07, at http://www.theaugeanstables.com/2007/11/20/western-civilization-is-not-really-a-civilization-westophobia-in-arab-culture/ and 'Westophobia: Why Do 'They' Hate America? Just Listen', 1/4/11, at http://www.crethiplethi.com/westophobia-why-do-they-hate-america-just-listen/islamic-countries/pakistan/2011/; Jonathan Sacks, *The Dignity of Difference: How to Avoid the Clash of Civilisations* (Continuum, London, 2002) and *The Home We Build Together: Recreating Society* (Continuum, London, 2007); Ziauddin Sardar, 'Reading the Qur'an in the Dark', *The Guardian*, 27/8/09; 'From Islamisation to Integration of Knowledge', in Ziauddin Sardar and Jeremy Henzell-Thomas, *Rethinking Reform in Higher Education* (IIIT, Herndon, 2017); Robert Skidelsky, 'Is Western civilisation in terminal decline?' *The Guardian*, 17/11/15 at https://www.theguardian.com/business/2015/nov/17/is-western-civilisation-in-terminal-decline; Richard Tarnas, *The Passion of the Western Mind: Understanding the Ideas that have Shaped Our World View* (Pimlico, London, 1996); Robert Trivers, Deceit

& Self-Deception: Fooling Yourself the Better to Fool Others (Allen Lane, London, 2011).

Writing Travel by James E. Montgomery

Primary sources discussed in this article, in the following order: 'Antarah ibn Shaddad, *War Songs*, translated by James E. Montgomery, with Richard Sieburth (New York, 2018; Bishr ibn Abi Khazim al-Asadi, *Diwan*, ed. 'Izzat Hasan (Damascus, 1960), Poem 10; Ma'mar ibn Rashid, *The Expeditions: An Early Biography of Muhammad*, translated by Sean Antony (New York, 2015); 'A'ishah al-Ba'uniyyah, *The Principles of Sufism*, translated by Th. Emil Homerin (New York, 2016); al-Tabari, *The History: General Introduction and From the Creation to the Flood*, translated by Franz Rosenthal (Albany, 1989); Abu l-'Ala' al-Ma'arri, *The Epistle of Forgiveness or A Pardon to Enter the Garden, preceded by Ibn al-Qarih's Epistle*, translated by Geert Jan van Gelder and Gregor Schoeler (New York, 2016); *The Travels of Ibn Jubayr*, translated by R. J. C. Broadhurst (London 1952); Ahmad Faris al-Shidyaq, *Leg over Leg*, translated by Humphrey Davies (New York, 2015); al-Biruni, *India*, translated by Edward Sachau (London, 1910); Al-Mas'udi, *Meadows of Gold*, translated by Paul Lunde and Caroline Stone (London, 1989); al-Muqaddasi, *The Best Divisions for Knowledge of the Regions*, translated by B. A. Collins (Reading, 2000); Ibn Fadlan, *Mission to the Volga*, translated by James E. Montgomery (New York, 2017); Abu Zayd al-Sirafi, *Accounts of China and India*, translated by Tim Mackintosh-Smith (New York, 2017); Buzurg ibn Shariyar, *The Book of the Wonders of India: Mainland, Sea and Islands*, translated by G. S. Freeman-Grenville (London, 1981); *One Hundred and One Nights*, translated by Bruce Fudge (New York, 2017); Geert Jan van Gelder, 'The Terrified Traveller: Ibn al-Rumi's Anti-Rahil,' *Journal of Arabic Literature* 27/1 (1996), pp. 37-48; Al-Jahiz, *The Book of Misers*, translated by R. B. Serjeant, reviewed by Ezzeddin Ibrahim (Reading, 1997); *The Assemblies of al-Harîri*, translated by Thomas Chenery (London, 1867); *The Assemblies of al-Harîri*: The Last Twenty-Four Assemblies, translated by F. J. Steingass (London, 1898); Ibn Battuta, *The Travels of Ibn Battuta*, edited by Tim Mackintosh-Smith (London, 2003).

Travel texts not discussed in this article that are informed by some of the varieties of travel mentioned include: Ibn Tufayl, *Hayy ibnYaqzan*, translated by Lenn E. Goodman (Chicago, 2009) (the spiritual ascent); al-Ghazali, *Path to Sufism and Deliverance from Error*, translated by R. J. McCarthy (Fons Vitae, 2001) (withdrawal from and return to the world); Usama ibn Munqidh, *The Book of Contemplation: Islam and the Crusades*, translated by Paul M. Cobb (London, 2008) (memoirs of a cavalier life of soldiery, diplomacy, hunting); Ibn Butlan, *The Physician's* Banquet, translated by Philip F. Kennedy (New York, in preparation) (travel to earn a livelihood); the sequence of poems composed whilst in captivity in Byzantium by the warlord Abu Firas al-Hamdani (d. 968), known as the Rumiyyat ('Poems from Rome,' the Greek and Arabic name for Byzantium), have not yet been translated into English; elite women sometimes travelled for the purposes of marriage, as when in 1087 Mah-i Mulk, the daughter of Sultan Malik-Shah, arrived from Isfahan to be married in Baghdad to Sultan al-Muqtadi (r. 1075-94). She returned home two years later, after a period of estrangement from the caliph: Ibn al-Sa'i, *Consorts of the Caliphs.Women and the Court of Baghdad*, translated by Shawkat M. Toorawa and the Editors of the Library of Arabic Literature (New York, 2017), pp. 63-64.

The best taxonomy of the 'travel of individuals in the medieval Islamic world' is provided by Shawkat M. Toorawa, 'Travel in the Medieval Islamic World: The Importance of Patronage as Illustrated by 'Abd al-Latif al-Baghdadi (and other littérateurs),' in *Eastward Bound: Travel and Travellers, 1050-1550*, ed. Rosamund Allen (Manchester, 2004), pp. 57-70, especially pp. 66-67. See also Houari Touati, *Islam and Travel in the Middle Ages*, translated by Lydia G. Cochrane (Chicago, 2010); Paul Zumthor, 'The Medieval Travel Narrative,' *New Literary History* 25 (1994), pp. 809-824 (translated by Catherine Peebles); *The Cambridge Companion to Travel Writing*, edited by Peter Hulme and Tim Youngs (Cambridge, 2002), for travel writing in English between 1500 and the present day; William Atkins, *The Immeasurable World: Journeys in Desert Places* (London, 2018), especially p. 280; *The Hajj: Pilgrimage in Islam*, edited by Eric Tagliacozzo and Shawkat M. Toorawa (Cambridge, 2106). For a full discussion of ships and sea-faring in early Arabic poetry, see James E. Montgomery, *The Vagaries of the Qasidah. The Tradition and Practice of Early Arabic Poetry* (Warminster, 1997),

Chapter 5, pp. 166-208; for al-Ma'mun's exploration of the Pyramids, see Michael D. Cooperson, *Al-Ma'mun* (Oxford, 2005).

Big, Bad Trump by Brad Bullock

Books mention in this article include: C. Wright Mills, *White Collar* (Oxford University Press, 1951); W.F. Whyte, *Organisation Man* (Simon & Schuster, 1956); Robert Bellah et al., *Habits of the Heart* (University of California Press, 1985); Amitai Etzioni, *The Moral Dimension* (Simon and Schuster, 1988); Samuel Huntington, 'The Clash of Civilisations?' (*Foreign Affairs*, vol. 72:3, 1993); George Ritzer, *The McDonaldisation of Society* (Sage, 1993); Theda Skocpol & Morris Fiorina, *Civic Engagement in American Democracy* (Brookings Institution Press, 1999); Robert Putnam, *Bowling Alone* (Simon & Schuster, 2000); Marc Hetherington & Jonathan Weiler, *Authoritarianism & Polarisation in American Politics* (Cambridge University Press, 2009); Peter Kilborn, *Next Stop, Reloville* (Times Books, 2009); Sherry Turkle, *Alone Together* (Basic Books, 2011); Jennifer Hochschild & Katherine Einstein, *Do Facts Matter?* (University of Oklahoma Press, 2015); Steven Levitsky & Daniel Ziblatt, *How Democracies Die* (Crown, 2018).

For election participation rates, see *United States Election Project* (http://www.electproject.org). Tables constructed and used here by the author are available upon request. I also used percentage of voter eligible population, since it corrects for certain anomalies, such as felons who have lost voting rights, but they are generally comparable to the VAP rates and do not alter these trends. The Pew studies include Andrew Perrin and Maeve Duggan, 'America's Internet Access: 2000-2015' (Pew Research Center, 2015); see also Pew Mobile Fact Sheet at http://www.pewinternet.org/fact-sheet/mobile/ (last accessed June 19, 2018).

For more about concepts like 'clicktivism' and 'slacktivism' start with Paulo Gerbaudo, *Tweets and the Streets: Social Media and Contemporary Activism* (Pluto Press, 2012) and Aishwarya Sawarna, 'Social Media and Activism' (*JR 17*, Xavier Institute of Communications, 2015).

Translations by Burçin K. Mustafa

Omar Sheikh Al-Shabab *From necessity to infinity, interpretation in language and translation*. (Cambridge: Janus Publishing, 2016); Mona Baker, *Translation and conflict a narrative account*. (New York: Routledge, 2006); Wilma Ann Bailey, *'You Shall Not Kill' or 'You Shall Not Murder'?': The Assault on a Biblical Text* (Minnesota: Liturgical Press, 2005); Alexandra.Lianeri, 2002. 'Translation and the establishment of liberal democracy in nineteenth-century England: constructing the political as interpretive Act.' In *Translation and power*, edited by Edwin Gentzler and Maria Tymoczko, 1-24. (Boston: University of Massachusetts press, 2002); Robert Stam and Louise Spence, 'Colonialism, racism and representation.' In *The post-colonial studies reader*, edited by Bill Ashcroft, Gareth Griffiths, and Helen Tiffin, 109-113. (London and New York: Routledge, 2007)

On Bin Laden tapes see: BBC. 2001. 'Bin Laden video to be released.' December 12, 2001. http://news.bbc.co.uk/1/hi/world/south_asia/1705788.stm; Bin Laden, Usama. 2008. 'Exhibit Number AF00007DVD United States v. Zacarias Moussaoui, Criminal No. 01-455-A.' US Government. 09:25 min. http://www.vaed.uscourts.gov/notablecases/moussaoui/exhibits/prosecution/AF00007DVD.html (viewed 06.07.2018). Theresa May's speech, 'Stronger Britain, Built On Our Values', can be accessed at: https://www.gov.uk/government/speeches/a-stronger-britain-built-on-our-values (viewed 06.07.2018). 'Jordan Peterson on Islam.' can be found on YouTube:
https://www.youtube.com/watch?v=jmp4h3B3j5M; and the 21 October 2011 cover story on Qaddafi of *The Sun*, can be accessed at: https://www.ultimate-guitar.com/forum/showthread.php?t=1489511; and Gerard Batten's reference to 'Mohammadans' can be found at: 'UKIP Leader Gerard Batten About Tommy Robinson, Infowars Interiew.' Uploaded on May 30, 2018. YouTube video, 09:51 min. https://www.youtube.com/watch?v=fvDo2ICkWKg

See also: Mohammad Abdel Haleem, Muhammad. 2005. *The Qur'an a new* (Oxford: OUP, 2005); David Altheide, *Creating Fear: News and the*

Construction of Crisis. (New York: Aldine de Gruyter, 2002); Susan Bassnett, *Translation studies* (London and New York: Routledge, 2008)

God Knows Best by Leyla Jagiella

The works mention in this article: Thomas Bauer, *Die Kultur der Ambiguitat Eine andere Geschichte des Islams*, (Verlag der Weltreligioinen, Berlin, 2011); Mehmet Kalpakli and Walter G. Andrews in *The Age of Beloveds,* (Duke University Press, Durham and London, 2004); Joseph Allen Boone`s *The Homoerotics Of Orientalism,* (Columbia University Press, 2014); Shahab Ahmed *What is Islam? The Importance of Being Islamic,* (Princeton University Press, Princeton and Oxford, 2015).

Empire and Freedom by Giles Goddard

Books referred to in this essay are: Jane Austen. 1992. *Northanger Abbey*. Ware: Wordsworth Editions; Reni Eddo-Lodge. 2017. *Why I'm No Longer Talking to White People About Race*. London: Bloomsbury Circus; The Honourable Lady Inglis. 1892. *The Siege of Lucknow*. London: James R. Osgood, McIlvaine & Co.; Shashi Tharoor. 2016. *Inglorious Empire*. London: Hurst & Company.

TS Eliot's poem 'Gerontion' can be found at: https://www.poetryfoundation.org/poems/47254/gerontion

The quote from Toynbee can be found at: https://www.brainyquote.com/quotes/arnold_j_toynbee_403872 while the quote from Voltaire can be found here: https://history.hanover.edu/texts/voltaire/volhisto.html

The Roy Strong quote was originally carried in *The Times* in response to a suggestion by Afua Hirsch in *The Guardian*. The quote can be found here: https://en.wikipedia.org/wiki/Afua_Hirsch

Dreaming by Nur Sobers-Khan

Quotes from ibn Sirin are taken from *Ibn Seerin's Dictionary of Dreams: According to Islamic Inner Traditions* by Muhammad M. al-Akili, foreward by Mahmoud M. Ayoub (Philadelphia: Pearly Publishing House, 1992), which purports to be a translation of the *Tasfir al-Ahlam*. The Intizar Hussian quote is from the introduction to the translation of his *A Chronicle of the Peacocks: Stories of Exile, Partition and Lost Memories*, translated from Urdu by Alok Bhalla and Vishwamitter Adil (Delhi: Oxford University Press, 2002). Other works mentioned: Saba Mahmood, *Politics of Piety: The Islamic Revival and the Feminist Subject* (Princeton: Princeton University Press, 2005); Shahab Ahmed, *What is Islam? The Importance of Being Islamic* (Princeton: Princeton University Press, 2016); Elizabeth Sirriyeh, *Dreams and Vision in the World of Islam: A History of Muslim Dreaming and Foreknowing* (London: I.B. Tauris, 2015) and *Sufi Visionary of Ottoman Damascus: Abd al-Ghani al-Nabulusi, 1641-1731* (New York: Routledge, 2005); Geert Jan van Gelder, *Close Relationships: Incest and Inbreeding in Classical Arabic Literature* (London, I.B. Tauris, 2005).

I haven't been able to thank most of the people whose conversations have shaped my ideas on the stories our dreams tell, mainly because I wasn't sure they would wish to be named publicly in a piece of writing arguing for dream interpretation as radical ontology, that discusses incest and cannibalism in the same breath as pilgrimage and mainly consists of thoughts that are not grounded in any academic discipline, merely in a self-confessed epistemological narrative aporia and disorder. But you know who you are, and please consider yourselves and your deepest, darkest internal stories duly thanked.

The Women of Rawabi by Sabrina Stallone

The works mentioned in this article include: Tina Grandinetti, 'The Palestinian Middle Class in Rawabi: Depoliticising the Occupation', *Alternatives: Global, Local, Political* 2015, Vol. 40(1): 63-78; Hanna L. Muehlenhoff, 'Victims, soldiers, peacemakers and caretakers: the neoliberal constitution of women in the EU's security policy', *International*

Feminist Journal of Politics, 19(2):153-167; Arpan Roy, 'Reimagining resilience: Urbanisation and identity in Ramallah and Rawabi', *City* 2016, Vol. 20(3): 368-388; Eyal Weizman, *Hollow Land. Israel's Architecture of Occupation* (Verso, London, 2007); and Léopold Lambert, Weaponised Architecture (PR-Barcelona, 2013). Lambert article on Rawabi, 'Architectural Prophecy of an Unequal State', published in 2017, can be accessed at https://thefunambulist.net/architectural-projects/palestine-report-part-4-rawabi-architectural-prophecy-unequal-palestinian-state.

The cited *Washington Post* article was written by William Booth and published on 25 May 2017. It can be accessed at https://www.washingtonpost.com/graphics/world/occupied/palestinian-metropolis-rawabi-rises-in-west-bank-as-israeli-occupation-turns-50/.

Postnormal Words by C Scott Jordan

Madeline Abright's, *Fascism: A Warning* is published by HarperCollins (New York, 2018); and Timothy Snyder's *The Road to Unfreedom: Russia, Europe, America* is published by Tim Duggan Books (New York, 2018). For more on postnormal times, go to www.postnormaltim.es, where a number of books and articles can be downloaded.

Antigone and Shamsie by Boyd Tonkin

Kamila Shamsie's *Home Fire* is published by Bloomsbury (2017). I have quoted from Robert Fagles's translation of Antigone (Sophocles, *The Three Theban Plays*: Penguin Classics, 1984). I have also consulted EF Watling's translation (Sophocles, *The Theban Plays*: Penguin Classics, 1963), and versions and adaptations by Friedrich Hölderlin (Hölderlin's Sophocles, translated by David Constantine: Bloodaxe, 2001), Jean Anouilh (*Antigone*, translated by Barbara Bray: Bloomsbury, 2000), Bertolt Brecht ('The Antigone of Sophocles', in Collected Plays: Eight: Methuen Drama, 2004), Tom Paulin (*The Riot Act*: Faber & Faber, 1984), Seamus Heaney (*The Burial at Thebes*: Faber & Faber, 2004) and Anne Carson (*Antigone*: Oberon Books,

2015). George Steiner's Antigones is published by Oxford University Press (1984) and Judith Butler's *Antigone's Claim* published by Columbia University Press (2000). On the Indo-Greek states see WW Tarn, *The Greeks in Bactria and India* (Cambridge Library Collection, 2010) and on Greek-Indian drama, ML Varadpande's *Ancient Indian and Indo-Greek Theatre* (Abhinav Publications, 1981) and Katharine B Free, 'Greek Drama and the Kuttiyatam', *Theatre Journal*, vol. 33, no. 1, March 1981. On recent global Antigones, see *Antigone on the Contemporary World Stage*, edited by Erin B Mee and Helene P Foley (Oxford University Press, 2011). 1205/6, respectively.

CONTRIBUTORS

● **Brad Bullock** is Professor of Sociology, Department of Sociology, Randolph College, Lynchburg, Virginia ● **Merryl Wyn Davies** is an anthropologist and writer well-known as the co-author of *Why Do People Hate America?* ● **Onaiza Drabu** is an anthropologist and writer based in Nairobi ● **Canon Giles Goddard** is the Vicar of St John's Church in Waterloo, London ● **Jeremy Henzell-Thomas** is a Research Associate and former Visiting Fellow at the Centre for Islamic Studies, University of Cambridge ● **Tam Hussein** is a television producer and a short story writer ● **Leyla Jagiella** is a cultural anthropologist exploring orthodoxy and heterodoxy in South Asian Islam ● **C Scott Jordan** is Assistant Director, Centre for Postnormal Policy and Futures Studies ● **Norhayati Kaprawi** is a Malaysian activist, filmmaker, writer, and visual artist ● **Hassan Mahamdallie** is an arts consultant and theatre creative ● **Nicholas Masterton** is an architect and researcher at Forensic Architecture ● **Shazia Mirza** is a well-known stand-up comedian ● **Misha Monaghan** works for the Muslim Institute and is also a YouTube food vlogger ● **James E. Montgomery** is Sir Thomas Adams's Professor of Arabic, University of Cambridge ● **Burçin K. Mustafa** teaches translation at Princess Nourah University, Riyadh and is a Research Associate at SOAS, University of London ● **Irna Qureshi**, co-founder of the Bradford Literary Festival, is writing her memoir ● **Samia Rahman** is the Director of the Muslim Institute ● **Shanon Shah** is Deputy Editor of *Critical Muslim* ● **Nur Sobers-Khan** is lead curator for South Asia at the British Library ● **Sabrina Stallone** is a Junior Fellow at the University of Amsterdam in the School for Regional, Transnational and European Studies ● **Boyd Tonkin** is a writer and journalist ● **Mozibur Rahman Ullah** was educated at Oxford University and Imperial College and is now an independent scholar and writer ● **Sahil Warsi** is an American anthropologist residing in the UK.